Sarah Boxer

Ultimate Blogs

Sarah Boxer, who was the first Web critic for *The New York Times*, is the author and illustrator of the cartoon novel *In the Floyd Archives: A Psycho-Bestiary*. She lives in Washington, D.C., with her husband and son.

ALSO BY SARAH BOXER

In the Floyd Archives: A Psycho-Bestiary

Ultimate Blogs

Ultimate Blogs

MASTERWORKS FROM THE WILD WEB

edited by Sarah Boxer

VINTAGE BOOKS
A Division of Random House, Inc.
New York

A VINTAGE BOOKS ORIGINAL, FEBRUARY 2008

Copyright © 2008 by Sarah Boxer

All rights reserved. Published in the United States by
Vintage Books, a division of Random House, Inc., New York,
and in Canada by Random House of Canada Limited, Toronto.

Vintage and colophon are registered trademarks of Random House, Inc.

Blog credits can be found at the end of the book.

Library of Congress Cataloging-in-Publication Data
Ultimate blogs : masterworks from the wild Web / edited by Sarah Boxer.
p. cm.
"A Vintage Books original."
Includes bibliographical references and index.
ISBN: 978-0-307-27806-7 (alk. paper)
1. Blogs. I. Boxer, Sarah.
AC5.U45 2008
006.7—dc22
2007037139

Book design by R. Bull

www.vintagebooks.com

Printed in the United States of America
10 9 8 7 6 5 4 3 2 1

For Harry & Julius

CONTENTS

INTRODUCTION

Sarah Boxer

"What are you working on?"

"An anthology of blogs."

"What?"

"An anthology of blogs."

"I didn't know you had a blog."

"I don't. It's an anthology of other people's blogs."

"How do you find good blogs?"

"I read. I surf. I look at blog contests. I follow links. I ask people I like about the blogs they like. I look at their favorites, and then at my favorites of their favorites."

"Is a good blog hard to find?"

"Yes. Very."

"What did you do before this?"

"I wrote for a newspaper."

"I love newspapers."

The truth is, I am one of those questioning me. I don't have a blogging bone in my body. I am not an exhibitionist. I do not crave friends I've never met. I hate gossip. The ding of new e-mail hitting my in-box fills me with dread. Instant messaging makes me feel like I've been cornered at a party with no drink. Yet here I am. I have spent the past year or so trawling for good blogs. I have opened a MySpace account as a fourteen-year-old boy. I have started my own blog—in fact two—and filled them with nothing.

Now the anthology is done, and, actually, I love everything in it: the writing, the thinking, the drawing, and the photos. And everything in it is bloggy to the core. None of these blogs would have been likely to sprout in any other form. They are masterpieces of blogging. That doesn't mean they're famous. Given that there are more than 80 million blogs out there, according to the Web-tracking site Technorati, with roughly 15.5 million of them active, "blogebrity" is quite a bizarre phenomenon anyway.

The most famous blogs—the Technorati Top 100 and the so-called Higher Beings in the Blogosphere Ecosystem, including Instapundit, Daily Kos, Boing Boing, and Engadget—are the ones that other blogs link to the most.* That is both the mark of their fame and how they became famous. In turn these blogs act as kingmakers, linking to lots of other sites. Some days the only writing you see on a blog is the equivalent of "Read this. . . . Take a look. . . . But, seriously, this is lame. . . . Can you believe this?" Then they lead you to other blogs, news articles, or maybe a few YouTube videos.

Because fame and links are one and the same, some bloggers will do practically anything—start rumors, tell lies, pick fights, create fake personas, brag about being prostitutes, and post embarrassing videos—to get noticed and linked. Bringing down a big-time journalist or politician is still the best way to hoist your blog to the top of the charts. But a simple mention from a popular blog like Boing Boing can also do the job. So, when a Higher Being gives the nod to an Insignificant Microbe, the lesser creature gives thanks and praise. And that, of course, brings greater glory to the alpha blogs.

Journalists are not deaf to the call of the wild. In 2006 Lee Siegel, a culture critic, *New Republic* editor, and National Magazine Award

---

* The Truth Laid Bear Blogosphere Ecosystem describes itself as "a list of weblogs ranked by the number of incoming links they receive from other weblogs on the list." As of late May 2007, there were about 95,000 blogs on the list. The top blogs had thousands linking to them; the lowest—the Insignificant Microbes—had no links. Technorati maintains a more comprehensive ranking system. In late May 2007 it was tracking 81 million blogs. Its system is also based on incoming links, but each linking blog can count only once.

winner (who incidentally coined the term *blogofascism* to describe bloggers' use of insult and intimidation to control opinion), was caught using a "sock puppet," a false blog persona, to flatter himself in the comments section of his blog. Under the name Sprezzatura, Siegel called himself brave and brilliant, and branded his attackers a "bunch of immature, abusive sheep."

The bloggers in this anthology are, for the most part, out of the fray. They write more than they link, and they're read more than they are linked to. Though it's true that a few of them are Large Mammals in the blog ecosystem (blogs with more than a thousand inbound links), most are the smaller, slimier creatures. Why favor the lowly over the linky? Because the thing you are now holding in your hand is a book, not a computer, and links and books are a deadly mix. You cannot click on a link in a printed book. And a book looks weird when its pages are littered with Web site addresses and very long quotes and quotes within quotes. So, no links here, folks.

And where are all the political blogs? Lots of people assume that a blog anthology must be filled with them, for these are the famous ones, the ones that have influenced elections and shamed big people out of their jobs. The blogs Little Green Footballs and Power Line helped set in motion Rathergate when they spread the word that some memos presented by Dan Rather on *60 Minutes II* about President George W. Bush's National Guard duty were fakes. The blogger Atrios publicized Trent Lott's racist remarks at Strom Thurmond's birthday party, leading to Lott's resignation as Senate majority leader. The Swift Boat veterans got lots of wind from right-wing bloggers questioning John Kerry's war stories. These bloggers are fast, fierce, and connected.

And few of them are in this book—once again for good reason. Most political blogs, and for that matter most gadgetry blogs, sports blogs, and gossip blogs, age quickly. Their posts get stale. Maybe that's why the books of some very good bloggers flop. A year ago Gawker, the popular media gossip blog, posted a list of blog-to-book deals under the headline "Not Even People on Your Blogroll Would Buy Your Book." (A blogroll is a blog's list of favorite sites.) That may be over-stating it. But it's fair to say that if you strip most blogs of their timeli-ness and their links, you are left with nothing. I did not want to fill the anthology with nothing.

Where then does that leave an anthology of blogs? If the blogs in here were not going to be timely, I figured, they had better well be timeless, and if they were not going to be linky, they had better well be self-contained. Who are these odd bloggers who don't swim with the quickie wiki crowd? (The term *wiki*, from the Hawaiian for quick, denotes any Web site that allows for collaborative writing or editing, like Wikipedia or the Wiktionary.) Are these bloggers then just plain old journalists, essayists, fiction writers, photographers, and cartoonists who have not found their publishers yet? No. First of all, many already have publishers. Second, their work is, one way or another, distinctly bloggy.

So, bloggy writing: It is conversational and reckless, composed on the fly for anonymous intimates. It is public and private, grand and niggling, smart-assed and dumb-assed. Bloggers won't help you catch up if you missed the last installment. They often begin midthought or midrant, in medias craze. They use their own trademark words—like *fugly* (the ugliness celebrities do best)—and give new meanings to old ones. A *troll* on the Web is someone who posts inflammatory things just to provoke an outcry. *Astroturfing* is creating a fake grassroots move-ment.

Bloggers are often loose-lipped and foulmouthed, free with their lives and free with the truth. They love run-on sentences and acronyms. They sprinkle their blogs with expressions like *WTF* (trans-lation: What the fuck?), *IMHO* (in my humble opinion), *LOL* (laugh out loud), *meh* (a verbal shrug), and *um*. They willfully misspell—like *teh* for *the*. They call the Internet *the internets*, cutely following George W. Bush's slip. If people wrote like this for publication, they'd probably be fired. And, indeed, there is a term for getting canned because of your blog: *dooced*, named for the blogger Dooce, now a stay-at-home mother (SAHM) or, as she puts it, a "Shit Ass Ho Motherfucker," who got fired for blogging about her employer.

Not every good writer can make good bloggy prose. Geoffrey Nunberg, a linguist at Stanford, admitted on NPR back in 2004, "I don't quite have the hang of the form." And, he said, many journalists who are now called upon by their editors to keep blogs are similarly stumped: "They fashion engaging ledes, they develop their arguments methodically, they give context and background, and tack helpful IDs onto the names they introduce." Guess what? They read like journalists, not bloggers.

Most bloggers don't care if they leave you in the dust. They assume that if you're reading them, you're either one of their friends or at least in on their gossip, their jokes, or the names they drop. They're not responsible for your education. They're like diarists, or like pamphleteers, or, as Mark Liberman, one of the founders of the blog Language Log, suggested, like Plato. ☺ Here's the beginning of Plato's *Republic:* "I went down yesterday to the Peiraeus with Glaucon, the son of Ariston, to pay my devotions to the Goddess, and also because I wished to see how they would conduct the festival since this was its inauguration." Huh? Who is Ariston? What Goddess? What festival?

Good news, though. Some bloggers out there actually write good bloggy prose that non–blog readers can read. They are the ones in this book. They are not only stunning writers (in the best electric sense), but use the Internet well too. Some use it as a writing prod. Some use it as a trash can. Some use it like a diary. Some use it like a pulpit. Some use it like a drawing pad. Some use it like a padded room. Some use it to reach out. Some use it to reach in. Some use it to get mad. Some use it to get even. (By the way, the women in this book are, generally speaking, a lot more open—and a lot angrier—than the men.)

These bloggers also have what you might call virtual charisma.

They are bold even when sharing their shame and their obsessions. Their writing is all bound up with their Internet identities. Anonymous or not, they are what they write. In the virtual world these are the town criers, the chiefs, and the village idiots. They are irreducible egos containing multitudes. And thanks to the Web, they now have as much claim to our attention as television's talking heads. Whether they tell the truth or not is another matter, but WTF. It would be hard to fake what they do, and it's kind of unbelievable that they live out in the open, fair game for all snipers. The only trick is finding them. And once you do, you'll see that because they are fearless they are magnetic. They could be writing about their dead mothers, clapping, or condoms. I would follow them anywhere. And I did.

I tried hard to classify the twenty-seven blogs in this anthology: by nationality (nineteen American, three British, one Guatemalan-American, one Iraqi, one Singaporean, one Russian(?), one South African); by sex (seventeen male, ten female); by age (a couple over sixty-five, seven in their forties, a dozen in their thirties, four in their twenties, one teenager, one dead); by genre (twenty-two nonfiction, one fiction, one poetry, two comics, one photography); by subject (culture, public policy, cosmology, seventeenth-century London, the Iraq war, fashion, family, the patriarchy, ideas that won't fly, motherhood, language, politics, personal stuff, rodents and crap, military life, animation and India, literature, classical music, muckraking, the Trojan War, and a whole lot of random stuff); by popularity; by type of blog name (eponymous, epithetical, prepositional, imperative, declarative).

And then I gave up trying to tame the wildness of the Web and decided the best order would be alphabetical. That way the blogs can speak to one another more freely and suggest their own interconnections without the constraint of categories. And, after all, there are twenty-six entries. Well, twenty-seven. Never mind that the letters F, K, P, Q, S, V, W, X, Y, and Z aren't represented.

A is for ANGRYBLACKBITCH (ABB). Her blog name (and her frequent invocation of it to refer to herself) is one of the blog's great charms. She never uses the words *I* and *myself.* Instead, it is always *a bitch* and *my ass*, tempered by an occasional (*wink*). She can show you just how black King Kong really is (wink).

B is for BECKER-POSNER, a cold shower of rationality for the overheated blogosphere. A Nobel laureate in economics (Becker) and a judge of the U.S. Court of Appeals (Posner) kick around some very heavy issues. Poverty. Immigration. Global warming. You may shiver at some of their cold conclusions, but boy, those guys are clear as ice.

C is for CLICK OPERA, the blog of a British pop singer living in Berlin and writing about pop culture, national psyches, and sex. He can find Sturm und Drang in German weather reports and paranoid fun in amigurumi. He's into Japanese music, Japanese women, and Japanese girls—not necessarily in that order.

C is also for COSMIC VARIANCE, a group physics blog. The blogger I've picked out of the group is a theoretical physicist who pities the poor animals in thought experiments and thinks of the visible matter of the universe as the "olive in the martini of dark matter."

D is for the DIARY OF SAMUEL PEPYS, the oldest blog in the book. Pepys (pronounced "peeps"), the seventeenth-century English diarist, joined the blogosphere about three years ago. He keeps track of every poop and periwig. A real bore sometimes. But then, just when you've had it, he has a fight with his wife or ducks into a tavern to "towze" Mrs. Lane.

E is for two epithetical blogs, EL GUAPO IN DC and EUROTRASH, one comic, one tragicomic.

El Guapo (the handsome one), a Guatemalan-American, chronicles his adventures around D.C. with his friend Miguel, a man who runs through boxes of condoms like candy.

Eurotrash, a Brit with a vicious bite, is best known for trashing a *New York Times* food writer thus: "You make my teeth want to vomit." As you'll see, she earned her bite the hard way. "Hey ho" is her favorite sigh.

G is for GET YOUR WAR ON and also for GO FUG YOURSELF, two blogs whose names are your commands. Both rank high in the blogosphere.

Get Your War On is a comic strip with clip-art characters chatting on the phone. Two days after the United States bombed Afghanistan, the first strip appeared: "Oh Yeah! *Operation: Enduring Freedom* is in the house! . . . *Operation: Enduring Our Freedom To Bomb The Living Fuck Out Of You* is in the house!!!" I mean, who said things like that a month after 9/11?

Go Fug Yourself proves that blogging is like junior high school. The "fuggers" are popular because they are snarky (that's snotty, catty, and wisecracking). They post pictures of celebrities and laugh at their "fugliness." Hey, they're just being helpful!

H is for HOW TO LEARN SWEDISH IN 1000 DIFFICULT LESSONS, a quiet, neat oasis on the Web. Francis Strand (a pseudonym) writes about his husband, his adoptive city (Stockholm), and his family back home in America in cool, beautiful sentences. Every entry ends with a short lesson in Swedish.

I is for I BLAME THE PATRIARCHY, best known for dissing blow jobs. When I asked permission to publish the "bj" posts, the author, Twisty Faster, was slow to reply. She was too busy posting scary shots of herself topless after a mastectomy. Finally she answered my request gallantly: "Why not? The Blow Job Wars are to Twisty Faster what 'Copacabana' is to Barry Manilow."

I is also for IN THE MIDDLE, written by an Iraqi man in the United States with one hell of a story about waiting for a plane.

I is also for IRONIC SANS, the blog of a guy who throws out ideas—for fonts, for ads, for cities, for bombs—the way other people throw out the trash.

I is also for IT'S RAINING NOODLES!, written by a nineteen-year-old student in Singapore who really likes pink, uses her real name, and cheerfully complains about her ex-boyfriend, his new girlfriend, bad grammar, bad courtship, and traditional Chinese medicine. She draws a cute puppy labeled "bitch" and a chainsaw labeled "pink," "fluffy," "harmless."

J is for JOHNNY I HARDLY KNEW YOU, named both for the anti-war song and the Edna O'Brien book. It is one of the dreamiest blogs on the internets. Spelling largely without capital letters, johnny floats between reality, dreams, and movies. The writing seems effortless: like falling down stairs or falling asleep.

J is also for JULIA {HERE BE HIPPOGRIFFS}, the journal of a thirty-six-year-old mother of one who has been through eleven miscarriages in her attempt to be the mother of more. Her logo includes a photo of a gargoyle gobbling a little person. Not your typical stay-at-home-mommy (SAHM) blog, all sweetness and snot.

L is for LANGUAGE LOG, a group language blog with lots of readers. From this group of linguists, I chose the lone lexicographer, who plucks the freshest words of the day and analyzes them until they scream for mercy and admit their pedigrees.

M is for MATTHEW YGLESIAS, a "proudly eponymous" political blog and the most popular thing in this book. He's so adept at finding fault with his friends (generally liberals) and finding merit in his enemies that there's now an Yglesias Award for pundits and politicians who do just that.

M is also for MICROGRAPHICA, an online cartoon that stars a small rodent and a piece of crap and reads like a tiny Beckett play. The artist says she loosens up by making the drawings inside one-centimeter-square frames and then posting them (irregularly) on Serializer, a cartoon Web site. "Being small means you can't add or fix anything," she explains. So does blogging.

M is also for MIDNIGHT IN IRAQ, a military blog written by a marine first lieutenant deployed to Fallujah in 2006. With over fifteen hundred "milblogs" in the world and a Web site that keeps track of them, you'd think finding a good one would be like shooting fish in a barrel. Wrong. Midnight is a rare blogger indeed.

N is for NINA PALEY, an animator. Mostly she blogs about the film she's making, *Sita Sings the Blues*, the story of the *Ramayana* told from Sita's point of view, and also, not so secretly, the story of Paley's own breakup in India. Her Lord Rama is a Blue Meanie crossed with Aladdin, and Sita looks like Betty Boop's Indian sister.

O is for OLD HAG, neither old nor hag. It's a literary blog hiding a published poet. On April 5, 2006, the poet was outed by a friend on the blog TMFTML (The Minor Fall, The Major Lift) who posted a nasty "review" of an Old Hag poem by one "Helen Vendler." The review was a hoax. The poem is the real thing.

R is for RADIO.URUGUAY, a photoblog with black-and-white pictures of Russia that are as pointedly dreary as other photoblogs are aimlessly colorful.

R is also for ROOTLESS COSMOPOLITAN, a blog about foreign affairs, soccer, and the war on terror, named after Stalin's slang term for Jews. The author, white and Jewish, grew up in South Africa working against apartheid. He's the only blogger I know who has compared the Holocaust to the Boer War.

T is for THE REST IS NOISE, a blog about classical music that illustrates how a passing shush in a concert hall can snowball into a grand investigation involving Mozart and Wagner.

T is also for THE SMOKING GUN, a muckraking site that is, in the words of Tina Brown, "where mortification lives." The editor of TSG, who claims it's not really a blog, makes Freedom of Information requests and then posts the haul on the Web—arrest records, celebrity mug shots, FBI memos—along with his salty comments.

U is for UNDER ODYSSEUS, the journal of Eurylochus, a soldier serving under Odysseus during the Trojan War. Written during the blogger's lunch breaks, UO is based on the *Iliad* and the *Odyssey* but borrows lines from neither. Maybe that's obvious. Here's Ajax reacting to the Trojan horse idea: "Oh, fuck the Horse, Odysseus! Do you really think the Trojans are going to fall for that?!"

Of course, this book is plenty skewed. These twenty-seven blogs are not exactly representative of the 80 million–plus blogs out there. They are funnier, more ambitious, better written, smarter, and (I think) more universally appealing. Many of the bloggers here have dual loyalties: two countries, two languages, or two modes (poetry and pulp, war and gaming, cartoons and epics). And for some reason they share some odd obsessions: superheroes, fonts, flying, shit, underwear, and the word *fuck*. Is that true of the whole blogosphere or is it just my taste in blogs?

This book, you'll notice, bucks the usual blogging format. On the Internet, bloggers' entries appear in reverse chronological order, like a pile of old mail—the newest stuff on top, the oldest at the bottom. Many bloggers also have long lists of their favorite blogs. And most of them have archives too, where you can find their old entries. None of that is here. The posts are in chronological order and appear without links or lists. And although I have tried to keep their flavor and the quirks of their punctuation, spelling, and grammar, I have corrected some errors.

Then there is the question of anonymity and truth. As I've said before, bloggers are loose with their lives and loose with the facts. Many bloggers include "About Me" pages on their blogs, which are often empty or filled with astrological information and lies. I have tried to suss out the fiction and say something about the real people behind the blogs in the minibiographies that appear after each entry. Sometimes I have succeeded. Sometimes I'm not so sure.

Ultimate
Blogs

ANGRYBLACKBITCH

ANGRYBLACKBITCH

PRACTICING THE FINE ART OF BITCHITUDE

http://angryblackbitch.blogspot.com/

FRIDAY, DECEMBER 02, 2005

King Kong . . .

A bitch is ready for the weekend! This bitch woke up today in frenzy. My ass has been invited to attend a ritzy event and, of course, waiting until the very last minute to decide what to wear!

Shit!

Somewhere between drama and meltdown a bitch remembered why my ass is usually anti-social.

2 cups coffee with Splenda and organic milk, followed by 1 Claritin, 2 pseudo Sudafed and cigs . . .

As a bitch jumped through the morning television in a desperate attempt to avoid multiple viewings of the Oprah/Letterman reconciliation (give a bitch a break, people) something caught my eye.

Peter Jackson of *Lord of the Rings* fame has remade *King Kong.*

Immediately, a bitch got pissed.

Why ABB Hates the King Kong *Story . . .*

A bitch has no hatred for Peter Jackson or his team of amazing folks. What this bitch hates . . . fucking cannot stand and thinks should be relegated to the same dark, murky hole in Hades that hopefully holds the entire body of black-face entertainment is the story.

King Kong, which was made famous as a 1930s film, is the story of a white, very white . . . extremely white and Aryan the way Ann Coulter wishes she was Aryan . . . woman who somehow ends up on a tropical, very tropical, WILD and untamed island populated by . . . NATIVES! Yep, natives who become entranced with this Aryan representation of civilized female beauty even though they have never set eyes on a white woman. Depending on the version, they either have always worshiped white women or simply begin to worship them once they set eyes on the blond bombshell that plops down on their island.

Now, they have a secret. A big fucking secret! There is a giant highly sexualized primate lurking on the island! Oh no! Jesus, why would a loving Gawd ever create such a beast? In the words of Wolf Blitzer . . . he's so black!

In order to pacify said giant black primate, the natives offer up sacrificial women. The giant primate then takes the women and leaves the natives alone for a while. 'Cause . . . well, you know . . . he's getting his freak on. And everyone knows that giant sexualized primates are soothed and calmed by the company of a terrified nubile woman.

Even though the regular offering of native women has pacified the giant primate, the natives know that this stunning white woman will put his ass over the top. Shit, they started coveting her right from the start! No way is their giant highly sexualized primate going to turn down a tryst with an unwilling blond beauty.

So, they capture the girl, tie her ass to a stake and offer her.

The giant primate, who represents society's notion that black men are obsessed with white women and are driven into uncontrollable frenzies by them, comes upon the blonde and . . . well . . . becomes obsessed with her and is driven into an uncontrollable frenzy.

It gets better!

The blonde, at first disgusted and terrified by the giant black primate, begins to fall under its spell. This is vital, because EVERYONE knows that the black man . . . oh, shit . . . no that would be the 'giant black primate' . . . has skills and, given enough time, can seduce pure untouched blondes with his sexual prowess!

Lets see . . . ummm . . . oh yes . . . blonde is freed, primate is captured, marketing blitz hits New York, blonde feels sorry for primate, primate is obsessing over blonde, primate gets loose . . . city is terrorized, blonde is kidnapped by obsessed primate, they get to the Empire State building and somehow the primate gets to the top. Makes sense since we're talking about a GIANT primate who just has to be used to climbing tall buildings and shit like that. Anyhoo . . . the primate, with blonde in hand, is shot and falls to the bottom. Terrorized blonde cries and primate dies with one . . .

large . . .

extremely large and black . . .

. . . fucking *GIANT* and BLAAAAAACK hand reaching out towards said blond symbol of white pure beauty.

Sigh.

Yeah, a bitch fucking hates this story. My ass knows that Hollywood can't and/or won't get its shit together regarding portrayals of minorities. But fuck this fucking shit!

Fuck everyone involved in bringing this historic insult back to the screen . . . to insult the fucking shit out of me again! Fuckers!

And as far as the portrayal of women . . . oh shit, that requires another post. [. . .] Between the portrayal of women and the resurrection of antiquated racial stereotypes, this black woman can find little good in the King Kong story. Which means that this remake will join the other blockbuster films of 2005 on the 'this bitch won't even watch it on cable' list.

Happy Friday, chil'ren . . .

posted by Shark-fu at 1:50 PM

MONDAY, MARCH 13, 2006

The myth of the black student who stole your spot at Yale . . .

This bitch had a fantabulous day off! The sun was shining, the birds were singing and my phone wasn't ringing . . . fantabulous indeed.

Thank you to my international readers for your concern over a bitch's safety. Yes, Missouri has been hit with some serious storms. This is the Midwest and we tend to have dramatic spring weather. Sadly, some lives have been lost. But rest assured that a bitch was blessed and did not face the full fury of nature here in St. Louis. We Midwesterners kind of take it all in stride . . . we cut our teeth on tornadoes and floods 'round here. But a bitch is touched that y'all care.

No, a bitch was not at O'Connell's Pub recently! But they do have yummy food. Mayhap a bitch will swing on by and get my St. Patrick's Day on. Anyhoo, whoever is out there looking like a bitch needs to cease . . . unless you're fine as hell, which only helps my brand image.

On to bitchitude!

The myth of the black student who stole your spot at Yale . . .
A certain Anonymous requested this bitch's opinion regarding minority preferences. Specifically, Anonymous said . . .

> I heard a white former South African once say: 'I was born and raised in Africa, I am an African. So when I become an American, am I not an African American? . . . Then why can I not get minority entrance points for college? . . . Am I not discriminated against?' . . . Since Black Africans won that conflict, maybe you would like to comment? From an historical perspective of course.

Well, a bitch only took one South African history course and that was years ago . . . but black South Africans having 'won' a conflict in South Africa doesn't have a damned thing to do with a white South African getting minority entrance points here in America . . . speaking from a historical perspective.

Having said that, a white South African who immigrates to America and feels that he is an African American can rock that identity all he wants to. Lawd knows checking African American on forms is beyond beneficial, sure as shit gets your foot in the front door and is the reason why so many top positions are held by African Americans.

Ummm . . . that's what my people call bullshit (wink).

Which brings a bitch to the underlying assumption that affirmative action is the reason some students don't get to go to State.

That's what we're talking about, right? The fear of a black person taking 'your' spot at Yale?

A bitch was pretty fucking pissed off when my ass showed up at a certain liberal arts college (no, not Yale . . . shudder and perish the thought) and realized that my ass had out tested most of the sorry assed motherfuckers raising hell about affirmative action.

Shit.

A bitch isn't trying to say my ass is wicked smart . . . shit, this bitch can't spell for shit . . . but my ass just wishes some of the assholes bitching about not getting in would look in the mirror and have a come-to-Jesus with their own ass about their GPA and those sorry assed SAT scores that really got them circular filed.

A bitch only got more pissed when my ass realized that some of the dumbest motherfuckers at school . . . and my ass means dumb . . . were legacies.

See, the dude who may have taken your spot at Yale is most likely not the brown and black students who make up less than 10% of the student body. He's that legacy admit . . . you know, Carter Silverspoon from Choate? . . . yeah, him and his forever unimpressive non-intellectual ass. College ain't a meritocracy, but that fact is better explored through a conversation with the heir to your right and not the black chick to your left.

My father went to college on the G.I. Bill and he went to grad school through an affirmative action program. He worked his ass off, was not academically prepared and struggled to get through. But he did it and he never let his chil'ren forget that struggle was mixed in with the blessing of an education. His daughters reaped the benefits of his efforts, attended strong public schools and had a much easier road to college as a result.

Sometimes affirmative action works.

Which brings us to this word 'fair.' Fair does not apply to college admissions. Most universities apply tons of qualifications and they don't exactly do it fairly.

My alma mater would have been majority Asian and international if 'fair' applied to college admissions.

Colleges seek to have a diverse population because diversity enriches the educational experience. International students, rural students, rich students, black students and so on add to the college experience. The problem comes when some students apply a sense of entitlement to college admissions . . . they then latch on to the most offensive 'got into school' practice and proceed to show their natural ass on *Dateline* by bitching about why they didn't get in and claiming that Keisha or Coretta or Michael took their spot.

A healthier . . . dare a bitch say more fair . . . rant would start with the legacies who took up 20% of the freshman class. Then you could move on down to the 50% of hyper-qualified students who didn't get accepted because said school had 'reached' a certain quota . . . then mosey on over to the 'daddy paid for this building' admissions . . . oh, and the 'our sports program is a revenue generator,' but don't hold your breath on that academic scholarship admission. The road is long and muddy as a motherfucker before you even get to the 10% that may or may not have been admitted with some racial preference . . . not that many are bothered by the 'may,' because a bitch wishes my ass had a dollar for every ignorant assumed-affirmative-action comment my ass heard while 'getting schooled.'

Yeah.

What was the original question? Oh, can a former white South African now white African American get special treatment when applying to college?

Sure, as long as an AngryBlackBitch can get my reparations paid in South African gold . . . honey.

posted by Shark-fu at 10:59 AM

Some thoughts on the documentary *F**K* . . .

C-Money and this bitch caught *F**K*, which is a documentary partici-
pating in the St. Louis International Film Festival.

Most of y'all know that a bitch adores ripe language. Shit, this bitch
has even been accused of having quite the potty mouth my damned
self (wink). So there was no way in hell my ass was going to miss
seeing this movie . . . even if it did start at 9:45pm on a school night!

F**K was fucking worth the late night viewage.

FUCK . . . and a bitch is going to uncensor the spelling of that shit
going forward . . . took me on a journey through the various uses of
the word. I was introduced to the diverse population of people that
freak out about it. The movie explored fear of *fuck*, the humor contained within *fuck*, the *power* contained within *fuck*, the impact of
censorship on culture, the FCC's split personality on how to handle
the word *fuck* and the culture war feeding off of naughty language
and behavior.

Whew!

And this was all done in fucking fantabulous detail.

The interviews were, however, the best part of the film.

They included but were not limited to Ice-T, Drew Carey, Bill Maher,
Dennis Prager, Billy Connolly (funny as hell . . . for real!), Alan Keyes
(total freak . . . and apparently rotting from within), Dr. Hunter S.
Thompson (Gawd, a bitch misses the hell out of that motherfucker!),
Michael Medved (still desperately seeking a Puritan revival), Janeane
Garofalo (SisterGirl was rocking some seriously fantabulous fashion

forward with a vintage twist eyeglasses), Ben Bradlee (of the Water-gate *Washington Post* Bradlees), and last but certainly not least Mr. Pat Boone.

Yes, Pat Boone.

A bitch can't name a single song of his and yet I do know that he was a 'somebody' sometime somewhere in the history of the 'used to be star fuckable' sorta-celebrities.

Even after seeing him in the movie this bitch probably couldn't pick him out of a lineup.

Doesn't matter . . . honestly, fuck it . . . Pat Boone still stole the show by giving this bitch a new naughty word!

Boone.

What?

Shit, Pat Boone said that he doesn't curse . . . he just replaces words like *fuck* with his name.

Boone!

Go boone yourself you motherbooner!

Get the boone out of my face, you boone-tool!

Gawd, this situation is booned up from the floor up!

Sigh.

Boone is fan-fucking-tabulous.

Thank you, Pat Boone, for being such a judgmental motherbooner!

A bitch is giving *FUCK* by Steve Anderson 4 out of 5 militant Afros.

posted by Shark-fu at 12:32 PM

A quick review . . .

Shall we?

Fantabulous!

This bitch couldn't avoid the coverage of the execution of a Saddam Hussein . . . and it got me thinking about the entire Saddam saga.

The Capture . . .
Saddam was found in a hole-esque bunker.

Okay, hold it.

Fuck that shit.

That was a motherfucking hole! Bunker my black ass. Saddam was pulled out of that nastified hole looking tore up . . . hair all crazy tore up. A bitch watched the telly as images of Saddam being inspected for . . . ugh . . . flashed across the screen.

Now, this bitch was surprised that they didn't just blow Saddam's ass away outside of the hole.

What?

Well, I was! But I quickly came to the conclusion that the United States must want a trial. Yeah, they must want some confirmation that Saddam was indeed the Dark Side and the new Iraqi government is indeed full of goodness that shines like a warm light and shall serve as an example to the region, which will facilitate the eventual democratization of the blah, blah and blah.

Oh, fuck it.

Ahem.

My ass came to the conclusion that they wanted a trial to demonstrate that Saddam was a tyrannical asshole. Which was known to our government . . . 'cause we used to be tight like that . . . way back in the day when Saddam was our tyrannical asshole.

So, bring on the made-for-television call to justice!

Not.

The Jerry Springer-*esque Trial . . .*

Postinvasion, war crime trials of known used-to-be-our-homeboy tyrants should go smoothly. There's an abundance of evidence . . . everyone wants to find the tyrant guilty . . . no need to fret about an impartial jury . . . hell, you've even got a fresh-off-the-motherfucking-presses judicial system that was written knowing that said tyrant might one day be brought before it.

But the trial of Saddam started to play out like the mutant love child of Maury P. and Jerry Springer! Assassinations . . . attempted assassinations . . . public rantings and fist wavings. [. . .]

Shit, we can't even get a well produced show trial out of these assholes!

Okay then.

Cough.

Anyhoo, surely the current puppet government is going to pull it together post conviction and get some mileage out of the execution of the tyrannical leader of the former puppet government.

Not so fast . . . think again!

To the Gallows . . .

A bitch was amazed by the coverage of the conviction . . . and the apparent confusion coming forth media-wise on the next steps.

And once the press got a hold of the law . . . and found out that Saddam was legally mandated to go to the gallows within 30 days of his conviction being upheld on appeal . . . well, you would have thought a hanging was on CNN's Christmas list!

The ever updated and yet still somehow breaking news headlines were full of bloodlust.

This bitch was waiting for Soledad O'Brien to host *Explaining Hangings—A Parent's Guide to Discussing Executions.*

Mercy.

But for sure they're going to pull it together, lead by example and administer justice with the kind of clarity of purpose Saddam never afforded his fellow Iraqis!

Certainly they . . .

We?

Ummm . . . they, if you believe *The West Wing*, have learned something and will take this moment to join together as one nation and bring an end to the . . .

Mission accomplished . . .

Oh, for the love of GAWD!

Who the fuck brings a camera phone to a hanging?

Jesus!

How the fuck did people fail to notice?

Pause.

And was a bitch the only person pondering *South Park* movie plot angles as the CNN Noose Ticker time clock wound down?

posted by Shark-fu at 12:20 PM

THURSDAY, JANUARY 04, 2007

Oprah gets her education on . . .

Did you know that Oprah opened up a school for young women in South Africa?

Of course you did!

Couldn't miss that shit with a map and a plan, could you (wink)?

A bitch has run the spectrum of emotions about Oprah's new school. My ass has separated my dislike of the star fucking that always accompanies shit like this (mark my words, someone is going to come up pregnant) from my honest respect for Ms. Oprah and what she has been able to accomplish.

Reaction #1–Jealousy is a sorry, sorry thang . . .
Shit.

Damn that Oprah!

A bitch has always wanted to open up a school of bitchitude here in St. Louis.

. . . sometime after the knee first jerketh . . .

Fuck that, this bitch's dream isn't married to Oprah's.

I can still open a school of bitchitude!

Reaction #2–Isolationism is like an infection . . .
Why South Africa? It's not as if we're running low on poor young women getting left behind.

. . . but reflection is a nice antibiotic . . .

Hell, I suppose the world is global and just because my ass thinks in terms of the community I live in doesn't mean anyone else has to.

Oprah is right about American students not having to pay tuition . . . although someone might want to hip her to the fact that taxes pay for public education (just ask folks living in Clayton . . . shudder). She's wrong about that iPod bullshit . . . some kids are spoiled materialistic little shits, but a lot of them are aspiring not acquiring.

But she is right about the fact that education is undervalued here despite its link to stability and prosperity.

I wonder why that . . . you know, the fact that not valuing education is illogical . . . why that wasn't inspiring to Oprah, because it inspires the hell out of me.

Some people see obstacles where a bitch sees a challenge.

Reaction #3–Enough with the star fucking . . .
Lawd have mercy. A bitch had to work hard to avoid all the celebrity hair flipping, serious face contorting whilst searching for the perfect quotable sorta-deep thought associated with the media blitz that was the Grand Opening of Oprah's Leadership Academy in South Africa.

Don't get me wrong . . . go on with your bad self, Oprah . . . but daaaaaaaaaammmmmmmn!

It's a school, right?

Just checking . . . because y'all are behaving as if it is a shrine.

Finally a bitch arrived here . . .
A bitch is inspired.

[. . .]

The education of young women, their empowerment, the development of leadership skills and the demonstration of what it takes to make that shit happen . . . that's what's on the table here.

A bitch happens to think that's a good thing (wink).

[. . .]

posted by Shark-fu at 12:40 PM

PAMELA MERRITT ■ ANGRYBLACKBITCH
http://angryblackbitch.blogspot.com/

AngryBlackBitch, also known as Shark-fu, is Pamela Merritt, age thirty-four. She grew up in St. Louis, Missouri, and lives there now, where she does marketing and sales for an independent newspaper. The "About Me" section of her blog is practically empty, in part on the advice of her family. The blog, she says, "seems to inspire extremes—racist responses, conservative backlash, cheers, and requests."

A coworker set up the blog for her as a birthday present. On February 10, 2005, she began her first post thus: "Okay, so after years of refusing to join the blogger world I am now drinking the Kool-Aid." Her blog name developed over time. "I often refer to myself as a bitch in conversation and started to incorporate it into my writing. For several months I played around with only using variations of it . . . *a bitch* and *this bitch*, but never *I*."

Her readers are "feminists, conservatives interested in a real debate, antiwar advocates, soldiers stationed abroad, Canadians (lots of Canadians), women of color, gays and lesbians, and a lot of moms who knit (even though I don't knit . . . I just think knitters dig me)." She reports that she is "currently pulling my Afro out writing my first book (nonfiction)," a modern interpretation of Thomas Paine's *Common Sense* from "a bitchitude perspective."

BECKER-POSNER BLOG

http://www.becker-posner-blog.com/

Is Sex Selection of Births Undesirable?

Becker

In China in 2005, 118 boys were born for every 100 girls born. This ratio is far above the normal biological ratio of about 106 boys to 100 girls. The sexual disparity in China has resulted from a combination of low birth rates, a preference in China for boys when parents only have one or two children, and the spread of ultrasound techniques in that country that allow the sex of fetuses to be identified and then aborted if parents do not like the sex. Similar trends have emerged in India and South Korea as well.

More sophisticated and expensive methods permit parents to raise their chances of a male baby even before a woman becomes pregnant. Considered most reliable is a method that involves in vitro fertilization, drugs to stimulate the mother's ovaries, surgery, and other steps. The total cost can exceed $20,000, so this method clearly is only available to richer persons.

Are there good reasons to object to sex selection, either by abortion or more sophisticated methods? On Feb. 1 the Committee on Ethics of the American College of Obstetricians and Gynecologists (the

ACOG) did issue an opinion objecting on the grounds that it is unethical for physicians to participate in sex selection by parents that was based not on potential for sex-linked genetic disorders, but solely on family balancing or personal preferences. This opinion about the ethics of sexual selection applied "regardless of the timing of the selection (i.e., preconception or post conception) or the stage of development of the embryo or fetus."

Such an opinion seems strange in light of the general support by physicians and the Supreme Court of abortions by parents "solely" to satisfy their personal preferences about timing or number of children. What is so different about sex-selected abortions that would lead the ACOG [. . .] to oppose abortions to satisfy parental desires for additional boys or girls while supporting the general right to abortion? The ACOG tries to provide an answer by claiming that sex selection through any method may "ultimately support sexist practices."

It is not clear what the ACOG means by "sexist practices," but all the evidence on sexual preferences in the United States and other richer countries indicates an overwhelming desire for variety—boys and girls—rather than a strong preference for either sex. So sex-selected abortions in these countries is unlikely to have much of an effect on the overall sex ratio, although it would affect the distribution of boys and girls in different families.

I concentrate my remaining discussion on the implications of sex-selected abortions in countries where it raises the number of boys relative to girls. China, South Korea, and other countries have tried to implement control over sex selection by making it illegal to use ultrasound techniques to select the sex of children. However, these regulations are notoriously difficult to implement since doctors may say "congratulations" when an ultrasound test reveals a boy, and remain silent when the fetus is a girl.

[. . .]

One might expect parents who abort fetuses of sexes they do not want to treat their children better than they would otherwise since they now are satisfied with the sexes of their children. In such cases, sex-selected abortions against girls would improve rather than worsen the average treatment of girls since parents would be happier with the girls they have than if they had girls who were not really wanted. It is no surprise, for example, that orphanages in China predominantly have girls (and some handicapped boys), given the preference for boys in the traditional Chinese culture.

What about the overall effects in a society of skewing the sex ratio of births toward boys? The fewer girls who are born presumably would be better off since they would be better educated, and in other ways better treated by parents who want them. This would be reinforced if the effect of sex-selected abortions is to lower the overall birth rate since it is well established that families with fewer children invest more in each one, girls as well as boys.

As children become adults in cohorts with a high ratio of boys, the advantage of girls and women increases since they are scarcer. It is claimed that young women in China are already at a premium as potential mates because strong sex-selection has been going on ever since the one child policy was introduced in the early 1980s. Prior to the spread of ultrasound techniques, sex selection occurred through sending girls to orphanages, neglect, and in some cases even engaging in female infanticide.

To be sure, if the value of girls as wives and girlfriends, and in other ways, rises because they are scarcer, then the value of boys as husbands and boyfriends tends to fall. However, it is not apparent why that should call for policies that prevent sex-selection techniques, unless the interests of men were motivating these policies. To use an analogy, a shift of demand in an economy toward services and away from manufacturing because of a shift in "preferences" toward ser-vices—as has occurred in the United States and other rich countries—

benefits women relative to men since women are more likely to work in services than are men. Yet no one would claim that society should prevent such preferences because they help (indirectly) one sex over another.

The great statistician and biologist R. A. Fisher used a celebrated biological analysis to explain why the sex ratio remains close to 50-50 in non-human species. An economic analysis based on incentives gives results that are related to Fisher's result. An improvement in the position of women due to a decline in the number of girls relative to boys leads to some correction in the sex ratio as parental choices respond in the long run to the more favorable position of girls. If women are in greater demand as wives and in the economy when they are in scarcer supply, some parents will decide that having girls has advantages, possibly through receiving generous bride prices when daughters marry. This would shift "preferences" toward having girls. The long run outcome would not necessarily be the biological natural ratio of a little more boy births than girl births, but it should be closer to that ratio than the current ratios in some Asian countries.

Posted by becker at 06:59 AM

Sex Selection—

Posner's Comment

I have little to add to Becker's convincing discussion. One small point worth noting, however, is a new technology for sex selection, described in an interesting article by Denise Grady in the February 6 *New York Times*. It is called "sperm sorting" and enables male or female sperm to be concentrated in semen, greatly shifting the odds in favor of producing a child of one sex rather than the other. The cost is only $4,000 to $6,000, which is much less than in vitro fertilization, since the "enriched" sperm can simply be inseminated in the woman rather than requiring in vitro fertilization. Sex selection by sperm sorting may actually be cheaper than ultrasound plus abortion, the conventional method; if so, and it comes to dominate, the ethics of sex selection will be separable from the ethics of abortion motivated by sex selection.

The key points that Becker makes, both of which I agree with, are, first, that sex selection by U.S. couples is unlikely to result in an unbalanced sex ratio; and, second, that in countries such as China and India in which there is a strong preference for male offspring, girls will be treated better if sex selection is permitted, since there will be fewer girls born to couples who did not want them. Of course, as there will be fewer girls, period, the net effect on total female utility is unclear: fewer reduces total utility but happier increases it. Since the net effect is uncertain, feminist opponents of sex selection should consider whether, if unwanted girls are born, there are feasible techniques for improving their treatment so that if sex selection is forbidden (assuming that that is feasible—Becker suggests that it is not), there can be reasonable confidence that net female utility will increase rather than decrease.

I also agree with Becker that there is a tendency to self-selection, since as the percentage of girls and women declines, men's demand for them rises, and, observing this, couples will tend to shift their reproductive selection in favor of girls. Since there is no reason why this tendency must overcome a preference for boys, an unbalanced sex ratio could persist indefinitely. But this is unlikely in rapidly developing countries such as China and India. A strong preference for male children tends to be found in societies in which there is a great deal of subsistence agriculture, a weak social insurance system, and a reliance on private violence (as in a revenge culture) to protect personal and property rights; all these factors increase the demand for male children. As these conditions (the first two of which are important in China and

India, and all three of which are important in Iraq, for example) change, the preference diminishes, as we observe in the wealthy societies of Europe and North America, where there is no longer a net preference for having male rather than female children.

[. . .]

The transition to a 50-50 sex ratio, even if inevitable, is likely to take a long time. Suppose at time 1 there is a large excess of male births, followed at time 2 by a dawning recognition that girls are more valuable than had been realized at time 1. Probably time 1 and time 2 will be separated by 20 or 30 years (or more, if there is a "values lag," as I suggested earlier), and so there will be at least one entire adult generation in which the sex ratio is skewed in favor of males. Should countries that face this imbalance worry about it to the extent of taking measures against it? We have a natural experiment, which can help us to answer the question, in societies that permit polygamy. The effect of polygamy (technically polygyny—multiple wives—but polyandry is virtually unknown) is to raise the effective ratio of men to women, since a number of women are removed from the pool available to the non-polygamous men. In a society in which there are 100 men and 100 women, but 10 of the women are married to one of the men, the male-female sex ratio, so far as the rest of the society is concerned, is 99 to 90. The result is to raise the average age of marriage for men and reduce it for women, reduce the percentage of married men and increase the percentage of married women, reduce promiscuity by increasing women's bargaining power, and possibly increase male emigration and female immigration. None of these effects seem likely to harm society seriously as a whole. In contrast, research that I discuss in my book *Sex and Reason* (1992) finds that the low effective male-female sex ratio of the black population in the United States (due largely to abnormally high rates of imprisonment and homicide of young black males) promotes promiscuity because there is more competition among women for men, and reduces the marriage rate and family formation.

In sum, sex selection, at least in favor of males, appears not to have negative external effects. It presumably confers net private benefits (like other preference satisfaction), or otherwise it would not be practiced. (There are no external effects in societies, such as that of the United States, in which sex selection is unbiased.) The case for forbidding it is therefore unconvincing (at least when sex selection is not implemented by abortion, to which there are independent objections) unless it can be shown to create a net decrease in female welfare.

Posted by Richard Posner at 09:54 PM

Gary S. Becker, a Nobel Prize–winning economist, and Richard Posner, a federal circuit judge, started blogging at the end of 2004 to "explore current issues of economics, law, and policy in a dialogic format." They were inspired by the notion of the blogosphere as a marketplace in Friedrich Hayek's sense—a network that "enables the instantaneous pooling (and hence correction, refinement, and amplification) of ideas and opinions, facts and images, reportage and scholarship."

Gary S. Becker, seventy-seven years old, earned his Ph.D. at the University of Chicago in 1955 and taught at Columbia from 1957 to 1968 while also working at the National Bureau of Economic Research. In 1970 he returned to the University of Chicago, where he still teaches today in the department of economics and the Graduate School of Business. For many years he wrote a monthly column for *BusinessWeek*. He was a pioneer in the application of economic thinking to issues traditionally considered the province of sociology: race, crime, and drugs. His influential 1981 book, *A Treatise on the Family*, was expanded and republished in 1991. He won the Nobel Prize in Economics in 1992 and the National Medal of Science in 2000.

Richard Posner, sixty-eight years old, graduated from Harvard Law School and clerked for Justice William J. Brennan, Jr. After government service in the Johnson administration, in 1968 he joined the law faculty at Stanford University, moving to the University of Chicago Law School the following year. In 1981 he became a judge of the U.S. Court of Appeals for the Seventh Circuit, where he remains, while teaching part-time at the University of Chicago Law School. He is a founding editor of *The Journal of Legal Studies* and the *American Law and Economics Review.* Posner has written prolifically on law and economics, and on such topical subjects as the Clinton impeachment and the Bush-Gore election fight in 2000. His most recent books are a seventh edition of his textbook-treatise *Economic Analysis of Law* and *The Little Book of Plagiarism.*

CLICK OPERA

http://imomus.livejournal.com/

MON., AUG. 28, 2006, 10:15 AM

Amigurumi: the slime of empathy

Your first thought on seeing one of the Japanese knitted dolls known as amigurumi might be "Aw, so cute! Hey, honey, look at this!" But, increasingly, experts are coming to see these knitted critters as something much more sinister. And it's precisely in their universal appeal that the danger lies.

The word *ami* comes from the Japanese word for stitch, *amimie. Gurumi* is an affectionate abbreviation of *nuigurumi,* a stuffed doll. Put them together and you get *amigurumi.* And this year, it's the word on Japan's woolen lips.

In the last few months the amigurumi industry has grown to an astounding 57 trillion–yen concern, outstripping even Japan's auto manufacturing sector. But look around the island nation's urban landscapes and you won't find a single amigurumi factory. These creatures are all handmade at home by anonymous crochet fanatics.

With that combination of economic clout and underground manufacture, it's no surprise that the notorious Japanese mafia, the yakuza, has taken an interest in the amigurumi industry. Some commentators believe it's now the sinister crime family who are pulling tight the eyethreads on these adorable teddies and tiny bunnies, using them to spread an ideology of right wing nationalism.

It's not hard to see why an amigurumi makes the perfect fascist trojan horse. Tapping into our most basic mammalian reflexes, the dolls bypass the rational thought control centers of the human brain, stunning our critical capacities and leaving us gasping "Ah ha ha, so cute!" Within seconds of exposure to an amigurumi, even the most intelligent person can become a dolt or, quite frankly, a blithering idiot.

Social psychologists call this phenomenon "the slime of empathy," and their research reveals that underworld powers are using this "slime" to break down personalities and reconstruct them to order.

Flashcard studies in the lab show that homeless people, millionaires, insurance assessors, quantity surveyors and mortuary slab attendants all have the same basic urge to adopt and protect an amigurumi. Given a chance to keep one, less than 1% of experimental subjects were able to refuse, and once they'd accepted the creatures they became extremely reluctant to separate from, discard or destroy them.

It's of little concern to a bank manager with an amigurumi strapped to his wrist that thousands of his customers are defaulting on their loans or stealing money from cash machines using doctored cards. All he cares about is his brown, fuzzy little bundle of empathy. And although he may be quite unaware that it contains a microphone passing his conversations to crime bigwigs, it's likely that he wouldn't care even if he did know. All that concerns him is whether his woolen sparrow "Tori" is hungry for crumbs, or wants a dust bath.

Even if they don't contain transmitters or other surveillance devices, the amigurumis are often coded to transmit ideology through their forms. [. . .] [One] is a two-faced amigurumi, which encourages duplicity. [. . . Another] doll clearly portrays in a positive light the kind of sexual pervert who hangs around children's parks. [. . . A] panda whose eyes are below its mouth [. . .] can only be the spawn of sinister genetic experiments. [. . .] Here's one the colour of right wing novelist Mishima's hair at the time of his attempted coup.

Whatever their theme, the brightly coloured dolls quickly become a habit. "The first amigurumi I saw was a shy negro rabbit in a bikini," confessed one addict, who wished to remain anonymous for this article, but is a homosexual. "I was so taken with it I had to track down who had made it. . . . Now Shinobu and I live together and make the dolls in a back room," he told me, adding, "Please use a false name for Shinobu in your article, or use his real name wearing a false moustache. . . . Hmm, that's a good idea for a doll."

[. . .]

FRI., DEC. 1, 2006, 12:00 AM

Pecha kucha is dead.

You heard me. Dead. Do you really need it spelled out in blood and sperm by a designer with a small but well-connected captive audience, 20 slides, and 20 seconds of slick narrative for each? What do you want, circle jerks and seppuku? Go home, you sick rubbernecking thrillseeker. It's over.

What do you mean, "What's pecha kucha, then?" I am stunned. Have you been wearing earphones all year? Are you one of those Prim Jims who doesn't know what's going on until *Time* magazine calls Mr Jean Snow in to explain it?

That's right, Jean Snow. Cool as jingle bells. Fast as the white stuff. He knows what pecha kucha is even if you don't, Mr Jones. His blog has exactly 470 references to it. He's the man who broke it all down for *Time* and *Metropolis*, way back ... must've been this summer. Went to his first pecha kucha night in October 2005. Of course,

PingMag were there from May 2005. No moss on those rolling stones.

Who's cooler than Snow and the Pings? Only Astrid Klein and Mark Dytham, Tokyo-based architects, really. They're so cool that they actually invented pecha kucha, back in 2003. It was a way to fill their Roppongi club, SuperDeluxe. I used to go there before pecha kucha existed, and I can tell you, there was just tumbleweed in that basement back then. Tumbleweed, crickets and a couple of blokes with rucksacks drinking Australian organic beer.

Pecha kucha changed all that. Now, on the last Wednesday of each month, there's just wall-to-wall fitted designers, and some guy at the front impressing the hell out of everyone. It's better than karaoke, because you speak instead of singing, and instead of some stupid video

of a girl wandering along a beach there are still pictures of products you can buy, or people in Mongolia showing you some really nice stickers on their cellphones.

The name comes from the Japanese phrase for the sound of people chattering. Pecha kucha, pecha kucha, pecha kucha—say it a few times, say it with friends, and it really will sound like conversation (but passersby will think you're an Ayurvedic sect). It's based on Show and Tell, and the *mukokuseki* [nationless] diasporans like to think of it as really Japanese, but actually nobody at Japanese schools does Show and Tell. It's just too individualistic, too Me-Me-Me.

[...]

Pecha kucha spread like bird flu. Which means that not

many people died of it, but it turned up everywhere. There are now pecha kucha nights in London, New York, Rotterdam, Berlin ... wherever there are unemployed designers desperate for an audience, in fact.

[...]

Have I ever been to a pecha kucha night? Jesus god no. I have better things to do with my time. (Although I've just spent six hours trying to come up with a theme

that would link the photos you see on this page. I couldn't think of one.) Anyway, didn't I mention that the whole thing was dead? But here's what my spy says. My spy is James Goggin, the designer who made my lovely Ocky sleeve. I've made him sound fashionably negative by cutting out all the positive things he said. He'll thank me for that eventually.

[...] "You provide your slides a week beforehand, they get them all in order along with professional little jazzy type animations announcing the next speaker as interstitial 'stings' (this really does give the impression now that pecha kucha is becoming more a branded franchise than an informal get-together or 'happening').

"I completely got the timing all mixed up in spite of my practising. Partly because I attempted to condense my hour-long [. . .] pop culture colour-theory lecture into the allotted 6 minutes . . . I belatedly realised that trying to relay the story of Apple's rainbow logo possibly being a homage to persecuted government scientist and godfather of modern computing Alan Turing, who killed himself by taking a bite from an apple injected with strychnine, into a single 20-second slide doesn't work. [. . .]"

I'll spare you the gory details of the sad, ugly, bloody death of pecha kucha. It's weepy, pants-round-the-ankles stuff. Just take my word for it: the whole thing was stone cold by August 32nd. But *The New York Times* will still make "Pecha Kucha" its Word of the Year. Just as soon as someone mails them twenty slides and a cassette tape about it.

This blog entry is also available as a pecha kucha presentation (mono mp3 file, 1.4MB, 2 mins, 58 secs).

The year in (anything but) music

If music didn't exactly die in 2006, it certainly felt sidelined, jilted, demoted, decentred, dethroned as the exemplary creative activity, the most vibrant subculture. Even the days of new movements like Freak Folk and new messiahs like Devendra Banhart felt far away and a million years ago. From where I stand (and I'm not standing here by accident), visual culture now occupies the central position music once did. I don't just say that because art fairs are booming, because art has become a better investment even than property, or because I spent three months as a performance artist and got gigs in as many galleries as rock venues. The signs are all around us.

It was the year when the megalithic mastodons of music toppled. Institutions like Tower Records and *Top of the Pops* crumbled and fell. David Bowie, whose 1972 *TOTP* appearance changed my life as it changed many others', crowned his year with a comedy song on the Ricky Gervais show *Extras*. And the death of Ivor Cutler, a staple of the John Peel show, reminded us again that the central pole of UK alternapop's big top still hadn't been adequately replaced, and perhaps never would be.

Meanwhile, new institutions came along to replace the old mastodons. Web 2.0 brought us YouTube and MySpace, which became the way most of us discovered and shared new music, and relived old. If someone mentioned a band, YouTube was the place I went first to hear their music. I even released a couple of YouTube singles myself. [. . .] Note, again, in the YouTube-ization of music, the sly upstaging of audio by visual content.

MySpace (which I refuse to have a presence on, but can't avoid consulting) continued the "famous for 15 people" trend. It was here we discovered new acts like No Bra [. . .] or Nobuko Hori or Joe Howe aka Germlin. [. . .]

Other friends, seeming to recognize the crisis in music, pushed at the boundaries, or the exit: Toog made a record using a bird as the main artist and threatened to do the same next time with a tree. Meanwhile Anne Laplantine gave up music to play Go, like Duchamp quitting art for chess. I completely understand Anne's decision. 2006 was the year I decided that roomtone was preferable to the endless flow of iTunes muzak.

[. . .]

When things are dead you spend a lot of time at the museum; I got interested in Enka, Cambodian Khmer cassette pop, Nyahbinghi reggae, and rediscovered the great Jake Thackray thanks to a brace of BBC 4 documentaries. There was also an outbreak of what I call epigone pop in the form of some shameless coffin-snatching by Charlotte Gainsbourg, who enlisted the usual suspects to pastiche her dead dad's style.

The death of Syd Barrett made one wonder whether the switched-on art student wouldn't have skipped straight to painting if he'd been born in 1980. [...]

My favourite new guitar band of 2006 was New Humans. But is "guitar band" really the right term for a project which "began out of bassist Mika Tajima's art practice and continues to be a large part of her investigation of space and minimalist concepts"?

The art world also seemed to annex the best pop music when Björk disappeared into the belly of whale-boyfriend Matthew Barney's new film, *Drawing Restraint 9*. Who knows if she'll ever re-emerge, and, when she does, whether there will even be such a thing as pop music left for her to cling to. [...]

Well, at least we still have eyes.

FRIDAY JAN. 19, 2007, 12:19 PM

Sturm und Drang

As the whole of Germany braced last night for the huge winter storm known here as Orkan Kyrill, I became fascinated with the live television coverage of the gusting winds (over 200 km/h on the north coasts) and heavy rain. First of all, I noticed how it took a local event of this magnitude to feel I was actually in Germany at all (I'm usually mentally in Japan, the UK or the US, selected parts of the city of Berlin, the internet). Secondly, I noticed the silly way all the reporters—mostly icily sexy blond mädchen—were shouting into big

fuzzy mic shields like enormous ruffling caterpillars, their hair flying out behind them. As the wind buffeted them, each in turn struggled, live on camera, to stay alive. There was something of Munch's *The Scream* about it all. But, in contrast to their usual icy reports on meetings at the Finanzministerium, this storm seemed to be flushing the mädchen with an unwonted élan vital. Next I noticed that the flat and banal quality of television video was being transformed, by wind and rain and water on the lens, into something else, something more exciting and artistic, a kind of radical subjectivity that harked back, perhaps, to something in Germany's 18th century past: the movement known as Sturm und Drang—storm and stress. Yes, this natural cataclysm seemed to be bringing something out in these "emergency girls": they seemed to be reaching back to the Geniezeit, the "era of genius"—that part of the German soul best encapsulated in the writings of young Goethe and Schiller. One of the reporters was even called Anke Genius! The Literary Encyclopaedia describes the Storm and Stress sensibility thus:

> In a nutshell, the central concepts of Sturm und Drang are ecstasy of emotion and passion; boundless affirmation of nature; the idolisation of the unique, creative and all-powerful individual (the "genius", the "Faustian" personality); the veneration of art as gospel, i.e., as creation of the genius. [...]

A radical subjectivity, a derangement of the senses, a sense of impending crisis, an awe in nature, a fascination with death—it was all there. Feeling my own genius rising up in me like a storm, I opened up iMovie and set shots of the "Sturm und Drang girls" to one of my own compositions, "I Refuse To Die".

We're all the weakest link, so . . . hello!

I had a couple of beers in Mitte last night with a friend visiting from London: a rather well-known design writer I'll call Mr X. There's

no reason to be so mysterious, really, except that sometimes social critique can become institutional critique and institutional critique can sour the milk and foul the nest.

Mr X and I are about the same age and share pretty much the same politics, so we spent most of our time agreeing. I want to sketch the substance of that consensus today, without really attributing too closely which of us said what—another reason not to name him, I suppose.

Mr X is a bit of a champion of my writing, and he started, as we walked through the gusty, mild evening towards ProQM, by asking whether my new album had been reviewed in the *Wire*. I told him it hadn't—none of my records ever have—and that I don't know why, really. Mr X was also curious about why my writing never appears in British newspapers or magazines, and again I couldn't answer other than say that, for some reason, only French and American publishers seem to want to publish me. I suppose this conversation, and the slight sense of perplexed hurt it triggered in me, set the tone for the evening.

[. . .]

We ended up sipping weissbier in the lobby of the Kino Hackescher Hof in Mitte. We talked about how little interest there is, in mainstream British culture, in design per se.

[. . .]

I ventured that this was partly because of bling culture: a lot of cultural coverage in the UK is really coverage of money, power and class in disguise. The super-rich invest in fine art and fashion, architecture and interior decoration, so those get covered as extensions of celebrity culture and the celebration of extreme concentrations of power and wealth (sometimes inaccurately called "aspirational" journalism). Graphic design has no bling angle, so it simply doesn't get covered. And yet in Italy or Japan (or Berlin, for that matter) things are different: the inherent loveliness of posters, flyers, graffiti, illustrations and so on seems prized, and there's commentary about it.

We agreed that a radical series like John Berger's *Ways of Seeing* couldn't really be made now in the UK. There isn't the same kind of strong ideology in either programme-makers or the audience for it. Which isn't to say that ideology is dead: far from it. British TV seems to be obsessed with the ideology of Social Darwinism. Shows like *Big Brother* and *The Weakest Link* are all about the elimination of losers, and involve their audiences in the choice of those losers. It's all very tally ho, a fox hunt. They're the result of the transformation of Britain from a society that was at least heading towards horizontality (in other words, low-Gini [Gini is a measure of income inequality]) in the 60s and 70s to one that's wedded at every level to inequality, unfairness, high-Gini—a "winner takes it all" society where income inequality is seen as something natural and even desirable.

Here in Germany you could never have shows as Social Darwinist as that, I ventured, because there really was the elimination of "the weakest link" here, within living memory, in the form of the extermination of gays, gypsies and Jews. In the same way, the surveillance excesses of the East German secret police have made it much harder to survey Germans. Britain's ubiquitous citizen surveillance would be unacceptable here.

And this, for me, is why guilt is good. It's guilt over things like surveillance and eliminating "the weakest link" which keeps the German state more liberal and benign than the UK state. It's lack of guilt that's the biggest current political problem in Israel, the UK and the US, and evidence of the return of guilt the most hopeful thing happening right now. [. . .]

Mr X thinks that etiquette, decency, fairness and good manners in Britain are in decline. I agree, but point out that anti-racism, for instance, is a new sort of etiquette. [. . .] But in general, I think, the problem with maintaining etiquette is that racial diversity and income disparity (along with declining social mobility) make it very hard to treat your neighbour as you'd like to be treated yourself. Income disparity is always justified with the carrot of opportunity—treat the rich as you'd like to be treated if you were as rich—hell, when you are as rich as them! But that illusion is hardly sustainable in the UK, unless you think you're going to win the lottery. So instead people bitch, and hate, and stick the knife in, and rob.

Of course, I contrast the UK with Japan, which may be heading in the same direction but is still massively more horizontal than the

UK, and has avoided the bitching, hating, knifing-and-robbing stuff so far. But I can't help wondering, as I bid Mr X farewell and head home past the posters for the new Hitler comedy, whether it isn't just that Japan has pre-eliminated its weakest links by never actually admitting anybody poor or racially other into the country in the first place?

Born in Paisley, Scotland, in 1960, Nick Currie has been making pop records under the name Momus (the Greek god of criticism) for two decades. He studied literature in Aberdeen and London. In 1981 he founded The Happy Family, a pop group including three ex-members of the Postcard Records group Josef K. Their first record, *The Man on Your Street*, was, in Currie's words, "a Brechtian concept album about a fascist dictator and the Red Brigades." In 1989 his single "The Hairstyle of the Devil" reached number two on the independent singles chart.

In 1999 Momus established his own label, Analog Baroque Records. (The four elements of the "analog baroque" style, in his description, are harpsichords, brevity, analog synthesizers, and wit.) In 2000 he made a documentary about the Manhattan art and music scene and a CD of pseudoethnological fieldwork called *Fakeways: Manhattan Folk*. In 2002 he moved to Tokyo and worked on a commission for the Museum of Contemporary Art, Los Angeles, a Flash piece for their online digital gallery about "a utopia where words are replaced by texture, color, and pure sound."

Momus, now forty-seven, has lived in Edinburgh, Athens, Montreal, London, Paris, New York, Tokyo, and Berlin, his current home. Some of his past admitted influences: Rabelais, Martial, Matthew Barney, and Stanley Kubrick. He writes a regular column for *Wired News* and has a sideline as a performance artist, telling stories in galleries and museums. He wears an eye patch because of an infection of amoebic keratitis caught from a contact lens.

COSMIC VARIANCE

http://cosmicvariance.com/

The universe is structured like a language

POSTED BY SEAN ON 22 MAY 2006 @ 17:53

A little while ago I went to see *Žižek!* a new documentary about charismatic and controversial Slovenian philosopher and cultural critic Slavoj Žižek. Part of the Žižekian controversy can be traced straightforwardly to his celebrity—not hard to get fellow academics ornery when you're greeted by admiring throngs at each of your talks (let me tell you)—but there is also his propensity for acting in ways that are judged to be somewhat frivolous: frequent references to pop culture, an unrestrained delight in telling jokes. I was fortunate enough to see Žižek in person, as part of a panel discussion following the film. He is a compelling figure, effortlessly outshining the two standard-issue academics flanking him on the panel. He adamantly insists that he had no control over the documentary of which he was the subject, indeed that he hasn't even seen it, but then reveals that a number of important scenes were admittedly his idea. In one example, the camera lingers on a striking portrait of Stalin in his apartment, which the cinematic Žižek explains as a litmus test, a way of interrogating the bourgeois sensibilities of his visitors. The flesh-and-blood Žižek, meanwhile, points out that it was just a joke, and that he would never have something so horrible as a portrait of Stalin on his wall. It ties into his notion that a film will never reveal the true person behind the scholar or public figure, nor should it; the ideas will stand or fall by themselves, separate from their personification in an actual human. I have no educated opinion about his standing as a thinker; see John Holbo, Adam Kotsko [. . .], or Kieran Healy for some opinions, or read [the] interview in *The Believer* and judge for yourself.

The movie opens with a Žižek monologue on the origin of the universe and the meaning of life. We can talk all we like, he says, about love and meaning and so on, but that's not what is real. The universe is "monstrous" (one of his favorite words), a mere accident. "It means something went terribly wrong," as you can hear him say through a distinctive lisp in this clip from the movie. He even invokes quantum fluctuations, proclaiming that the universe arose as a "cosmic catastrophe" out of nothing.

I naturally cringed a little at the mention of quantum mechanics, but his description ultimately got it right. Our universe probably did originate as a quantum fluctuation, either "from nothing" or within a pre-existing background spacetime. Mostly, to be honest, I was just jealous. As a philosopher and cultural critic, Žižek gets not only to bandy about bits of quantum cosmology, but is permitted (even encouraged) to connect them to questions of love and meaning and so on. As professional physicists, we're not allowed to talk about those questions—referees at the *Physical Review* would not approve. But it's worth interrogating this intellectual leap, from the accidental birth of the universe to the richness of meaning we see around us. How did we get there from here, and why?

It's the possibility of addressing this question that I take to be the most significant aspect of the "computational quantum universe" idea advocated by Seth Lloyd in his new book *Programming the Universe*.

Lloyd is a somewhat controversial figure in his own right, but undoubtedly an influential physicist; he was the first to propose a plausible design for a quantum computer—i.e., a computer that takes advantage of the full quantum-mechanical wavefunction of its elements, rather than being content with the ordinary classical states.

To Lloyd, quantum computation is a hammer, and it's tempting to see everything interesting as a nail—from black holes to quantum gravity to the whole universe. The frustrating aspect of his book is the frequency with which he insists that "the universe is a quantum computer," without always making it clear just what that means or why we should care. What is the universe supposed to be computing, anyway? Its own evolution, apparently.

[...]

My own personal reconstruction of the problem that Lloyd is suggesting we might be able to solve by thinking of the universe as a quantum computer, although in slightly different words, is precisely that raised by Žižek's monologue: Why, in the course of evolving from the early universe to the end of time, do we pass through a phase featuring the fascinating and delightful complexity we see all around us?

Let's be more specific about what that means. The early universe—at least, the hot Big Bang with which our observable universe began—is a very low-entropy state. That is, it's a very unlikely configuration in the space of all the ways one could arrange the universe—much like having all of the air molecules accidentally be located in one half of a room (although much worse). But entropy is increasing as the universe evolves, just like the Second Law of Thermodynamics says it should. The late universe will be very high-entropy. In particular, if the universe continues to expand forever (which seems likely, although one never knows), we are evolving toward heat death, in which matter cools down and is dispersed thinly over space after black holes form and evaporate. This is a "natural" state for the universe, one which will essentially stay that way in perpetuity.

However. While the early universe is low-entropy and the late universe is high-entropy, both phases are simple. That is, their macro-states can be described in very few words (they have low Kolmogorov complexity): the early state was hot and dense and smoothly distributed, while the final state will be cold and dilute and smoothly distributed. But our current universe, replete as it is with galaxies and planets and blogospheres, isn't at all simple; it's remarkably complex. There are individual subsystems (like you and me) that would require quite a lengthy description to fully specify.

So: Why is it like that? [...]

Lloyd's suggested answer, to the extent that I understand it, arises from the classic thought experiment of the randomly typing monkeys. A collection of monkeys, randomly pecking at keyboards, will eventually write the entire text of *Hamlet*—but it will take an extremely long time, much much longer than the age of the observable universe. For that matter, it will take a very long time to get any "interesting" string of characters. Lloyd argues that the situation is quite different if we allow the monkeys to randomly construct algorithms rather than mere strings of text; in particular, the likelihood that such an algorithm will produce interesting (complex) output is much greater than the chance of randomly generating an interesting string. [...]

So the force of the idea that "the universe is a quantum computer" lies in an understanding of the origin of complexity. Think of the different subsystems of the universe, existing in slightly different arrangements, running different quantum algorithms. It is much easier for such subsystems to generate complex output computationally than one might guess from an estimate of the likelihood of hitting upon complexity by randomly choosing configurations directly. [...]

Of course I don't really know if any of this is true or interesting. [...] But big ideas are fun, and concepts like entropy and complexity are far from completely understood, so perhaps it's permissible to let our imaginations run a little freely here.

The reason why this discussion of quantum computation and the complexity of the universe fits comfortably with the story of Žižek is that he should understand this (if he doesn't already). Žižek is a Lacanian, a disciple of famous French psychoanalyst Jacques Lacan. Lacan was a similarly controversial figure, although his charisma manifested itself as taciturn impenetrability rather than voluble popular appeal. One of Lacan's catchphrases was "the unconscious is structured like a language." Which I take (not having any idea what I am talking about) as a claim that the unconscious is not simply a formless chaos of mysterious impulses; rather, it has an architecture, a grammar, rules of operation much like those of our higher-level consciousness.

One way of summarizing Lloyd's explanation of the origin of complexity might be: the universe is structured like a language. It is not just a random configuration of particles typed out by tireless monkeys; it is a quantum computer, following the rules of its algorithms. And by following these rules the universe manages to generate configurations of enormous complexity. Examples of which include science, poetry, love, meaning, and all of those aspects of human life that lend it more interest than we attach to other chemical reactions.

Of course, it's only a temporary condition. From featureless simplicity we came, and to featureless simplicity we will return. Like a skier riding the moguls, eventually we'll reach the bottom of the hill, and dissolve into thermal equilibrium. It's up to us to enjoy the ride.

The Cash Value of Astronomical Ideas

POSTED BY SEAN ON 16 AUGUST 2006 @ 16:13

Can't . . . stop . . . blogging . . . must . . . resist . . .

So you may have heard that Pluto is still a planet, and indeed we have a few new ones as well! Phil Plait, Rob Knop, Clifford [Johnson], and Steinn [Sigurdsson] have all weighed in. Hey, it's on the front page of *The New York Times*, above the fold!

The problem is that Pluto is kind of small and far away. Those aren't problems by themselves, but there are lots of similar-sized objects that are also out beyond Neptune, in the Kuiper Belt. As we discover more and more, should they all count as planets? And if not, shouldn't Pluto be demoted? Nobody wants to lose Pluto among the family of planets—rumors to that effect were previously enough to inspire classrooms around the globe to write pleading letters to the astronomical powers that be, begging them not to discard the plucky ninth planet. But it's really hard to come up with some objective criteria of planet-ness that would include the canonical nine but not open the doors to all sorts of unwanted interlopers. Now the Planet Definition Committee of the International Astronomical Union has proposed a new definition:

> 1) A planet is a celestial body that (a) has sufficient mass for its self-gravity to overcome rigid body forces so that it assumes a hydrostatic equilibrium (nearly round) shape, and (b) is in orbit around a star, and is neither a star nor a satellite of a planet.

It turns out that, by this proposed definition, there are twelve planets—not just the usual nine, but also Ceres (the largest asteroid, between Mars and Jupiter), and also Charon (Pluto's moon, but far enough away that apparently it doesn't count as a "satellite," but as a double-planet), and UB313, a faraway rock that is even bigger than Pluto. I'm not sure why anyone thinks this is an improvement.

The thing is, it doesn't matter. Most everyone who writes about it admits that it doesn't matter, before launching into a passionate defense of what they think the real definition should be. But, seriously:

It really doesn't matter. We are not doing science, or learning anything about the universe here. We're just making up a definition, and we're doing so solely for our own convenience. There is no pre-existing Platonic nature of planet-ness located out there in the world, which we are trying to discover so that we may bring our nomenclature in line with it. We are not discovering anything new about nature, nor even bringing any reality into existence by our choices.

The Pragmatists figured this out long ago: we get to choose the definition to be whatever we want, and the best criterion by which to make that choice is whatever is most useful and convenient for our purposes. But people have some deep-seated desire to believe that our words should be brought in line with objective criteria, even if it's dramatically inconvenient. (These are the same people, presumably, who think that spelling reform would be really cool.) But as Rob says, there is no physically reasonable definition that would let us stick with nine planets. That's okay! We have every right to define *planet* to mean "Mercury, Venus, Earth, Mars, Jupiter, Saturn, Uranus, Neptune, and Pluto, plus whatever other large rocky bodies we find orbiting other stars." Or whatever else we want. It's completely up to us.

So we really shouldn't have to tear up a century's worth of textbooks and illustrations, and start trying to figure out when the shape of some particular body is governed by hydrostatic equilibrium, just to pat ourselves on the back for obeying "physically reasonable" definitions. But it looks like that's what the IAU Planet Definition Committee wants us to do. Of course that's what you'd expect a Planet Definition Committee to suggest; otherwise why would we need a Planet Definition Committee?

Now if you'll excuse me, I have change-of-address forms to fill out.

[. . .]

Dark Matter Exists

POSTED BY SEAN ON 21 AUGUST 2006 @ 11:52

The great accomplishment of late-twentieth-century cosmology was putting together a complete inventory of the universe. We can tell a story that fits all the known data, in which ordinary matter (every particle ever detected in any experiment) constitutes only about 5% of the energy of the universe, with 25% being dark matter and 70% being dark energy. The challenge for early-twenty-first-century cosmology will actually be to understand the nature of these mysterious dark components.

A beautiful new result illuminating (if you will) the dark matter in galaxy cluster 1E 0657-56 is an important step in this direction. [. . .]

A prerequisite to understanding the dark sector is to make sure we are on the right track. Can we be sure that we haven't been fooled into believing in dark matter and dark energy? After all, we only infer their existence from detecting their gravitational fields; stronger-than-expected gravity in galaxies and clusters leads us to posit dark matter, while the acceleration of the universe (and the overall geometry of space) leads us to posit dark energy. Could it perhaps be that gravity is modified on the enormous distance scales characteristic of these phenomena? Einstein's general theory of relativity does a great job of accounting for the behavior of gravity in the Solar System and astrophysical systems like the binary pulsar, but might it be breaking down over larger distances?

A departure from general relativity on very large scales isn't what one would expect on general principles. In most physical theories that we know and love, modifications are expected to arise on small scales (higher energies), while larger scales should behave themselves. But, we have to keep an open mind—in principle it's absolutely possible that gravity could be modified, and it's worth taking seriously.

Furthermore, it would be really cool. Personally, I would prefer to explain cosmological dynamics using modified gravity instead of dark matter and dark energy, just because it would tell us something qualitatively different about how physics works. (And Vera Rubin agrees.) We would all love to out-Einstein Einstein by coming up with a better theory of gravity. But our job isn't to express preferences, it's to suggest hypotheses and then go out and test them.

The problem is, how do you test an idea as vague as "modifying general relativity"? You can imagine testing specific proposals for how gravity should be modified, like Milgrom's MOND [Modification of Newtonian Dynamics], but in more general terms we might worry that any observations could be explained by some modification of gravity.

But it's not quite so bad—there are reasonable features that any respectable modification of general relativity ought to have. Specifically, we expect that the gravitational force should point in the direction of its source, not off at some bizarrely skewed angle. So if we imagine doing away with dark matter, we can safely predict that gravity will always be pointing in the direction of the ordinary matter. That's interesting but not immediately helpful, since it's natural to expect that the ordinary matter and dark matter cluster in the same locations; even if there is dark matter, it's no surprise to find the gravitational field pointing toward the visible matter as well.

What we really want is to take a big cluster of galaxies and simply sweep away all of the ordinary matter. Dark matter, by hypothesis, doesn't interact directly with ordinary matter, so we can imagine moving the ordinary stuff while leaving the dark stuff behind. If we then check back and determine where the gravity is, it should be pointing either at the left-behind dark matter (if there is such a thing) or still at the ordinary matter (if not).

Happily, the universe has done exactly this for us. In the Bullet Cluster, more formally known as 1E 0657-56, we actually find two clusters of galaxies that have (relatively) recently passed right through each other. It turns out that the large majority (about 90%) of ordinary matter in a cluster is not in the galaxies themselves, but in hot X-ray-emitting intergalactic gas. As the two clusters passed through each other, the hot gas in each smacked into the gas in the other, while the individual galaxies and the dark matter (presumed to be collisionless) passed right through. [...] As hinted at in last week's NASA media advisory, astrophysicists led by Doug Clowe (Arizona) and Maxim Markevitch (CfA) [Center for Astrophysics] have now compared images of the gas obtained by the Chandra X-ray telescope to "maps" of the gravitational field deduced from weak lensing observations. Their short paper is astro-ph/0608407, and a longer one on lensing is astro-ph/0608408. And the answer is: there's definitely dark matter there!

It's still quite possible that the acceleration of the universe can be explained by modifying gravity rather than invoking a mysterious new dark component. One of our next tasks, then, is obviously to come up with experiments that might distinguish between dark energy and modified gravity—and some of us are doing our best. Stay tuned, as darkness gradually encroaches upon our universe, and Einstein continues to have the last laugh.

Sean Carroll, forty-one years old, is a theoretical physicist at the California Institute of Technology, where he works on dark matter and dark energy, the physics of inflationary cosmology, modifications of Einstein's general relativity, and the origin of time asymmetry. Carroll received his Ph.D. in Astrophysics from Harvard in 1993 and did post-doctoral research at MIT. His lecture notes from a course he taught there on general relativity were later expanded into the textbook *Space-time and Geometry: An Introduction to General Relativity* (Addison-Wesley, 2003). In 2003, inspired by the blog then kept by Michael Bérubé, a literature professor, Carroll started his own blog, Preposterous Universe.

In 2005 Carroll joined four other theoretical physicists to launch a group blog, Cosmic Variance. Among physics blogs, he says, it is the largest, with the most links on the Internet. On a typical day the site gets about three thousand visits—from students, researchers, physicists, journalists, and plain old people who want to read about cosmology and gravity. That, he admits, is tiny compared to the one hundred thousand hits of the big politics and technology blogs, but it's a lot bigger than the audience for a cosmology paper in *Phys. Rev. D.*

In a post in November 2006 titled "Love and Blogging," Carroll announced that he had gotten engaged to another science blogger, the woman behind Cocktail Party Physics. Carroll, according to his fiancée, "is nothing if not romantic." She wrote that while they were looking at the waves at sunset on the Pacific coast "he put his arms around me and whispered, 'Wouldn't it be fascinating to take a Fourier transform of those waves?' "

DIARY OF SAMUEL PEPYS

http://www.pepysdiary.com/

WEDNESDAY 23 MAY 1660

[. . .] [W]e weighed anchor, and with a fresh gale and most happy weather we set sail for England. All the afternoon the King walked here and there, up and down (quite contrary to what I thought him to have been), very active and stirring. Upon the quarterdeck he fell into discourse of his escape from Worcester, where it made me ready to weep to hear the stories that he told of his difficulties that he had passed through, as his travelling four days and three nights on foot, every step up to his knees in dirt, with nothing but a green coat and a pair of country breeches on, and a pair of country shoes that made him so sore all over his feet, that he could scarce stir. [. . .] Then the difficulty of getting a boat to get into France, where he was fain to plot with the master thereof to keep his design from the four men and a boy (which was all his ship's company), and so got to Fecamp in France. At Rouen he looked so poorly, that the people went into the rooms before he went away to see whether he had not stole something or other. [. . .] About bed-time my Lord Bartlett (who I had offered my service to before) sent for me to get him a bed, who with much ado I did get to bed to my Lord Middlesex in the great cabin below, but I was cruelly troubled before I could dispose of him, and quit myself of him. So to my cabin again, where the company still was, and were talking more of the King's difficulties; as how he was fain to eat a piece of bread and cheese out of a poor boy's pocket; how, at a Catholique house, he was fain to lie in the priest's hole a good while in the house for his privacy. After that our company broke up, and the Doctor and I to bed. We have all the Lords Commissioners on board us, and many others. Under sail all night, and most glorious weather.

FRIDAY 25 MAY 1660

By the morning we were come close to the land, and every body made ready to get on shore. The King and the two Dukes did eat their breakfast before they went, and there being set some ship's diet before them, only to show them the manner of the ship's diet, they eat of nothing else but pease and pork, and boiled beef. [. . .] Great expectation of the King's making some Knights, but there was none. About noon (though the brigantine that Beale made was there ready to carry him) yet he would go in my Lord's barge with the two Dukes. Our Captain steered, and my Lord went along bare with him. I went, and Mr. Mansell, and one of the King's footmen, with a dog that the King loved, (which [dirted] the boat, which made us laugh, and me think that a King and all that belong to him are but just as others are), in a boat by ourselves, and so got on shore when the King did, who was received by General Monk with all imaginable love and respect at his entrance upon the land of Dover. [. . .]

FRIDAY 9 JANUARY 1663

Waking in the morning, my wife I found also awake, and begun to speak to me with great trouble and tears, and by degrees from one discourse to another at last it appears that Sarah has told somebody that has told my wife of my meeting her at my brother's and making her sit down by me while she told me stories of my wife, about her giving her scallop [a scallop-shaped lace band on a dress] to her brother, and other things, which I am much vexed at, for I am sure I never spoke any thing of it, nor could any body tell her but by Sarah's own words. I endeavoured to excuse my silence herein hitherto by not believing any thing she told me, only that of the scallop which she herself told me of. At last we pretty good friends, and my wife begun to speak again of the necessity of her keeping somebody to bear her company; for her familiarity with her other servants is it that spoils them all, and other company she hath none, which is too true, and called for Jane to reach her out of her trunk, giving her the keys to that purpose, a bundle of papers, and pulls out a paper, a copy of what, a pretty while since, she had wrote in a discontent to me. [. . .] She now read it, and it was so piquant, and wrote in English, and most of it true, of the retiredness of her life, and how unpleasant it was; that being wrote in English, and so in danger of being met with and read by others, I was vexed at it, and desired her and then commanded her to tear it. When she desired to be excused it, I forced it from her, and tore it, and withal took her other bundle of papers from her, and leapt out of the bed and in my shirt clapped them into the pocket of my breeches, that she might not get them from me, and having got on my stockings and breeches and gown, I pulled them out one by one and tore them all before her face, though it went against my heart to do it, she crying and desiring me not to do it, but such was my passion and trouble to see the letters of my love to her, and my Will wherein I had given her all I have in the world, when I went to sea with my Lord Sandwich, to be joyned with a paper of so much disgrace to me and dishonour, if it should have been found by any body. Having torn them all, saving a bond of my uncle Robert's, which she hath long had in her hands, and our marriage license, and the first letter that ever I sent her when I was her servant, I took up the pieces and carried them into my chamber, and there, after many disputes with myself whether I should burn them or no, and having picked up, the pieces of the paper she read to-day, and of my Will which I tore, I burnt all the rest, and so went out to my office troubled in mind. Hither comes Major Tolhurst, one of my old acquaintance in Cromwell's time, and sometimes of our clubb, to see me, and I could do no less than carry him to the Mitre, and having sent for Mr. Beane, a merchant, a neighbour of mine, we sat and talked, Tolhurst telling me the manner of their collierys in the north. We broke up, and I home to dinner. And to see my folly, as discontented as I am, when my wife came I could not forbear smiling all dinner till she began to speak bad words again, and then I began to be angry again, and so to my office. Mr. Bland came in the evening to me hither, and sat talking to me about many things of merchandise, and I should be very happy in his discourse, durst I confess my ignorance to him, which is not so fit for me to do. There coming a letter to me from Mr. Pierce, the surgeon, by my desire appointing his and Dr. Clerke's coming to dine with me next Monday, I went to my wife and agreed upon matters, and at last for my honour am forced to make her presently a new Moyre gown to be seen by Mrs. Clerke, which troubles me to part with so much money, but, however, it sets my wife and I to friends again, though I and she never were so heartily angry in our lives as to-day almost, and I doubt the heartburning will not [be] soon over, and the truth is I am sorry for the tearing of so many poor loving letters of mine from sea and elsewhere to her. So to my office again, and there the Scrivener brought me the end of the manuscript which I am going to get together of things of the Navy, which pleases me much. So home, and mighty friends with my wife again, and so to bed.

SUNDAY 28 JUNE 1663

(Lord's day). Early in the morning my last night's physic worked and did give me a good stool, and then I rose and had three or four stools, and walked up and down my chamber. Then up, my maid rose and made me a posset [a drink made of hot milk curdled with wine or ale], and by and by comes Mr. Creed, and he and I spent all the morning discoursing against to-morrow before the Duke the business of his pieces of eight, in which the Treasurer makes so many queries. At noon, my physic having done working, I went down to dinner, and then he and I up again and spent most of the afternoon reading in Cicero and other books of good discourse, and then he went away, and then came my brother Tom to see me. [. . .]

MONDAY 29 JUNE 1663

Up betimes and to my office, and by and by to the Temple, and there appointed to meet in the evening about my business, and thence I walked home, and up and down the streets is cried mightily the great victory got by the Portugalls against the Spaniards, where 10,000 slain, 3 or 4,000 taken prisoners, with all the artillery, baggage, money, &c., and Don John of Austria forced to flee with a man or two with him, which is very great news. Thence home and at my office all the morning, and then by water to St. James's, but no meeting to-day being holy day, but met Mr. Creed in the Park, and after a walk or two, discoursing his business, took leave of him in Westminster Hall, whither we walked, and then came again to the Hall and fell to talk with Mrs. Lane, and after great talk that she never went abroad with any man as she used heretofore to do, I with one word got her to go with me and to meet me at the further Rhenish wine-house, where I did give her a Lobster and do so touse her and feel her all over, making her believe how fair and good a skin she has, and indeed she has a very white thigh and leg, but monstrous fat. When weary I did give over and somebody, having seen some of our dalliance, called aloud in the street, "Sir! why do you kiss the gentlewoman so?" and flung a stone at the window, which vexed me, but I believe they could not see my touzing her, and so we broke up and I went out the back way, without being observed I think, and so she towards the Hall and I to White Hall, where taking water I to the Temple with my cozen Roger and Mr. Goldsborough to Gray's Inn to his counsel, one Mr. Rawworth, a very fine man, where it being the question whether I as executor should give a warrant to Goldsborough in my reconveying her estate back again, the mortgage being performed against all acts of the testator, but only my own, my cozen said he never heard it asked before; and the other that it was always asked, and he never heard it denied, or scrupled before, so great a distance was there in their opinions, enough to make a man forswear ever having to do with the law; so they agreed to refer it to Serjeant Maynard. So we broke up, and I by water home from the Temple, and there to Sir W. Batten and eat with him, he and his lady and Sir J. Minnes having been below to-day upon the East India men that are come in, but never tell me so, but that they have been at Woolwich and Deptford, and done great deal of business. God help them. So home and up to my lute long, and then, after a little Latin chapter with Will, to bed. But I have used of late, since my wife went, to make a bad use of my fancy with whatever woman I have a mind to, which I am ashamed of, and shall endeavour to do so no more. So to sleep.

WEDNESDAY 5 AUGUST 1663

All the morning at the office, whither Deane of Woolwich came to me and discoursed of the body of ships, which I am now going about to understand, and then I took him to the coffee-house, where he was very earnest against Mr. Grant's report in favour of Sir W. Petty's vessel, even to some passion on both sides almost. So to the Exchange, and thence home to dinner with my brother, and in the afternoon to Westminster hall, and there found Mrs. Lane, and by and by by agreement we met at the Parliament stairs (in my way down to the boat who should meet us but my lady Jemimah, who saw me lead her but said nothing to me of her, though I ought to speak to her to see whether she would take notice of it or no) and off to Stangate and so to the King's Head at Lambeth marsh, and had variety of meats and drinks, but I did so towse her and handled her, but could get nothing more from her though I was very near it; but as wanton and bucksome as she is she dares not adventure upon the business, in which I very much commend and like her. Staid pretty late, and so over with her by water, and being in a great sweat with my towsing of her durst not go home by water, but took coach, and at home my brother and I fell upon Des Cartes, and I perceive he has studied him well, and I cannot find but he has minded his book, and do love it. This evening came a letter about business from Mr. Coventry, and with it a silver pen he promised me to carry inke in, which is very necessary. So to prayers and to bed.

SAMUEL PEPYS ■ DIARY OF SAMUEL PEPYS
http://www.pepysdiary.com/

Samuel Pepys (pronounced "peeps"), best known as a diarist, was born in London in 1633, the fifth of eleven children (only three of whom survived into adulthood). He was sent away to grammar school during the English Civil War (1642–1651) and then attended St. Paul's School and Cambridge University. After graduating, he worked as secretary to Edward Montagu, the Earl of Sandwich, who was closely linked with Oliver Cromwell and his son Richard. Pepys married Elizabeth St. Michel. When he started the diary, at age twenty-six, he and Elizabeth were living in London, where Pepys often sampled the city's music and women. (He once wrote that he stood in a "strange slavery" to the beauty of both.)

Pepys, who died in 1703 and whose journal was discovered more than a hundred years later, joined the blogosphere on January 1, 2003, when Phil Gyford, a Web designer and programmer, who worked in the 1990s as a model maker for Aardman Animations (including some work on the Wallace and Gromit movie *A Close Shave*), had the idea of publishing the diaries of Samuel Pepys as a blog. "I thought I'd like to read his diaries, as I live in London, but knew I'd never get 'round to it," said Gyford, who is now thirty-six years old. "It occurred to me that the diary format was virtually identical to Weblogs, and I was surprised to find no one had created a Pepys diary Weblog yet."

EL GUAPO IN DC

El Guapo in DC

I am El Guapo. The most Guapo man in all of DC. Mucho Amor

http://www.elguapodc.blogspot.com/

WEDNESDAY, FEBRUARY 22, 2006

Rumors: Not Guatemalans!

There are evil rumors going around about El Guapo. I'm not sure who is responsible for these rumors, perhaps that cabron Miguel, but I can not pin this solely on him. Not yet anyway.

I've been receiving e-mails. Not the regular e-mails that I receive from you, my amigos, but e-mails offering particular types of services. Services, that although I appreciate the thought of it all, I don't need.

Moments ago I received an e-mail that made me write this post. It was from a nice girl named Areli Farrington. I do not know this woman, but she seems to think that I would benefit from Viagra pills for $3.75 a pill.

Mi amor, perhaps you do not know about me, El Guapo. I am Guatemalan. Does this make you realize the error of your e-mail? Did you perhaps think that I was Argentinean?

If so, please, do not let this error occur again. I beg of you.

As a Guatemalan male, I was blessed by whatever supreme power blessed all Guatemalans with virility. This is a widely known fact. If you go around giving the Viagra pill to Guatemalans I'm afraid that the entire female population in the United States would be overworked by our love making. The women would be too tired to work. Guatemalans do not want the US economy to falter because of our loins. After all, we need to send dinero home!

Argentineans, unfortunately, did not have this same blessing. Guatemalans were given the gift of amazing love making abilities and the Argentineans were given, well, they have nice hair. Their facial hair is lacking what we Guatemalans can offer, but they try. Bless their little hearts.

But El Guapo, surely the Argentineans are very good at something. They are good at soccer, no?

Yes. They are very good at soccer, but only number two, maybe three in Latin America. Argentina will forever be Brazil's little bitch when it comes to soccer. When it comes to love making, they have much learning to do from the Guatemalans. Much learning. Having pretty hair will only get you so far in life. Perhaps Argentineans would be well served to contact Ms. Areli Farrington for some Viagra?

Ms. Farrington, lo siento that your e-mail will not garner you some business, but hopefully you will be able to focus your marketing skills towards the Latin population that needs help. I understand how you got Guatemala confused with Argentina. Those four syllable country names can confuse even the best of us.

Rule of thumb is this: Guatemala starts with "G" and we are GREAT. Argentina starts with "A" and they are Average. Easy no?

Mucho Amor,

El Guapo

Virginia: A little trip con Miguel

"El Guapo. El Guapo, wake up!"

I close my eyes tighter because for some reason I think he'll go away. He doesn't. He never does. Porque? I'll tell you why. Miguel is what they call a bona fide dirty cabron. There he is in all of his unshaven glory to bother me with something that is sure to be a complete waste of my time.

What! Que quieres?

"I'm out of condoms."

Have you ever stared at someone and realized, as you bit the sides of your mouth, that they will never fully understand anything you say to them? Si? God bless him.

I already gave you all my condoms you dirty, dirty son of a goat. I'm out. No tengo mas. What the hell are you doing over there? You're like a machine. Go to CVS.

No way. I'm not going back there anymore. Nunca mas. I can't afford their prices anymore. I'm tired of this El Guapo. I'm spending almost $200 a month. Why are condoms so expensive? Everywhere I go I see the signs about being safe, and HIV, and unwanted pregnancy, and herpes, and this and that, it's such a waste. If the government is so worried about all of these things, why don't they just make it so that condoms are cheaper?

Son of a bitch, Miguel just pretty much described a government subsidy for condoms. For a split segundo, and please trust me when I say that it was just a fleeting moment, I actually thought about telling Miguel about government subsidies. But you know what? This is just too much for him right now.

Miguel, I think it's time that I take you to a place that sells condoms at a better price. Miguel, I'm going to introduce you to Costco.

We got on the blue line at McPherson Square and off we went to Pentagon City's Costco. Miguel was full of questions, but I put my hat over my eyes and tried to grab a quick nap.

Once we got there, Miguel looked at me in amazement. He took off his hat and said, "That's a coffin."

Si, they sell everything here.

"It has a Lady of Guadalupe on it. That's a Latino coffin. This place sells coffins for Latinos."

Si, they even sell coffins for Latinos.

"You knew about this place and you never told me?"

Miguel, let's not worry about that right now. Let's get you some condoms.

I don't usually go to Costco very often because 1) It's located outside of DC in Virginia; 2) I'm afraid of Virginia; 3) Virginians live there; 4) I don't trust the blue-and-orange-line crowd. They all have beady eyes.

I take him to the condom aisle and he immediately grabbed a box in amazement.

"This is my kind! Forty condoms for $9.69? Is this a broma?"

All of a sudden my man does a little salsa dance in the middle of the store while a Virginian mother with beady eyes held her children closer. Then I see Miguel starts to do some kind of calculation with his finger and simultaneously places two boxes at a time in the cart. He stops at 10 boxes, walks away, and then goes back for two more.

Miguel, that's a lot of condoms. We can come back.

He ignores me because he's upset that I've never told him about Costco.

The cash register was interesting. He places all of the boxes in front of the cashier (I show her my membership card) and smiles with content. The cashier laughs along with a couple of other employees as they look over at my amigo's purchase. The whole scene is comical and even I break a smile while looking away and rubbing my eyes.

"Yes. So what? I fuck a lot."

You can't take this chico anywhere . . .

Mucho Amor,

El Guapo

Friday

"Here. Gracias."

What is this?

"A check. For the money you lent me."

You're giving me a check?

"Si. For the money you lent me."

A check. You're giving me a check. For the money I lent you. Miguel, I lent you $15. Can't you give me cash?

"El Guapo! Stop being such a drama queen! It's the same damn thing, coño!"

I am going to have to walk to the bank and get charged for seeing a teller because you couldn't give me cash.

"Just deposit the damn thing at the ATM so you don't have to pay a fee. Stop being simple."

I don't like doing that. They only credit your account the next day. Sometimes in two days. It's annoying. I don't like that.

"El Guapo, do not get annoyed with me because of your anal retentive nature! You lent me money and I'm paying you back. I do not wish to owe mi amigo money. Money ruins relationships."

Okay . . . Fine! Gracias! Gracias for paying me back. Gracias for paying me back with a check. I'll deposit it tomorrow.

"De nada. Wait, what?"

I said, gracias! I'm not even being sarcastic. En serio, gracias for paying me back. I had forgotten all about it.

"You're going to deposit it tomorrow?"

Si.

"No, don't deposit it tomorrow. Don't deposit it before Friday. Actually, only on Friday afternoon just to be safe. Gracias hermano. I will see you later."

Miguel pats me on the shoulder and walks out eating a banana yogurt. My last one . . .

Friday . . . For fifteen dollars. Why not?

Mucho Amor,

El Guapo

P.S.: Thank you to my friend who helped me determine the difference between *lent* and *leant*. I was right. You were wrong. Guatemala in the house!

New Underpants

I was almost beaten up by a bunch of 13-year-old kids today.

No soy the pugilist I once was, but I'm pretty certain that if one 13-year-old tried to fight me, I could hold him down by his shoes with wheels. However, when there are 6 shoes with wheels, that can be a bit of a problem.

"What the fuck are you looking at nigga'?"

Ay Dios . . . I looked up from my paper to see who was unfortunate enough to have these words thrown at them. Then I realized that the angry eyes which belonged to the young, angry voice were being directed at me.

"That's right nigga'. I'm talkin' to you!"

Ay Dios . . . I bit my lower lip to take in the situation. There I was, a gorgeous Guatemalan, who up until that point was having a pretty good day. Then, I find myself getting surrounded by half a dozen kids in oversized winter coats.

A couple of scenarios flashed through my mind and one of them involved me breaking into a Latino Jackie Chan segment with Chris Tucker in the back of the bus yelling nonsense. Another involved me waking up in the hospital with my face beaten to a pulp and mi madre praying her rosary beads. My face . . . Mi beautiful Guatemalan face . . . Should I rely on my wit in situations like this? Maybe I could make these caballeros laugh at my Latino observations.

"Answer me motha' fucka'!"

Perhaps I could find a better time to make someone smile. These kids were just in the mood to fight.

"He don't understand what you sayin' Arnie."

Arnie . . . This kid's name is Arnold. No wonder he's angry.

"What's the matter bitch? All you understand is tacos and burritos?"

Yo quiero Taco Bell.

I realized the words coming out of my mouth and wanted them to go right back in. Get back in!!! What the hell was that? Yo quiero Taco Bell? That was the best that I could do when I'm about to get jumped by a couple of teenagers in black marshmallow jackets? Why Dios? Why now? Why must I do my impression of the Mexican Chihuahua, why? Then, it happened. I saw it start in the back and filter through the group. I even heard an old woman (who should have had my back in the first place) try to contain a chuckle. Then the kid with the angry mouth cocked his head, pressed his lips together and winced his eyes in a playful fashion.

Playful fashion. This is a good thing, yes?

"Yeah money. I want some Taco Bell too. We're getting off here!"

And so, it was. They left.

Pobre Arnold. Going through life angry that his parents named him Arnold. Don't be angry Arnold. Don't be angry.

Now I just need new underpants.

Mucho Amor,

El Guapo

Depeche Mode Part I

Sometimes I don't like Miguel. Not because I sometimes think that he is actually certifiably crazy, but because of the situations he causes for me.

This weekend was interesante for me. Miguel made me come out with a couple of girls that he met because, as he says, "I need some gringas on my mind." Whatever. I've been blowing him off for so long that it didn't make much sense for me to stay indoors.

So I find myself in a group house full of East coast educated women with colorful tapestries on the walls and Depeche Mode on the iPod. I looked at the ladies in the room and noted their very black mascara and ill-washed hair. One had black and white leggings with a short skirt and a one side longer than the other haircut. It was that type of crowd, they were cute, but I wondered how in the name of everything holy did Miguel get hooked up with them.

Then I realized why. I looked up at mi amigo and noticed that he became very chatty. He was using his hands a bit too much and really being more annoying than normal. One of his new amigas, a quiet one, wearing all black, was also rubbing her nose. I understand. They found each other through a love of snow. How romantic. Miguel has always loved the nieves, but I wasn't aware that he was playing with the snow too. Oh well, it is his nose. Who am I to judge?

Then the woman with the black and white leggings suddenly began dancing, well, "dancing" in front of me while I sat on a futon covered by yet another colorful tapestry. I smirked and wished that there was a TV I could watch or maybe a baseball bat that could hit my head. She was nice looking and everything, but the Depeche Mode and nose rubbing was beginning to make me nervous. I politely smirked.

"You're shy aren't you? You're the silent type. I like that."

Baby, I'm not silent. I just don't want to be around when the music stops. Then she straddled me while still gyrating her hips and arms. Interesante. Depeche Mode chicks dig me. It is the mustache. Then, she kissed me. It was not a good kiss. Mostly because I did not want to kiss her and mostly because it was a kiss full of teeth. Her teeth clanked against mine and I could feel my face tighten as I felt her wetness.

"There, that will cheer you up a bit."

I didn't know what the hell she meant by that. Did a dentist teach her to kiss? Why would that cheer me up? God, is this what being single is going to bring me? Sitting in an ill-lit room with Depeche Mode in the background?

Then I tried to put that moment out of my mind and listened to the words of the music and watched Miguel Latin dance with the women to Depeche Mode. This man will dance to anything as long as he can move his hips.

The laughing, the dark lights, the tapestries, the music. They were all becoming one. The nose scratching was making me dizzy. I needed to go to the restroom.

The restroom had a picture of a pink teddy bear that seemed to smile at me. I did my business and washed my hands. Then, I looked at myself in the mirror. I was looking particularly good looking today. Look at that mustache! Perfectly trimmed. I think I'll just stay in here and look at myself. That bear, I can see it in the mirror. It waves at me and winks at me. I like that bear.

"What are you doing?"

Just looking at myself in the mirror. Have you seen me?

"Yeah, you're hot. Come out here and dance."

No. I rather get punched in the back.

"Well, I'm going to pee."

Go ahead.

This scene repeated itself several times. Several girls came into the bathroom and talked to me while they relieved themselves. One tried to kiss me, but I was having none of it. All I would allow them to do was speak with me and wash their hands. The mirror was mine.

Then the kisser came in.

"Ah. Didn't do what I thought it would. I was hoping it would relax you, but out there."

I'm just going to look at myself in the mirror.

"Yeah . . . I've never seen someone trip in the bathroom before. At least you're not freaking out."

How can I freak out? I have a mirror in front of me. And that bear. That bear is so nice. Waving at me.

Then, I realized it. The tooth grinder put something in my mouth when she kissed me. I had felt something, but just thought it was my imagination. No. I was "tripping" on something. No wonder I was starting to enjoy Depeche Mode . . .

To be continued . . .

Mucho Amor,

El Guapo

Depeche Mode Part II

I could see words. They were coming out in different colors depending on the sound they made. Any kind of a hard C or K came out in an orange hue. The Y sound was a teal color. I wasn't as much hearing what people were saying, but more translating through the colors coming out of their mouths. It was surreal, but funny. I liked it.

As the short-on-one-side-haircut girl spoke to me in her prism of colors I put my hand against the wall to hold myself up. Seeing colors come out of someone's mouth isn't for the weak. As I placed my hand on the wall I noticed the wall ripple against my hand as if someone had thrown a pebble into a pond. The ripples spread throughout the bath-room and the bear kept waving at me through his new plaster pool.

"Dude, you are seriously tripping."

Pisada . . . Who does this to someone? A drug through a kiss? What color could I hurl at her to make her know how I did not approve of this? The walls kept increasing in their movement and I was getting dizzy. The bear was starting to get afraid as well and showed it by jumping up and down.

I looked down at her legs which would normally soothe me, but her black and white leggings turned into running zebras jumping as fervently as the little bear on the wall.

The music filtered through the door in a gray-blue tone and that is how I shall forever associate the sound of Depeche Mode. It sounds horrible sober and it looks horrible through my newfound color lan-guage.

The little bear was angry. He was doing flips now. Backward and frontward flips. I no longer wanted to look at myself in the mirror because my mustache was doing strange things. I saw the light of the bathroom ceiling. I actually saw each beam of light come down and rest on my body. Each individual beam dancing on my body declaring it his.

To feel light is one thing, but to see it, well, I needed out.

I rushed out of the house to go home. Every time I blinked a wave of psychedelic colors, psychedelic waves, haunted my vision. I tried not to blink. I didn't want to blink. Too much color. Dry eyes . . .

Each step I took created a wave on the sidewalk and I had to steady myself on the bleeding cars parked on the street because the sidewalk was acting like a bucking horse. Waves of cement rippling higher and higher bringing my knees to my chest. Where was I? I needed to get home, but the waves were too big. They were getting too violent. I don't have sea legs.

I saw a bench that seemed to be withstanding the onslaught of cement waves and I stumbled towards it. I could see that the ground had become a stream of monkey skulls opening and closing their mouths in no particular order. Each step I took would send the monkey skulls scattering across the street as if I were parting the Red Sea. I was kicking monkey skulls away because I was afraid they would bite. Get away monkey skulls!

The bench provided me shelter and the wooden planks grew to protect me from the monkey skulls. I looked over my new bench boat and breathed a sigh of relief that the monkey skulls wouldn't get to me.

The moon was out, but there were no stars. The moon spoke with me. Soothing colors came from the moon, and I eventually fell asleep on my bench boat and dreamed of hiking to find a God. I didn't go high enough, because I could only hear him. Yellows and pinks, all yellows and pinks.

I woke up at Miguel's place with him passed out on the floor. I wasn't angry, but I was perturbed. He must have carried me home.

I opened up his fridge, ate all his flan, then left.

And while I was able to see speech, light beams and a waving teddy bear, the running on monkey skulls is something I would rather soon forget. A beautiful Guatemalan like myself shouldn't be running on monkey skulls.

Mucho Amor,

El Guapo

El Guapo in DC is written by an anonymous male twenty-something Guatemalan-American born in Washington, D.C. He says he has a mustache and it is glorious. He writes his blog without accents because "it takes three to four extra keystrokes to get the accents in there." The blog, he reports, "is currently on siesta."

EUROTRASH

[Eurotrash]

["the whole detached-irony thing is very 1999"]

http://www.upsaid.com/eurotrash/

MARCH 24 2004

A Waaaafer thin mint, madam?

This unspeakable piece of codswallop pretty much sums up the worst of New York journalism for me.

Humourless. Pretentious. Smug. [. . .]

[T]his restaurant review [of Jean-Georges Vongerichten's Spice Market] made me want to burn something. I disliked Amanda Hesser by the second sentence when she used the phrase 'olfactory amuse-bouche'. By the end of the piece I wanted to grab her and make her wear clothes from Old Navy and eat Big Macs for the rest of her life.

Take a peek:

> [. . .] *Waitresses in silky persimmon-color smocks, open at the back, sweep through. Howard Stern and a girlfriend amble by. You are in a James Bond movie, a high-end bar in Bangkok.* [. . .]

I imagine you are probably working on a novel, Amanda. Everyone else in New York is. One word of advice. Stop. You make my teeth want to vomit. The last time you took the subway was in 1983. You once read a Kurt Vonnegut novel and pretended you understood it. You laugh like a hyena, but you crave approval. Your clothes are nice, though. I don't know. I don't know you from Adam. I'm sorry. You just made me angry. It's nothing personal. I bet you're really nice.

[. . .] This is a Vongerichten fantasy.

What the fuck are you talking about? [. . .] What are you trying to say? What's the fucking food like? Nice? Who fucking knows? Oh. OK. You're setting the scene here. I get it. Sorry. Didn't mean to go off on one.

Here we are. Some food descriptions. Hurrah!

And in that fantasy, fat tapioca pearls loom large [. . .] simmered with Thai chilies, Sichuan peppercorns, cinnamon and chipotle, then paired with slivers of raw tuna in a cool coconut broth. [. . .] The dish is eaten with a spoon.

A spoon? A fucking spoon? Really? Wow. A real spoon? One of those stick things with a little bowl-shaped thing on the end? One of them? A 'spoon'? Fuck me. Who'd have thought, eh? A spoon. I've heard it all now, I tell ya. Fascinating and informative.

Between the wings, your chopsticks make their way to slices of mango, there for relief.

Do they? Do they really, Amanda? Do my chopsticks make their way to the mango, Amanda? Of their own accord, Amanda? Or do my hands make them go there? I shall ponder this. You are thought-provoking.

A blood orange mojito is fresh tasting and herbal. [. . .] It is difficult not to slug it back. Order a Pattaya if you are feeling the need for discipline. [. . .]

When I feel the need for discipline, Amanda, I'll hire a dungeon-master. You see, you're just talking rubbish here, aren't you? What the fuck do you mean by 'discipline'? Are you so incredibly intellectual that you have forgotten the meaning of words? That's cool!

In the next sentence, you tell me that you are 'reveling' over some ginger rice. I'll give you the benefit of the doubt and assume you weren't folk dancing round the table, here. It's rice and it tastes great. You can say that, you know. It's allowed. You don't have to thumb that thesaurus quite so hard, girl.

OK. I'm sorry again. I know you can't just write a review that says 'The food was great, go there'. I'm not stupid. But equally, I don't want to have to read the early drafts of your novel when I want to know if a new restaurant is any good. You are over-egging the pudding, if you'll pardon my pun. Less really *is* more a lot of the time, especially when it comes to journalism.

And of course, everything I'm saying is just bollocks anyway. I'm a foreigner, I'm not rich and glamorous, I don't even pretend to read Kurt Vonnegut, so what the hell do I matter? You're not writing for *me* are you? If you met me you would probably just point and laugh and I wouldn't blame you. I dress badly and my shoes are crap. I'm not your target audience. So carry on. Do that thing you do. Ignore me.

But I did read a Dave Eggers book once, you know. . . .

Heh. Just kidding.

The fat lady has well and truly sung.

I know I've been a little quiet recently, but that's because I've been wrestling with my soul. That and a nasty case of gastroenteritis when I got back from London.

Anyway. About my soul.

My first job in journalism was way back in 1992, as a cub reporter on an evening newspaper in the boil on the arse of civilisation known as Gloucester. I was fresh from journalism school and I was young and eager and very poor. The gig paid a mighty nine thousand of your British pounds per annum, and most of that went on the rent for my squalid bedsit (my fellow tenants included a few mentally ill souls, a man who told me to be careful because there were black people living in the trees who wanted to stab me, and a couple of people with learning difficulties who worked in Primark as trainee managers), and paying off a loan for my beige second-hand Ford Fiesta.

My first boss was a horrendously deranged harpy called Jane. She was one of the loudest, nastiest, most psychologically damaged people I have ever met, let alone worked for.

And she had a cracking case of halitosis which meant when she stalked up to you in the newsroom to flay your tormented soul with some well-screeched foulness, you had to choose between crying with the humiliation, and vomiting as the hell's maw that was her breath enveloped you in its vile caress.

These days, bullets bounce off me, mostly. Back then I was young and full of fear. Most days the bullying was so awful I would go home and cry. In the mornings I would throw up just contemplating the ordeal ahead. After about a year, she left to join another newspaper and I think the collection for her going away present just about topped five quid. I gave a symbolic penny. Wish I'd shoved it up my arse beforehand, now.

But, evil cow from hell that she was, Jane left me with a very important legacy. After she'd waddled her hefty hate-filled living corpse out of our newsroom, I realised that never, ever, EVER again would I do a job that made me that miserable, ever again.

Fast forward to today. When I quit my job. A job that until recently I really loved, even if it did drive me a bit crazy at times. Recently they decided to, well, reconfigure it a bit to include some un-fun stuff that I really didn't want to do. I objected, but they were well within their rights to tell me to do it. And I'm sure they thought I would cave in and do it in the end.

But alas, they reckoned without the psychological scarring I received at the hands of Jane. I'd like to say I thought long and hard about my decision, but that's not true. The spectre of Jane screeched its fetid horror over my shoulder and that was enough.

So there we are.

JULY 23 2006

Any resemblance is purely unaccidental. Alas.

When my mother died, my father immediately jetted back from his mistress in the Caribbean to discover to his horror, that in a more sane(ish) than not moment (although my sister can tell a hell of a story about this), Mum had separated the tenancy on their family home and made a will, leaving her half of it to her three children, in equal shares.

My parents were still married, because—hey! Why go through the expense of divorcing someone who's going to drink themselves to death any day now! You go, Daddio!

For a man so utterly dependent on his sense of control, the news of my mother's pre-fatal legal manoeuvre was the equivalent of a smack in the face with a wet fish—oh yeah, while someone's cutting off your balls at the same time.

And so, after he flew in, he called us over to the family home, whereby he 'informed' us that even though our mother had seen fit to will us her half of the property ('How dare she!' was implied), all goods and chattels within it were his property and his alone. He then handed us blocks of Post-It notes and told us that anything we wanted, we could put a Post-It note on 'requesting' it, and he would 'consider' our 'request'. I can't remember whether this was before 'hello', or not. And to be fair, it was before he invoiced us for her funeral.

Anyway, as a result, I have just three things that ever belonged to my mother: a Le Creuset frying pan and a cheap casserole dish she gave me when I went to university for the second time (first time, it really would not have been worth it as I spent three years living on dry Shredded Wheat), and a tackily framed black and white photo of her, taken in Jersey, when she was 16.

She'd run off to Jersey to escape her depressed widowed mother and the memory of a Galway slum and those eight dead brothers and sisters. And perhaps for one of the first times in her life, she was happy. And she was unquestionably, utterly beautiful.

The picture is taken, I guess in 1956/7 by a chap she was chastely 'dating' (No sex please! We're Irish!) while she worked as a housemaid in a hotel in Jersey. She's on top of a lighthouse of all things, wearing a white sleeveless peasant blouse, a full skirt and one of those celtic hippie belt long things that I can't remember the name of, but that I think my sister still has. She has a cheap plastic bangle falling over her left wrist. And she's almost daring to smile.

It's long before she married my father. Obviously.

Anyway, last night I got home drunk and sad, and I found myself crying and clutching this photo, of a beautiful, hopeful, passionate, desperate, alcoholic, loving, wounded, hateful, clever, funny, angry, nasty, inspirational, generous, occasionally wonderful woman, and I was so desperate to see nothing of her about me. Just like when I was a kid, when my misguided sense of wishful-thinking, combined with a belief in a God who never existed, led me to pray pointlessly on my knees every night for a good few years, that I was really adopted.

I saw my brother in her eyes, her hair, her colouring and in her intensity and intellect and sensitivity. I saw my sister in the shape of her face, her lips, her colouring and her creativity, vulnerability, unexpected wisdom, and hope. And in both of them, I saw the truly loving parents they are, and the parent she might have been.

I look absolutely nothing like my mother when she was young. Which is why I used to hope I was adopted. I think I had a secret sense of superiority to my brother and sister—they looked like her. And they also looked like Dad. I didn't look like either. Surely I was the cuckoo in the nest? And I would be the one who was rescued, saved, delivered by my imaginary real parents.

But last night, I finally saw a resemblance. And it was very unappealing—and it wasn't about her good points, either.

But it gave me an idea for a story. And a couple of ideas on top of that, for the real world.

So maybe she's reaching from beyond the grave.

Or maybe I was just drunk. It does run in the family, after all.

JULY 24 2006

My mother told me.

When I was born in Belgium, my sister was 12-and-a-half months old.

After I got home from the hospital we had our own rooms across the hall from each other. My sister's cot was on wheels, and apparently when I'd wake up and howl in the mornings, my parents could rest easy. Because my sister (probably already awake, but being pleasantly quiet and rather well-adjusted about the whole thing) would stand up in her cot and nudge herself against the bars so that she could jog the whole thing across the hallway and into my room, landing it next to mine. Then she'd happily babble to me until I calmed down and we could spend the next hour or so happily babbling to each other, until my parents got up.

That speaks volumes about my sister and, less flatteringly, me. My sister always thinks she's not the clever one in the family, but any one-year-old who can figure out how to drive her cot around the house is pretty damn near genius, in my opinion.

Growing up, my sister and I usually shared a room—not for space reasons, but because, well, we belonged together—even if we did occasionally squabble and draw lines dividing the room into our own halves that neither was allowed to cross, ON! PAIN! OF! . . . something or other. We had bunk beds that were bright red and covered with nylon sheets that my self-absorbedly oblivious parents had no idea and cared less, would cause my sister and her eczema years of torment. Ach, never mind. Have another gin and bitter lemon, you bastard. The kids'll be asleep soon and we can get back to throwing staplers at each other.

Weirdly, my brother had bunk beds too, even though he almost never had friends round to stay and was shunted off to boarding school at an early age, where he pretty much disappeared from our lives for the longest time. His bunk beds were beige.

A few years after we landed in England, and my brother had been sent off to his institutional hell, my father moved out of the master bedroom and into my brother's room, in the lower bunk bed. The top one was in the 'spare room', I've just remembered. And that's a different story for another time.

My father lived in that child's bunk bed for almost the rest of his married life with my mother. And space was certainly not an issue.

I can't remember when, but at some point after Dad decided to live in his son's bunk bed, Mum ditched their manky old marital bed and bought this incredibly expensive, huge, iron-framed, gorgeous bed. Ah, the irony.

My father never spent a night in it. He had his bunk bed, you see. And his utter contempt for my mother.

As she drank herself to death, my mother pissed herself, shat herself, threw up, and generally gave up existence in that bed. I occasionally changed her incontinence nappy and rubbed anti-rash cream on her vagina—framed with her wispy, greying pubic hair—in that bed. I led her off it so she could squat on a commode, because she couldn't fucking find the ensuite bathroom two fucking feet away.

And that's only a fraction of what my sister was doing for Mum at the time. I can't bear to think of what images are burned on her brain because I didn't have the guts or maturity to face any of it myself.

Anyway, when Mum died, I was off on a jaunt to Amsterdam with a 6'4" 21-year-old skydiver from South Africa. I'm finding a pattern here (and yes, Freddie—I do plan to get to your epic contribution to this story!).

So we got to the Rijksmuseum (I'm pretty sure I've told this bit already, so I won't go on) and the phone rings and Mum's dead and we go back to the hostel and smoke a joint and he holds me. For the longest time. He was actually quite a good chap. He deserved better than me cutting him dead shortly afterwards. But I had my own shit to deal with.

My brother and his wife had found Mum dead, in the hallway outside her bedroom, sitting on a chair. It bothers me now that I can't picture which chair it was. I think maybe I knew at some point (the little three-legged Spanish one? The African tall-backed one? The bizarrely displaced church pew?) but now I'm not sure. So I can't even picture my mother's pathetic death, dammit.

Whatever. As her routine in those days was pretty much 'wake-up (wherever/whenever), drink, smoke, sit under the table for a bit, drink, drink, drink, drink, drink, smoke, smoke, smoke, smoke, combine the two until unconscious, maybe wake up, then head for bed at some point, wake-up, repeat the above', again, I don't know whether my mother was heading for her bed—her big, expensive, futile, virginal bed—or away from it, when she found temporary respite (on whichever fucking chair it was) and then death.

But what I do know is that after she died, my father gave her bed to one of his mistress's children.

And even at my therapised, counselled, medicated, educated, psychobabbled, self-hugging vagina-monologuing advanced age, I can't picture the scene of me ever meeting him again. Because above everything else, everything fucking else, I just can't get the fuck over that one.

AUGUST 07 2006

I don't have an amusing title for this one.

Picture me.

11-years-old, walking home from school, clutching my hockey stick and my school bag. And I was ONE. CORNER. FROM. HOME. Amazing, eh? I was at the crossroads of Kingsley Way and Holne Chase. I lived one 'block' as Americans would say, up. At the corner of Milton Close and Holne Chase. (I've google mapped it with varying accuracy many a time. As one does.)

As I crossed Kingsley Way on the left side, there was a bench under a cherry tree on my right as I began the trudge up the gentle hill to my home. Only two houses between me and mine. Sitting on the bench was a man. Grey-haired, handsome, and well-dressed, he was in his mid-40s (I surmise now), and as I passed him, he stood up and asked me if I could help.

Pathetic as this may sound, he asked me to stop and see if I could help him find the balloon that his two children had lost in the cherry tree, as they were really upset about losing it.

I was 11. Catholic. My parents were either alcoholic, insane, depressed, [or] obsessed with their own pain. [. . .]

The man asked me to stand on the arm of the wooden bench under the tree to look for the balloon. I complied. And it was then that I (didn't, actually, at the time, but did later that night) realise that he was stroking my thighs. I was trying to be a good little girl, and searched desperately for the balloon. I couldn't find it. I was, yet again, a stupid, crap, awful piece of rubbish who should have been aborted, at this new failure. At that point he removed his hand, and asked me where I lived. I pointed to my house, clearly visible, and even to my bedroom window, which we could both see from the bench.

So he suggested we go and 'meet' his son and daughter, named 'Sarah and David'—nice choice, this was a very Jewish neighbourhood—who were playing tennis in Littleton Playing Fields, just around the corner.

Aware of my earlier failure to please, I was only too eager to atone. And so I led him, unwittingly on my part, probably planned on his, to the most isolated entrance to the park. Just around the corner. On Linden Lea, I think it was called.

And there, we had a marvellous view of the tennis courts across the park, while he got me to stand on another bench and try and spot 'Sarah and David' playing tennis. He had bad eyesight, you see, and he'd apparently left his glasses at the office. Having always been berated as a failure, I was only too desperate to help someone. And probably, have someone tell me thanks.

And I stood on that bench, and he lifted my skirt while I scanned the courts intently for his son and daughter, and he took down my knickers (both pairs, the ungainly enormous blue games knickers designed to protect our dignity on the hockey field, and the normal little girl things I had underneath). And throughout the whole thing, I did know that I wasn't awfully sure that what he was doing was right—but then I had a dim inkling by then that most of what my parents did wasn't exactly right—so I didn't really have a normality register to measure this by.

But I was desperate to find his kids, because then, I would have helped someone, like a good little Catholic girl, and I wouldn't be the most appalling, sick, evil child in the world. Hopefully. Maybe Mum and Dad would finally approve of me.

[. . .]

And then he, and I will phrase this carefully, because I don't want shedloads of child p_rn spam [sic], well, he did the kind of things that men who search for child p_rn [sic] want to do to 11-year-old girls. [. . .] But he didn't rape me, which is, totally, like, a HUGE plus. Dontcha think? In fact, at some point, he stopped abruptly, let me go and sent me off out of the park.

What a gentleman.

[. . .]

As for the aftermath of all this—again, it's a story for another time. But it's fucking priceless.

Eurotrash, age thirty-nine, is an Irish-Canadian who was born in Belgium and raised in London, where she lives now. She said, "I went to a posh school, did a law degree, then a postgrad journalism degree and worked on local papers, then a global scum-tabloid news agency before deciding to go Zen and give it up and go off and benefit people somewhere. Before I could do that my sister decided to have a baby, my dad ran off with his mistress, and my mother drank herself to death."

Subsequently, Eurotrash worked for the Reuters news agency. Then she moved to New York City to work for *Star* magazine. "A year and a half later," she writes, "I wanted to almost (but only almost) kill myself, so I left. Then all sorts of shit happened, mostly revolving around a broken heart, so I came back to England."

Eurotrash began her blog in 2003. The post that got the mainstream media's attention was her skewering of Amanda Hesser, a *New York Times* food writer. "A storm in a teacup to me," Eurotrash said. Shortly afterward, Hesser was no longer doing reviews. "Life in New York. Hey ho."

In addition to her blog Eurotrash is thinking about writing a book about "the various nutters who hang around the BDSM [bondage, discipline, and sadomasochism] scene." In 2007 she wrote for Nick Denton's media blog, and she was, she said, "the resident atheist shiksa over on Jewess," a blog. She says her real name is Geraldine Allison Winnifred Mary Hayward. "But no one ever called me that apart from my dead angry mother." Her friends call her Delly.

GET YOUR WAR ON

http://www.mnftiu.cc/mnftiu.cc/war.html

PUBLISHED 10/9/01

PUBLISHED 5/29/06

I agree with Thomas Friedman: When it comes to Iraq, the next six to nine months are really going to be *crucial*.

I'm sick of that line. Like any other six to nine months in Iraq *won't* be crucial? It's like saying, "The next six to nine slugs that enter your bullet-ridden skull are going to be *crucial*. Seriously, dude: Try to pay attention to those particular bullets."

You know how people have been saying that "six-to-nine months" line for years now? Do you think maybe they weren't referring to *consecutive* months?

PUBLISHED 7/31/06

For the last time: Do we like Lebanon or not? I thought we supported their government, and their "air-freshener tree revolution" or whatever it was called, but now it looks like we're trying to *prevent* a cease-fire.

We like Lebanon. In fact we *love* Lebanon. That's why we want Israel to attack the shit out of it until the population starts resenting Hezbollah for the mess they're in.

Goddamn, I love violent paths to peace. *Because then I can wish for peace without feeling like a wimp!*

PUBLISHED 9/18/06

"In the first days after the 9/11 attacks I promised to use **EVERY ELEMENT OF NATIONAL POWER** to fight the terrorists, wherever we find them. One of the strongest weapons in our arsenal is the **POWER OF FREEDOM.** The terrorists fear freedom as much as they do our firepower." (George W. Bush, 9/11/06)

 Hmm. Is the Pentagon aware that terrorists fear freedom as much as our firepower? Because I'm looking at the FY 2006 military budget and we seem to be spending a shitload of money for something that's not even scarier than *freedom.*

You know what they say: *"Freedom without firepower is like a pleasant, abstract concept without the attendant mechanisms of violence which may actually undermine it."*

Goddamn! When did they start saying *that?*

"The (9/11) attacks were meant to **BRING US TO OUR KNEES, AND THEY DID,** but not in the way the terrorists intended. Americans united in prayer, came to the aid of neighbors in need, and resolved that our enemies would not have the last word." (George W. Bush, 9/11/06)

 I remember coming to the aid of my neighbors on 9/11, but I'm pretty sure I wasn't *on my knees.* They're not that type of neighbors.

No, you jackass, that's not when you were on your knees— you were on your knees when we were united in prayer. Remember?

Oh, right. May I assume that after Bush's speech, we were all on our knees united in front of the toilet?

Hey, infidel, can I have the last word?

No!!!

PUBLISHED 10/23/06

"Whatever your opinion of the outcome (last Tuesday), all Americans can take pride in the **EXAMPLE OUR DEMOCRACY SETS FOR THE WORLD** by holding elections even in a time of war." —President Bush, 11/11/06

 Yeah, I think we really blew the world's mind when we held elections last week.

 The world was all like, "How is America gonna pull off *actually holding elections?* Don't those crazy kids know it's a *time of war?*" And America was all like, "Check out this intense example we're setting! *Plunk!* I just totally pulled a lever! DEAL WITH IT!"

 Holy shit, I know why Bush thinks it's a big deal we held elections— somebody told him Iraq invaded *us.*

"In his first day in the capital of a country that was America's wartime enemy during his youth, President Bush said today that the American experience in **VIETNAM** contained lessons for the war in **IRAQ**. Chief among them, he said, was that '**WE'LL SUCCEED UNLESS WE QUIT**.'" (*The New York Times*, 11/17/06)

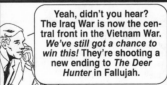 I don't get it: Is Bush saying that if we don't quit Iraq, there's still time to succeed against. . . the *Viet Cong?*

Yeah, didn't you hear? The Iraq War is now the central front in the Vietnam War. *We've still got a chance to win this!* They're shooting a new ending to *The Deer Hunter* in Fallujah.

 I guess that makes sense: We're fighting Charlie in Iraq so we don't have to fight him over here. I wonder if Cheney has his deferments planned out?

GET YOUR WAR ON   **91**

I hate "Surge!" "Surge" sounds like a goddamn waterpark in Ohio or some shit. I liked it better a few weeks ago, when the cool thing to say about Iraq was "*Go big, go long, or go home.*" Now *that's* a phrase that makes me sound like I know what the fuck I'm talking about when I utter it.

I think they should combine every recent Iraq-related phrase into one ultimate phrase, like: "*Surge big, surge long, or clear-and-hold home.*" That sounds good!

Don't forget Thomas Friedman's stupid new goddamn phrase: "*Ten months or ten years.*" Throw that in: "*Surge ten go big, surge long go years ten, or months clear ten-and-hold home!*" You know—all of a sudden (*sniff*). . . I actually think we can win this motherfucker.

Are you looking forward to the new year?

Hell yes! 2006 was a bullshit year. It felt like the first year in the War on Terror in which nothing really big happened—things just sort of pooped along. You know, I think I'm actually getting *bored* with this generation-defining, high-stakes battle for the future of civilization.

You know, for something so boring, you'd be surprised at how much it's gonna cost.

PUBLISHED 1/8/07

How many additional troops would have to go to Iraq before it affected you personally?

Hmm. I don't really know anyone in the military, so. . . maybe, like, a million troops? Maybe if they recruited a million more troops I would know one of 'em? And then maybe I'd *finally* bother learning the difference between a battalion and a brigade. Right now, I define both words as: "*a large group of armed strangers.*"

See? That's why I think they should call up *fifty* million troops. Not to mention, we would totally win the *FUCK* out of the war then.

GET YOUR WAR ON

DAVID REES ■ GET YOUR WAR ON
http://www.mnftiu.cc/mnftiu.cc/war.html

In the fall of 2001, David Rees was working as a temporary fact checker at *Maxim* magazine when Operation: Enduring Freedom began and *Vanity Fair*'s editor Graydon Carter pronounced irony dead. The lack of satire and dissent in the post-9/11 popular culture inspired Rees to create "Get Your War On," an Internet cartoon about the War on Terrorism. "GYWO" is notable for its liberal use of profanity and public-domain clip art.

Although it began as a personal, cathartic exercise, "GYWO" became an Internet phenomenon after Rees forwarded the first few strips to his friends. It now appears in every issue of *Rolling Stone*. "GYWO" was adapted for the stage by the Rude Mechs, a Texas theater company. That production went on tour and had an off-Broadway run in early 2007. Sales of two "GYWO" anthologies have raised almost $100,000 for land mine removal in western Afghanistan.

Mr. Rees, now thirty-five years old, grew up in Chapel Hill, where he played soccer and was dragged to church every Sunday morning. He is a graduate of Oberlin College. Mr. Rees's other comics include "My New Fighting Technique Is Unstoppable" and "My New Filing Technique Is Unstoppable," which appeared every Thursday in *The Guardian* until his editor, according to Rees, "realized the strip was neither amusing nor popular."

GO FUG YOURSELF

go fug yourself

fugly is the new pretty

| HOME | ARCHIVES | FAQ | E-MAIL | MEET THE FUGGERS | MEDIA | ADS/CREDITS |

http://gofugyourself.typepad.com/

FEBRUARY 14, 2005

Grammy Awards: Pre-Party Fug Carpet

How to make your own Grammy dress, courtesy of Blu Cantrell:

1) Find your grandmother's old shawl—you know, the one she used to wear when she rocked you to sleep as a baby, and which was left to you in her will.

2) Cut that shit UP. If a garment doesn't look like a feral cat mauled you on the way to the party, then it's no good.

3) Grab that tablecloth you've always loved and wrap it around your ass. Hope fervently that it doesn't quite make it all the way around—the better to flash some thigh, my dear.

4) Keep the tablecloth there by wrapping a swath of gold lamé around your waist and safety-pinning it.

5) Sneak over to Crazy Cat Lady's house and skin twelve of her pets; stitch them into a coat/shawl type thing as carelessly as possible. It'll be fine—she's got ten other cats, and besides, wouldn't these beasts prefer photographic immortality to a life in her stuffy old apartment, watching soap operas on the magic noisemaking box and eating

Friskies? So what if this coat's going to get stepped on by Kanye West and then probably sexed on by Usher and his regular posse of eighteen, before being stuffed into the back of the closet along with all your old shirts that don't expose any of your stomach. So WHAT? It will look GREAT hanging from your arm—kind of like you're a modern-day cavewoman.

6) Voilà! Pair with aggressive earrings, and you're ready to spend the entire night tugging at various parts of your ensemble to ensure they're in place. It's every girl's dream.

Posted by Heather at 11:38 AM

DECEMBER 11, 2006

The Fug Wears Prada

Oh, Anne Hathaway. Generally, I have no beef with you. You have lovely, shiny hair and seem to have no problem sharing the screen with older actresses who rock harder than you do (see Streep, Meryl and Andrews, Julie). You did the best you could in *The Devil Wears Prada*, even though your part was basically Whiny Entitled Girl Who Doesn't Know How Good She Has It. I also appreciate that, by all accounts, you seem to understand what "adequate" means, and you probably know how to spell it. So I feel a little bad about this:

From the waist up, you look lovely. But the balloon skirt is a problem. You start to look a little . . . well, a little . . . My grandma had a doll that sat on top of her toilet. Her crocheted gown belled out to cover the extra roll of toilet paper that lived up there. As a child, this fascinated me. Why didn't the toilet paper in my house have outfits? Why didn't everything in my house have outfits: the spatulas, the drinking glasses, the cat? "Because that would be tacky," my mother told me. "But Grandma's toilet paper has an outfit," I protested. "Your grandma is an eccentric and fascinating woman," my mother replied, "but my toilet paper does not need a dress."

Between you and me, I think if my mother could find a black satin cocktail dress in the appropriate shape to cover a roll of Scott [. . .] she might change her mind.

Posted by Jessica at 07:59 AM

MAY 04, 2007

Phugtom of the Opera

When I was little, I loved Sarah Brightman. *Loved* her. Primarily because I was a musical-theater nerd who didn't really care about the actual quality of the musical (hence: saw *Cats* three times), and I saw Sarah as the original Christine in *Phantom of the Opera,* which then-hubby Andrew Lloyd Webber wrote just for her, and I loved it because she was so pretty with her hair and the costumes and the yearning and all that. Plus, in England they often (or at least used to) release songs from hit musicals onto the pop charts. So in addition to being on the West End, Sarah was *also* all over my very favorite show EVER, *Top of the Pops* (rest in peace, little buddy), and I was constantly presented with opportunities to watch the video of the musical's title song, in which a masked man boats a beautifully dressed Sarah across a dry-ice river while they sing about how the Phantom of the Opera invades your mind. It was all very romantic. Never mind that the boater was a man in a mask that was a) strangely *not* the same mask they

use in the musical, but some sort of red and gold full-face version that would be more at home in my nightmares, and b) said masked man was psychotic and wanted to lock her up in a basement. Although when you're nine, there's also something very romantic about being locked in a dungeon while you happen to look gorgeous and can make a man weep with your perfect voice, while the rest of the world ceases to turn on its axis until you are found. Hot.

Ahem. Anyway. There are still things I love about Sarah Brightman. Like, I'm pretty sure she's had some good plastic surgery over the years, and she divorced ALW after getting what she needed out of him, which is good because otherwise she might have been associated with things like *Sunset Boulevard*.

But what I find most charming about her is her modesty and sense of occasion.

Scarlet platform stripper shoes and a dress made from denuding Big Bird's equally gigantic redheaded half-brother? Oh, Sarah, *when* will you get a little confidence and stop living life as a wallflower?

Posted by Heather at 02:52 PM

JESSICA MORGAN AND HEATHER COCKS ■ GO FUG YOURSELF
http://gofugyourself.typepad.com/

Who are the authors of Go Fug Yourself? "We're not a pair of gay men, and, yes, Heather and Jessica are our real names," they insist. Jessica Morgan, who worked on *Growing Up Gotti* and *30 Days* in her pre-blogging life, is thirty-two, and Heather Cocks, who worked on *America's Next Top Model*, is thirty. "GFY is currently our full-time job. We started the blog to amuse ourselves and our friends . . . but it's really taken off." Their book, *The Fug Awards*, will be out this year.

The word *fug*, they explain, comes from *fugly*, a contraction of *fantastically ugly*–"or an F-word more prurient, if you like, but we are clean and delightful young ladies who don't engage in that kind of filth, dammit." *Fugly* is different from plain old *ugly*. "Fugly," they say, "is a self-inflicted state, and no one seems to excel at dwelling in the depths of fug quite like pretty people with money to spare and little sense of how to spend it. Celebrities are always skipping around in public wearing things that are phenomenally perplexing," like, say, miniskirts and UGG boots together.

Next to Heather's name on the "Meet the Fuggers" page of their Web site is a picture of Joan Collins in a silky nightgown lying on her stomach with one high heel kicking up behind her. Next to Jessica's name is a picture of young Shannen Doherty as she looked playing Brenda Walsh in the television show *Beverly Hills 90210*.

HOW TO LEARN SWEDISH IN 1000 DIFFICULT LESSONS

HOW TO LEARN SWEDISH IN 1000 DIFFICULT LESSONS

http://www.francisstrand.blogspot.com/

MONDAY, JANUARY 09, 2006

Can there be anything more harrowing than parenthood?

Not that I can figure.

The thing is, when my little brother and his wife brought Owen home from the hospital to start his life in the big bad outside world, the doctors and nurses told them to watch out because he seemed a little jaundiced. And then, after a couple of days, he had become even more so, and the pediatrician said that he better go back in the hospital. And it turns out that Owen, poor little baby, is a rather severe hemophiliac. Which is quite treatable. But that is poor solace.

My brother told me they cried, they felt guilty, and then they had to face it, a three-step process that no doubt will be repeated for the rest of their lives. And me, I just felt sick and all I could think of was Owen, and of something my sister wrote to me, about how becoming a parent changes your life not in the way you think, but more in that you become so very vulnerable just because your children are so vulnerable. I can only imagine, since I lay awake all night thinking about my brother and his suffering for his son, and worrying about Owen, who is so very little, so very vulnerable.

But, the first reaction in my family is to be stoic. When my brother called to tell me all of this, he sounded a bit hoarse, but his voice was steady.

"The doctor said he can never be a boxer," he said.

We laughed.

The Swedish word for the day is *blödarsjuka*. It means *hemophilia*.

—by Francis S.

TUESDAY, JANUARY 24, 2006

If anyone asks me if I believe in ghosts, I tell them it's not that I believe in them, it's more that I just don't *not* believe in them.

But the truth is that my heart, the irrational part of myself, most definitely believes in them, no matter how skeptical the rest of me is. I remember when I was nine or ten, I would play the piano and wonder if the ghost of Bach was listening, and if he was insulted. Or if I played well enough would he appear and tell me how good I was (he never showed up, definitely a testament to my poor fingering, overuse of the damper pedal and tendency to play so fast that the notes would get all tangled up in knots and I'd have to start over again, which drove my father mad).

Just last weekend, when the husband was in Gothenburg over Saturday night, as I finally turned out the light and pulled the covers up tight to my chin, feeling very alone in bed, I wasn't worried about someone breaking into this vast apartment, I was actually worried that I would open my eyes to find a nasty spirit floating above me. Or something like that.

Not that I've ever actually seen a nasty spirit floating above me, or for that matter a spirit of any kind above, below or beside me.

The problem is that no matter how hard I try, I can't will myself to really not believe, no matter what I say about not believing and not not believing.

I think it's time that I just give in and tell people, well, I've never seen any but yes, I suppose that I believe in ghosts.

Do you?

The Swedish word for the day is *Spökslottet,* which is the name of a mansion not far from Odenplan, and means *the ghost castle.*

—by Francis S.

SATURDAY, FEBRUARY 18, 2006

The husband and I had lunch with the priest last week at a peculiar restaurant with three counters for three different types of semi-hemi-demi fast food. *"Pinnar eller bestick?"* the girl behind the counter asked, and I held up the line for a minute, unable to decide whether to go for *chopsticks or regular utensils* (there, you've got your Swedish phrase for the day). Which was stupid, because wooden chopsticks always work so much better than plastic forks and knives for eating just about anything.

We sat down to our little cardboard cartons of food and dug in, and the conversation meandered onto the subject of funerals.

"The most horrible are the ones where it's just me, the organist and the funeral director in the back or outside smoking cigarettes," the priest said.

The husband and I were taken aback. Do they even have a funeral for someone if no one comes?

"Yes," she said, and sighed. "All the time. I just had one yesterday. It's unbearably sad. Instead of speaking to the people who have come, I speak to the person who has died. It's one of the worst parts of my job. And I think I couldn't stand it if I didn't believe in God."

We sat silently for just a second or two, amid the clatter all around us. And then we moved nimbly on to the topic of the husband's trip to Spain, or the book I was reading, I don't actually remember what it was.

—by Francis S.

As I sat in the dentist's chair at 8:15 this morning, the left side of my mouth not quite numb enough to prevent me from feeling the dentist's drill and nearly flying out of the chair and seriously injuring the dentist, but managing to restrain myself to a pathetic whimper, the kind you make when your mouth is full of dental instruments and your eyes are tearing, I thought to myself how interesting it is that torture seems to be all the rage on American TV these days, and how curious a mirror television is, held up to American culture.

Of course, by all the rage, I mean one episode of a TV show [*Lost*] that we saw a couple of weeks ago: A character, whose backstory is that of a former Iraqi military officer forced to torture a fellow Iraqi officer by his American captors, tortures another character in a situation in which TV viewers are nudged into thinking that the torture is probably a good thing under the circumstances.

Isn't TV wacky?

Anyway, it gets my conspiracy-theory juices flowing, making me wonder if the producers of *Lost* have been hanging out with Alberto Gonzales, the latest in a long line of nutcase—uh, I mean, *outstanding* Republican U.S. Attorneys General that would include John Ashcroft and Ed Meese (who famously said in the 1980s: "I don't know of any authoritative figures that there are hungry children. I've heard a lot of anecdotal stuff, but I haven't heard any authoritative figures. . . . I think some people are going to soup kitchens voluntarily. I know we've had considerable information that people go to soup kitchens because the food is free and that that's easier than paying for it. . . . I think that they have money").

Actually, it doesn't really get me thinking conspiracies, it gets me thinking that there really is no excuse for torture. That's why they call it torture.

My mouth is still kind of sore.

The Swedish word for the day is *häftapparat*. It means *stapler*.

—by Francis S.

Spring has been so cold and graceless this year, it wasn't until this past weekend that we made it out to Bird Island for the first time for the season. It was windy and raw on the island, but here and there little purple anemones had bravely sprung up in the woods, about the only sign of spring that I could see.

When I walked out to the end of the island on Monday morning, I came upon the smoking remains of a bonfire from the night before, a celebration of Valborg, one of those witchy pagan holidays that Swedes have kept right alongside the more familiar Christianized and political ones that the rest of Europe also celebrates.

Back in town, it was just as windy and raw, and there had been a big gathering of kids just outside our apartment on Odenplan, a group called Reclaim the City. I'm not altogether sure who they want to take it back from and who they then want to give it to, but they are supposedly against motor traffic, violence, racism and other bad things, but also apparently believe that windows need to be smashed in order to redistribute sporting goods to needy athletes. Which they did at Sergels Torg and not at Odenplan, for which I am thankful.

But really, why ever did I think that Stockholm was a laughably safe place to live? It seems that Odenplan is a magnet for the more, um, energetic Swedes in Stockholm.

The Swedish word for the day is *kravaller*. It means *riots*.

—by Francis S.

I called my beloved little brother the other day to confirm the rumor that he and his wife had bought an apartment on the Upper West Side, and in the background, amid the noise of the baby and the household, I could hear a police siren: a slow long wail, as opposed to the more rapid quacking of the police sirens here.

Swedes love the way police sirens in the U.S. sound. Someone, I don't remember who, once said to me: "When you go there and hear them in person they sound exactly the way they do on TV!"

Yes, I said, they certainly do.

Aren't Swedes just the cutest things?

The Swedish word for the day is *hörselskadad*. It means *hearing impaired*.

—by Francis S.

Are you superstitious? I'm not terribly superstitious, but I do have a few little quirks that amount to superstition. Like with the rip-off-a-page calendar sitting on the desk next to the computer I am writing this on, for which I feel it is tempting fate to rip off a page before I've actually completed the day, as if it could contribute somehow to an untimely death. My untimely death, mainly. [. . .]

The Swedish word for the day is *vidskeplig*. It means *superstitious*.

—by Francis S.

Hallå? I said into the phone. I was calling A., the TV producer, but every time I called, I kept getting connected to some place with lots of French people talking in the background. Just what I needed as I was trying desperately to keep up with Christmas, which seems to be leaving me breathless this year with all the venison dinners, madrigal concerts, rock concerts, *glöggs*, Lucia processions, and shopping that have taken over my life in the past two weeks.

Five minutes later, A. called.

"Did you just try to call me and get connected to a French bakery?" she asked me.

Well, yeah, I guess that's what it was, I told her.

She laughed an evil little laugh. "I have my phone set up to forward to a bakery in Paris when it's someone I don't know," she said.

But you know *me*, I said, indignant.

"I just couldn't get to my phone fast enough," she said. "Isn't it funny?"

It's kind of mean, I told her.

"I know," she said, ignoring the fact that I was speaking in my sourest voice. "I have this side to me that sometimes I can't believe I have," she said. And she laughed that evil laugh again, forcing me to laugh with her. Because, well, it is kind of funny.

The Swedish phrase for the day is *jag skulle vilja prata med....* It is a most formal way to begin a phone call if you don't know who you are talking to, and means *I would like to speak with....* The appropriate way to answer the phone—unlike in the U.S., where one simply says "hello"—is to simply state your full name, or even just your surname. I think my favorite way of answering the phone is the way the Italians do it, with a *pronto.*

—by Francis S.

As we returned from Christmas in the Midwest, on the plane from Chicago to Stockholm I suddenly noticed that it was Dec. 29 (Central European Time, it was still only Dec. 28 in Illinois). Which meant that it was eight years to the day since I'd moved to Sweden. Strange to be on a plane again and remembering it all: my worldly possessions travelling separately in a container somewhere between Washington, DC and Stockholm, the excitement I felt (I wasn't even scared, which astonishes me), the nearly overwhelming lust and love for the man who would become my husband, who was waiting for me at Arlanda airport. I had arrived some five hours later than expected, since my flight from Reykjavik to Stockholm had been cancelled and I had to go through Copenhagen instead, making it three flights in all to get here. I remember talking at Keflavik airport in Iceland to an American woman who had lived in Sweden for fifteen years, which seemed like forever.

At New Year's, the mother of the popstar [Frances S.'s friend] asked me: "Will you die here?"

And then she smiled, embarrassed a little that she had put it that way.

My favorite Finn, who was part of the conversation, hummed a bit of the Swedish national anthem, which ends with the phrase "I want to live and die in the North."

I could only answer, well, yes, probably.

It's strange to think I will never leave, but it becomes less and less likely that I will abandon Sweden as the years pass.

And fifteen years seems like no time at all anymore.

Still stranger is to think of growing old and dying here. Will the husband and I end up in an old people's home, together or separately? Will I revert to English in my dotage? Who will come to visit me? And who will put flowers on my grave?

The Swedish word for the day is *alltid*. It means *always*.

—by Francis S.

Francis Strand (a pseudonym) is a forty-six-year-old American who has lived in Stockholm since 1999. Now a magazine editor, he has been a groundskeeper, a librarian's assistant, a technician on a psychiatric ward, a waiter, an assistant director for a press association, a public relations associate, a communications director for a nonprofit, and a managing editor for a graphic design magazine. His blog won a 2005 Bloggie award for best gay-lesbian-bisexual-transgender blog and a 2005 Satin Pajama AFOE European Weblog award for best writing. He recently contributed to *Boys to Men* (Carroll & Graf, 2006), an anthology about growing up gay. He is married to a Swedish man and is fluent in Swedish but notes: "I no doubt sound like a five-year-old on occasion."

I BLAME THE PATRIARCHY

I Blame The Patriarchy
the patriarchy-blaming blog that never misses dinner

http://blog.iblamethepatriarchy.com/

Judgmental Sex Pedantry

PUBLISHED BY TWISTY JUNE 14, 2006

Flea—how I admire Flea; no erudite dildopreneur was ever so hilarious—actually gets email asking for sex advice. I can only imagine the degree to which such a thing enhances her quality of life. My envy is pronounced. I myself am never called upon to opine on intimate matters. Which is probably just as well, since my reply to every question would undoubtedly be "Dump him!"

Anyway, in response to one such email, Flea has a post up containing second-party information on how to perform a blow job without gagging.

Flame me if you will, but I posit nevertheless that no woman, since the dawn of the patriarchal co-option of human sexuality, has ever actually enjoyed this submissive sexbot drudgery. There's a reason that deep-throating a funk-filled bratwurst makes a person retch.*

* Reason: It's fucking gross.

Today's unrelated photo: Season's Greetings from the aftermath of yesterday's razing of the tar-paper shack three doors down from the Twisty Bungalow.

How dare I presume to impugn the sanctity of a woman's right to the blow job? I do so mostly on accounta I will get a big bang out of the impassioned arguments defending it.

Patriarchy Defeated By Fellatio; We Can All Go Home Now

PUBLISHED BY TWISTY JUNE 16, 2006

I sorely underestimated the magnitude of the bang I was going to get out of all the comments in defense of blow jobs. Holy moly! What fun! Hitherto-unplumbed depths of commentarian grossness were fathomed. Hetero porn models were advocated. Quaint Freudian notions were invoked. Status quos were defended. Defensively. Some of you seized the opportunity to acquaint the group with your erotic autobiographies (don't quit your day jobs!). Some of you even argued that blow jobs are the dudely equivalent of cunnilingus. But then someone actually used the word *cum*. I had to call in a haz-mat team to fumigate my office.

And that's not the only price I paid for my critical stance on Boo-Ya Nation's favorite pastime. One blogger has likened me to bible-thumping zipper-cunt Dawn Eden: "Both of you need to stop delivering broad-based pronouncements on other people's sexual practices on the basis of what you personally object to."

I am chastened. I'd forgotten that when it comes to sex, it is the duty of the radical feminist to shut the fuck up. Sex, which, along with religion, is the new religion, is sacrosanct territory. It is anti-feminist to point out the ideological problems with certain patriarchal sexbot traditions because so many women enjoy patriarchal sexbot traditions. It is, in fact, offensive to suggest that getting off has any untoward political ramifications at all. I mean, we're talking about getting off. It's the feminist nirvana. Anything goes as long as someone gets off, and besides, it's none of my beeswax.

Like Germaine Greer always says, if you wanna nail your nutsack to a breadboard and call it sex, it's A-OK with me!

I must have been insane to question the degrading sexual theatrics that are every woman's birthright, when the mastery of these theatrics is her invitation to life's rich feast. It is a well-known fact that most women spring from their beds every morning singing, "O I hope I can blow some dude today!" That poor dumbass who wrote to Flea asking for help in controlling her gagging was just an anomaly.

We all know that in a patriarchy (and by "patriarchy" I mean a social order in which all women are subject, by universal agreement, to all men), on accounta the power differential, all relationships with men are inherently inequitable.

Except, it turns out, relationships wherein women suck cock! That's when patriarchy miraculously recedes into the aether and male privilege becomes a distant memory! No woman was ever so free as the woman with a mouth full of throbbing gristle! How could I have been so blind? Less blaming and more cocksucking, that's my new motto! Mystery solved! The struggle is over!

Comment of the Week

PUBLISHED BY TWISTY JUNE 21, 2006

Remain calm. This post is a lament on commentarian sloppiness. It is not about blow jobs. At least not much. If I mention them here it is only to give my example comment some context. If you have something to say about blow jobs, send it to *Penthouse*.

Recently I wrote an essay in which I seditiously suggested, like I do in every other essay I write, that the dominant culture imposes inequities on human beings according to their sex. I used heterosexual fellatio to illustrate this sweepingly radical notion. This essay generated a pestilence of asinine responses, both here and on other blogs. Behold a randomly selected sample, the gist of which has been nearly universal among my fearsome cocksucking detractors (I have kept the typo intact for that authentic commentarian flava):

> Um, who kneels these days? I prefer a comfy chair with the patriarch standing at attention before me. Why should't I be comfortable? Like frisee, keep the bjs off your plate if you don't care for them, but don't outlaw them for the rest of us!

Let us now go where no blog post has gone before: to the stream-of-consciousness musings with which I was afflicted after having read this sample comment and its many identical brethren, published here for the first time ever on the World Wide Web:

First I experienced revulsion, which is understandable since the remark commences with "um". Wherefore this mania for beginning a written sentence with preverbal grunts? It is grueling enough slogging through 16,723 comments saying "Where do you get off expressing an opinion on your own blog, you prudey asexual?" without having to endure 5th grade speech viruses ironically affected by adults engaged in a limp effort to convey condescension.

I then experienced amazement that a woman could, in 2006, take pride in publicly announcing that she happily sucks off someone she refers to as "the patriarch."

Then I experienced revulsion again.

Then I thought, "How can a blow job be on a plate? God help us all, the metaphor is dead!"

Then I wondered why people who have clearly omitted reading my essays insist on responding to them. This bizarre conduct absolutely mystifies me. The logical thing to do, when you haven't read an essay, is to not comment on it. Lest you look like an ass. I know this from years of experience of not reading essays and not commenting on them. Many's the time I've been asked, "Twisty, what is the recipe for success in the cutthroat world of not looking like an ass?" My answer? "Not reading essays and not commenting on them, Grasshopper. It's a winner!"

Yet our commenter, like so many before her, has, in her haste to lead an unexamined life, not only made erroneous assumptions concerning the actual content of my post, but has elected to publish her response to this mythical content on the blog, thereby diluting the sterling quality of the discourse.

For instance (I mused), in drawing out of thin air the supposition that I desire to "outlaw" her favorite pastime, she misconstrues my observations on the universal ramifications of patriarchal intrigue as some kind of official decree threatening the venerable American institution of cocksucking. She has, in other words, leapt to the conclusion that I endeavor to control her, presumably because I am a mutant who can bend people to my will just by writing stuff.

At this juncture I greatly enjoyed a reverie based on a scenario wherein I could bend people to my will just by writing stuff. Whereupon I thought, "If my magnificence was such that I actually could outlaw stuff merely by expressing an opinion on an obscure blog, would I really squander my superpower on some pedestrian hetero sex act? Hell no. I would outlaw Austin traffic, worship of dead Jews, and all supercilious parroting of the directives of the status quo."

And then the dinner bell rang.

Torture

PUBLISHED BY TWISTY NOVEMBER 24, 2006

If you're anything like me—and why wouldn't you be?—you've been whipped into something of a froth by reports of "Bush's mysterious new programs" targeting "Fifth Columnists" (supposed terrorist collaborators, disloyal fraternizers, kids who refuse to say the Pledge of Allegiance, what have you), AND how Halliburton has been awarded yet more contracts to build prisons to house the inevitable influx of the aforementioned traitors, not to mention those poor sods who, once they've been tortured by Rummy's patented techniques, can't ever be released for the rest of their lives on accounta they know too much about Rummy's patented techniques.

Anyway, I've been ruminating on the subject of torture, and one thing has led to another, and, as was inevitable, I've started stewing about women's underwear.

I mean to say that in report after gruesome report on torture tactics sanctioned by the Secretary of Defense and employed by American sociopath-imperialist forces in hell-holes like Guantánamo and Abu Ghraib, one reads ceaselessly of "snarling military dogs," "stress positions," "deprivation of light and auditory stimuli," "20-hour interrogations," "sleep deprivation," "forced to perform tricks while tethered to dog leash," "waterboarding," and "forced to wear women's underwear on head."

Every news source reports this women's-underwear-on-head situation without batting an eye. That it counts as torture strikes nobody as odd. [The online magazine] *Salon* (its gripping series "The Abu Ghraib Files" uses images from the Army's own investigation to chronicle the enormity of prisoner abuse from October to December, 2003) reports that women's-underwear-on-head was (and undoubtedly still is) "standard operating procedure." According to *Salon*, "The Fay report [a U.S. military internal affairs report] found that there was 'ample evidence of detainees being forced to wear women's underwear.' Fay concluded that the use of women's underwear may have been part of the military intelligence tactic called 'ego down,' adding that the method constitutes abuse and sexual humiliation."

All right-thinking Americans—people who would feast for 47 days and 47 nights if Donald Rumsfeld were finally tried for war crimes— accept without comment that, although the physical duress it entails must be something on the order of "comfy chair," panties-on-the-noggin represents an act of degradation so extreme it appears to be a breach of the Geneva Conventions.

While it's true that most of the prison photos show women's underwear used in conjunction with one or more of the other more sadistic tactics, few media reports fail to accord the undies at least equal billing. A military CID [Criminal Investigation Division] caption of Abu Ghraib photo reads "Detainees [sic] is handcuffed in the nude to a bed and has a pair of panties covering his face." Here the syntax

reveals that "handcuffed in the nude" is deemed the equivalent of "panties covering his face." Now consider, if you will, the caption I found accompanying this same picture at notinourname.net: "A naked prisoner, chained to his matress-less [sic] bunk, is forced to wear women's underwear on his head." Not "a naked prisoner, women's underwear on his head, is shackled spread-eagle to a bare bunk." By virtue of its position as the sentence's predicate, the brutality of the panties is clearly the statement the caption's author wishes to make about the subject, revealing, I contend, the aspect of the photograph to which the writer has experienced the greater emotional response.

The prisoners themselves have expressed a marked sensitivity to the humiliative superpowers of women's panties, recalling their under-wearian experiences in what is to me surprisingly (given all the other godawful shit they'd endured) vivid detail. Back at *Salon*, detainee H— says, "They gave me woman's underwear that was rose color with flowers on it." Another detainee says, "[The] American police [. . .] he put red woman's underwear over my head." Taken in context, their statements suggest they actually view underwear-on-head on a par with being suspended above the floor from shackled hands for 5 hours.

I am not arguing that forcing prisoners of war to wear women's underwear on their heads is not an act of torture. Clearly it is torture. What interests me is the reason it is torture. How is it that nobody has anything but the utmost sympathy for a fellow shown with a pair of girly skivvies on his head? By what demented code does a swatch of soft pink cotton become an instrument of torment? What makes this particular cruelty stand out from a field of persecutions so squalid they can only have proceeded from massively deranged minds crammed with snuff films and bongwater?

Duh, it's universally and unanimously acknowledged that there is no lower life form than a human female, no bit of her more base than her cunt, and no tangible symbol of that cunt more handy than a pair of her knickers. Clearly, on this point our sadistic American military jailers and their unfortunate captives agree. When you wanna totally humiliate, degrade, and dehumanize a dude, just call him a girl.

Military intelligence sadists realized, incidentally, that putting women's underwear on female prisoners' heads didn't have quite the same resonance, so it was a case of "show us your tits or we'll rape you" for the women they arrested on suspicion of, what else, prostitution.

Twisty Faster describes herself as a queer pro-choice atheist and aesthete and "a spinster aunt." To people outside the blogging world, she is Jill Posey-Smith, forty-seven years old. This is her online biography: "Twisty grew up on a farm in Texas. One day she went to St. Louis, Missouri. There she was drugged and held prisoner without any decent tacos for twenty-five years. Eventually she was able to reach escape velocity, whereupon she hoofed it back to Texas pronto. She now divides her time between a bungalow in North South Austin and a ranch in the Texas Hill Country.

"Twisty's pop culture credentials include coming of age in one of today's most popular decades, the seventies. She studied E Lit at Washington University in St. Louis for a while, toiled as a bartender for a while, wrote songs and played guitar in a couple of loud rock bands, and wrote songs and played Casio in one quiet Casio band. For a while, Twisty was a restaurant critic at a Midwestern news weekly [the *Riverfront Times* in St. Louis]. Her unorthodox views regarding provel 'cheese,' combined with her effete and pompous style, earned her a prestigious James Beard Award nomination in 2003."

Twisty cheerfully explains what her blog is not: It "is not a feminist primer" nor "a forum for patriarchy-enthusiasts to air their grievances against uppity women," she says. "If your feminist college roommate wouldn't sleep with you, don't come cryin' to me." And she offers a few disclaimers: "I represent neither all women nor all feminists as an elected spokesperson. Neither does any other woman of your acquaintance (this includes your wife, your girlfriend, that stripper friend of yours, and the characters on *Sex and the City*). . . . Therefore, if you have a beef with Andrea Dworkin that you feel invalidates feminism as a whole, I couldn't care less."

IN THE MIDDLE

In The Middle

Raed Jarrar's Blog

http://raedinthemiddle.blogspot.com/

THURSDAY, AUGUST 10, 2006

Back from the Mideast

I just came back from a short trip to Jordan and Syria. The trip to
Syria was so fast, but I managed to visit some Lebanese refugee camps.
[. . .] On more than [one] occasion, I got shouted at because I live in
the US.

[. . .] The trip to Jordan was more productive and organized. I
managed to put together a couple of meetings with Iraqi parliamentar-
ians representing the major groups in the parliament. One meeting was
with two MPs, one representing the biggest Sunni group, and the other
representing the biggest Shia group in the parliament. They gave the
US delegation that accompanied me a strong and united message
against the US presence in Iraq. It was a clear Sunni/Shia demand to
end the occupation and set a timetable for withdrawing the US troops.
[. . .]

I came back to DC for a day, then I took the bus to New York to
watch *Fear Up: Stories from Baghdad and Guantanamo*, and participate in some discussions.

The next day, I went to JFK in the morning to catch my JetBlue plane to California. I reached terminal 6 at around 7:15 am, was issued a boarding pass, and checked all my bags in, and then walked to the security checkpoint. For the first time in my life, I was taken to a secondary search. My shoes were searched, and I was asked for my boarding pass and ID. After passing the security, I walked to check where gate 16 was, then I went to get something to eat. I got some cheese and grapes with some orange juice and I went back to gate 16 and sat down in the boarding area enjoying my breakfast and some sunshine.

At around 8:30, two men approached me while I was checking my phone. One of them asked me if I had a minute and he showed me his badge. I said: "sure." We walked some few steps and stood in front of the boarding counter where I found out that they were accompanied by another person, a woman from JetBlue.

One of the two men who approached me first, inspector Harris, asked for my ID card and boarding pass. I gave him my boarding pass and driver's license. He said "people are feeling offended because of your t-shirt." I looked at my t-shirt: I was wearing my shirt which states in both Arabic and English "we will not be silent." [. . .] I said "I am very sorry if I offended anyone, I didn't know that this t-shirt would be offensive." He asked me if I had any other t-shirts to put on, and I told him that I had checked in all of my bags and I asked him "why do you want me to take off my t-shirt? Isn't it my constitutional right to express myself in this way?" The second man in a greenish suit interfered and said "people here in the US don't understand these things about constitutional rights." So I answered him "I live in the US, and I understand it is my right to wear this t-shirt."

Then I once again asked the three of them: "How come you are asking me to change my t-shirt? Isn't this my constitutional right to wear it? I am ready to change it if you tell me why I should. Do you have an order against Arabic t-shirts? Is there such a law against Arabic script?" So inspector Harris answered "you can't wear a t-shirt with Arabic script and come to an airport. It is like wearing a t-shirt that reads, 'I am a robber,' and going to a bank." I said, "but the message on my t-shirt is not offensive, it just says 'we will not be silent.' I got this t-shirt from Washington DC. There are more than a 1000 t-shirts printed with the same slogan. [. . .] It is printed in many other languages: Arabic, Farsi, Spanish, English, etc."

Inspector Harris said: "We can't make sure that your t-shirt means 'we will not be silent'; we don't have a translator. Maybe it means something else." I said: "But as you can see, the statement is in both Arabic and English." He said "maybe it is not the same message." So based on the fact that JetBlue doesn't have a translator, anything in Arabic is suspicious because maybe it'll mean something bad!

Meanwhile, a third man walked in our direction. He stood with us without introducing himself, and he looked at inspector Harris's notes and asked him: "is that his information?" Inspector Harris answered "yes." The third man, Mr. Harmon, asked inspector Harris: "can I copy this information?" and inspector Harris said "yes, sure."

Inspector Harris said: "You don't have to take off your t-shirt, just put it on inside-out." I refused to put on my shirt inside-out. So the woman interfered and said "let's reach a compromise. I will buy you a new t-shirt and you can put it on on top of this one." I said "I want to keep this t-shirt on." Both inspector Harris and Mr. Harmon said, "No, we can't let you get on that airplane with your t-shirt." I said "I am ready to put on another t-shirt if you tell me what is the law that requires such a thing. I want to talk to your supervisor." Inspector Harris said, "You don't have to talk to anyone. Many people called and complained about your t-shirt. JetBlue customers were calling before you reached the checkpoint, and customers called when you were waiting here in the boarding area."

It was then that I realized that my t-shirt was the reason why I had been taken to the secondary checking.

I asked the four people again to let me talk to any supervisor, and they refused.

The JetBlue woman was asking me again to end this problem by just putting on a new t-shirt, and I felt threatened by Mr. Harmon's remarks as in, "Let's end this the nice way." Taking in consideration what happens to other Arabs and Muslims in US airports, and realizing that I will miss my flight unless I covered the Arabic script on my t-shirt as I was told by the four agents, I asked the JetBlue woman to buy me a t-shirt and I said, "I don't want to miss my flight."

She asked, "what kind of t-shirts do you like? Should I get you an 'I heart New York' t-shirt?" So Mr. Harmon said, "No, we shouldn't ask him to go from one extreme to another." I asked Mr. Harmon why does he assume I hate New York if I had some Arabic script on my t-shirt, but he didn't answer.

The woman went away for 3 minutes, and she came back with a gray t-shirt reading "New York." I put the t-shirt on and removed the price tag. I told the four people who were involved in the conversation: "I feel very sad that my personal freedom was taken away like this. I grew up under authoritarian governments in the Middle East, and one of the reasons I chose to move to the US was that I don't want an officer to make me change my t-shirt. I will pursue this incident today through a Constitutional rights organization, and I am sure we will meet soon." Everyone said okay and left, and I went back to my seat.

At 8:50 I was called again by a fourth young man, standing with the same JetBlue woman. He asked for my boarding pass, so I gave it to him, and stood in front of the boarding counter. I asked the woman: "Is everything okay?" She responded: "Yes, sure. We just have to change your seat." I said: "But I want this seat, that's why I chose it online 4 weeks ago." The fourth man said, "There is a lady with a toddler sitting there. We need the seat."

Then they re-issued me a small boarding pass for seat 24a, instead of seat 3a. They said that I can go to the airplane now. I was the first person who entered the airplane, and I was really annoyed about being assigned this seat in the back of the airplane too. It smelled like the bathrooms, which is why I had originally chosen a seat which would be far from that area.

It sucks to be an Arab/Muslim living in the US these days. When you go to the Middle East, you are a US tax-payer destroying people's houses with your money, and when you come back to the US, you are a suspected terrorist and plane hijacker. [. . .]

Road trip, road map, and the little thug

[. . .]

The t-shirt incident opened my eyes to a bitter reality in the US. There are many underground racist movements that are coming out in public now to spread their fascist ideologies. Many anti-Arab, anti-Muslim, anti-immigrant, and anti-Semitic groups are pretty active online and offline spreading their ideologies of hate and exclusivity. [. . .]

Look what this soldier/national guard who served in Iraq wrote me:

> Hey ******* get the **** outta my country if you dont like whats going on stand up for your weakling self obviously your countrymen cant stand up for whats theirs i guess neither can you what a bunch of pathetic fools you know nothing about life and freedom if i run across you in my daily tasks i will kill you GET THE **** OUT OF MY COUNTRY IF YOU DONT LIKE IT HERE

Mr. brian m. seems to be still active in the army/national guard. What is more shocking and scary than his email is the fact that he doesn't even feel that he should hide his threats or his name. He sends me emails from his personal and army addresses, with his full name, threatening to kill me while he's on duty! After googling mr. Brian's name and finding much information about him, I wrote him back saying "The US is my country now, as much as it's yours, or maybe a little bit more. I will do my best to make this country, our country, a better place. This may include putting people like you in jail. . . ."

Then I asked him, based on my 10 minutes' googling of his name, whether he was the same brian who is 32 and lives in Danville, PA [. . .] the same brian [. . .] who called his mom, [. . .] when he got injured in Baghdad while searching for WMDs. So, it seems that he freaked out after my email and decided to write me back, apologize and beg for forgiveness.

I welcome your thoughts on this matter . . . should I file a police report against this little thug or not? I'm going to write the Office of the Chief of Public Affairs, 1500 Army Pentagon, Washington, DC, 20310-1500 to ask whether they support such behavior in the army.

SUNDAY, DECEMBER 31, 2006

Saddam: the execution scene

As I predicted a year and a half ago, Saddam was executed because of the relatively minor case of Al-Dujail. I was against Saddam's execution for two major reasons: The first is that I am against capital punishment in general whether it is against a former gangster like Tookie Williams or a prisoner of war and a former dictator like Saddam, and the second is that I have always believed that the only people who have the right to change Saddam's political regime and interrogate him are Iraqis, not illegal foreign occupiers.

The way that Saddam was executed added some more points to my argument. I would have never guessed that Saddam would be killed on the morning of Eid (the equivalent of Easter for Christians in terms of religious importance), and I would have never expected that it would be carried out by sectarian militiamen. On a day when Muslims are supposed to sacrifice a lamb in honor of God's mercy, Saddam's unprofessional executioners made him look like a sacrificed victim of vengeance.

There are two videos showing the execution scene: the official one (which is the one that hit the news some 6 hours after the execution took place), and another more graphic one that was "leaked" to the media.

The second video can be found here. It shows Saddam's last minutes and it doesn't stop where the official one does. It shows Saddam with the noose around his neck standing for some seconds while a group of men chant Shia slogans and others praise Muqtada Al-Sadr and Muhammad Baqir Al-Sadr (the godfather of PM Al-Maliki's Al-Dawa Party). Then it shows someone cussing and shouting "go to hell," then Saddam falling while saying the sentence every Muslim has to say before death: "I bear witness that there is no god except Allah, and that Muhammad is the messenger of Allah." In fact, he wasn't even given the chance to complete his sentence.

The execution scene shows some militiamen in civilian outfits covering their faces [. . .] holding and moving Saddam, who refused, while handcuffed and shackled, to cover his face. The execution scene did not at all resemble a State execution; rather, it looked like a chaotic sectarian act of revenge interrupted by shrieking militiamen who received him from the US forces less than 30 minutes before killing him.

Saddam was given the chance to look like the calm and brave leader who didn't fear death, and who claimed to love and defend Iraq and the Islamic nation until the last second. At the same time, his executers, hiding their faces, demonstrated themselves as vengeful thugs supported by the occupation and representing only their political party and sects.

It takes a lot of stupidity to lose moral authority to a former dictator with a noose around his neck. It takes a lot of stupidity to turn Saddam's execution into an event dividing Iraqis further instead of uniting them. It takes a lot to turn Saddam from a former dictator to a symbol of resistance and pride. I can go as far as comparing this to how much stupidity and hard work John Kerry put into losing the elections to an inept president like Bush.

RAED JARRAR ■ IN THE MIDDLE
http://raedinthemiddle.blogspot.com/

The first appearance of Raed Jarrar in the blogosphere was not as the author of a blog but rather as its intended audience. Back in 2002, an Iraqi man who called himself Salam Pax (a pseudonym made of the Arabic word *salam* and the Latin word *pax*, both meaning peace) started blogging about life and then war in Iraq. He called the blog Where is Raed? because his friend Raed Jarrar, who was in Jordan working on a master's degree in architecture, wasn't responding to his e-mails. Jarrar noticed and soon started blogging on Pax's site. In 2003 he struck out on his own with In the Middle, a blog of political analysis and news about Iraq.

A twenty-nine-year-old architect and political analyst based in Washington, D.C., Jarrar was born in Baghdad and has spent most of his life in Iraq. After the U.S. invasion, he became director of CIVIC Worldwide in Iraq, which he describes as the only door-to-door casualty survey. He also established an organization to facilitate reconstruction projects that would be carried out by local communities in Baghdad and the nine southern provinces. His master's thesis was about postwar reconstruction.

In 2005 he moved to California, where he translated and consulted for a project on Iraq's marshlands and worked with California Peace Action to urge Congress to outlaw permanent U.S. bases in Iraq. In Washington he has been active as director of global exchange for the Iraq Project, which tries to bridge the gap between Iraqi leaders and U.S. Congress members.

Jarrar writes about Iraq for *Foreign Policy in Focus*, a publication of the Institute for Policy Studies, and has been a talking head on CNN, CNNI, Al-Jazeera, Al-Alam, the BBC, and many radio stations, including member stations of Pacifica, BBC, NPR, CBC, CBS, and FOX.

Ironic Sans (It seemed like a good idea on paper)

http://www.ironicsans.com/

MARCH 20, 2006

Idea: Pre-pixelated clothes for Reality TV shows

I don't watch much Reality TV, but I've seen enough of it to notice an on-going phenomenon: Someone wears a garment with a trademarked logo or artwork on it, and the producers have to pixelate it beyond recognition in post-production. Of course no Reality TV star wants their shirt, which displays their well-chosen article of self-expression, senselessly pixelated so nobody can see it. But no Reality TV producer wants to deal with the headache of removing said article of self-expression to avoid trademark violations. The pixelation process seems like an awful lot of trouble to go through for something that could have been avoided with a little pre-planning.

So I'd like to introduce my new line of pre-pixelated clothing for Reality TV shows. If you're going to be on a Reality TV show, you can buy one of these fine products and save someone a lot of headaches later. In fact, if you live in an area where a Reality TV show is taping, you should think about getting one of these shirts in case you get caught in the background of a shot. And if you're heading to audition for a Reality TV show, maybe you should wear one of these shirts to the audition so they know that you're really serious about Reality TV.

Available here in these and other fine styles:

---//---

Random Acts of Emphasis

I flew Delta this *weekend,* and found myself LOOKING through their in-flight magazine while *waiting* to take off. I noticed something in their magazine that I've noticed before—they randomly ITALICIZE things for no apparent reason. And *sometimes* they use all caps for no apparent REASON.

I *SUPPOSE* THEY THINK IT ADDS VISUAL INTEREST. ITALICS AND CAPITALS ARE *TREATED* AS DESIGN ELEMENTS. AND THAT'S FINE. BUT IT MAKES FOR *CONFUSING* READING WHEN THEY USE IT IN EVERY *HEADLINE.* WHEN I READ, I MENTALLY

EMPHASIZE THE ITALICIZED AND CAPITALIZED WORDS. I THINK THE SKY *MAGAZINE* PEOPLE FORGET THAT. AT *LEAST* THEY DON'T ADD **BOLD** INTO THE *MIX.*

―――――――― // ――――――――

FEBRUARY 27, 2006

Michelangelo's *David* meets David's *George Bush*

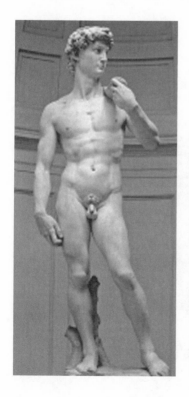 

While traveling on business through Houston's Bush Intercontinental Airport, I was struck by this statue of George Bush (the senior George Bush) in one of the terminals. What struck me was the eerie similarity between this statue and Michelangelo's *David*. The 8-foot-tall George Bush was sculpted by David Adickes, the Houston artist whose busts of all the presidents grace two different President Parks.

I can't help but wonder if the similarity is intentional. Michelangelo's *David* depicts the second king of Israel, with a sling over his shoulder that he used to slay the giant Goliath of the Philistine army who threatened to destroy Israel. With that in mind, if Bush represents David, who represents Goliath in this scenario?

———————————— // ———————————

JUNE 6, 2006

Georgia O'Kleenex

This is what I saw when I reached for the last tissue in the box.

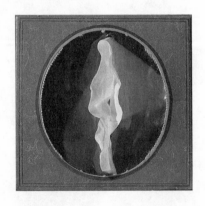

———————————— // ———————————

Idea: A . . . commercial I'd like to see

A guy is showing his girlfriend his brand new flat screen TV. He's beaming with pride showing it off. "Honey, this is the best flat screen TV money can buy. It's a 1080p HDTV with dual HDMI inputs, and digital audio output. It's got a 1200 to 1 contrast ratio. It has four different memory card expansion slots for viewing digital photos or playing MP3s, and it auto-uprezzes from 480 and 720 sources with bicubic interpolation. The blacks are ink black. The whites are paper white. And the color is as vivid as real life. Baby, I'm telling you. This is the Cadillac of televisions."

Then we see the Cadillac logo, and their latest fancy car rotating slowly against a black background. "Cadillac. We set the standard."

This could be a whole series of commercials like this featuring different luxury products. Clocks. Fine wines. Pianos. Each one would have a person—maybe the product's owner, or a salesperson, etc.—extolling the virtues of the product, and finally calling it "the Cadillac of" whatever it is. Everyone knows that "the Cadillac of . . ." is frequently used to express that an item is at the top of its class. So why shouldn't Cadillac capitalize on that? I'm surprised they haven't already.

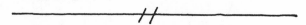

Idea: Use "apparent" when it's not simply "alleged."

In America, a person is considered innocent by the law until he is proven guilty. When the media cover a case where someone has been accused of a crime but not convicted, they follow the same guideline.

And they should. If the news calls someone an arsonist, for example, but he is later determined to be innocent, the news could get in trouble for defamation or slander. So the word *alleged* is used.

Dictionary definition of *alleged:* "asserted without proof or before proving." That's great. The media shouldn't go around convicting people before they've had their day in court. But what if there is proof, but the legal process hasn't yet taken its course? What if the suspect was caught red-handed? Sure, there might be circumstances not yet known that would shine a completely different light on the situation. But when there is known evidence, maybe *alleged* isn't the right word. I propose *apparent.*

Dictionary definition of *apparent:* "manifest as true on the basis of evidence that may or may not be factually valid."

Let's look at some stories in the news. In Orange County, Florida, police have arrested a man for running an "alleged pot-growing operation." News footage shows a dozen or so large marijuana plants found in his home. Now, sure, I suppose it could turn out that they're plastic plants and nobody realized it. Or that someone else put them there to frame him. But given the evidence on hand, I think it's weak to call this simply an alleged pot-growing operation. It looks like an apparent pot-growing operation to me. This acknowledges that the evidence still may be shown to be invalid, but it calls the situation what it actually is.

[...]

(Note: This paragraph not for the squeamish) And in Hong Kong, tragedy struck a woman who had previously reported domestic violence. This time, she didn't survive. According to reports, she called emergency services, screaming that there had been a murder, and then she got cut off. Police arrived in her home to find her and two others hacked to death. The article headline calls this an "alleged murder." Surely it's safe to call it an "apparent murder," isn't it?

I understand the need to err on the side of caution. But the word *alleged* has an actual meaning. It's not just a catch-all word to keep you out of trouble. There is another word that is just as cautious, and is often more appropriate. Apparently, not everyone sees it that way.

A museum recommendation and a recommendation for the museum

Part I: A Museum Recommendation

On Thursday I had a chance to attend a preview of a new exhibit called Magritte and Contemporary Art, which opens tomorrow at the

Los Angeles County Museum of Art. Of course the art is impressive, including more than 60 works by Magritte, and another 60 or so by artists including Barbara Kruger, Andy Warhol, Jeff Koons, etc. But the exhibit installation is one of the best examples of museum space enhancing the artwork that I've ever seen. Designed by John Baldessari, the museum space is transformed into a surreal experience worthy of the artwork it contains. The floor is a carpeted Magritte-esque sky. The ceiling is covered with images of freeways. The guards all wear suits and bowlers, like they've stepped out of a Magritte painting. [...]

Part II: A Recommendation for the Museum

[...] LACMA needs to check their cash registers. When I made a purchase, I received a receipt with the name of the museum misspelled. How long has it been like that? Someone should be paying more attention to detail.

```
LOS ANGELES COUNTY MUSUEM OF ART
        5905 Wilshire Boulevard
        Los Angeles, CA   90036
```

————————— // —————————

JANUARY 08, 2007

Idea: Word balloons as quotation marks

I noticed the other day that word balloons have the same basic shape as quotation marks. It's interesting because both are used to convey that a person is speaking. That got me thinking of an instance where word balloons could be used as quotation marks, as a design element.

It would probably be weird to have

them as part of a font set, but maybe it would look neat used for a pull quote in an article about comic books. [...]

For the example above, I thought it looked weird with open word balloons, so I made them solid black. And double-quotes looked odd to me, too. I decided a solid single-quote word balloon worked best. For actual use, a typographer or graphic designer could probably play around and find other variations that work even better.

---//---

Idea: Paintings of descriptions of the paintings

If I had the time, the means, and the resources, I'd make a series of large paintings of those little cards that describe paintings in museums. They would be paintings of the cards that describe themselves. For example, I'd do a painting in oil on canvas that describes itself as being an oil painting on canvas. Then I'd hang it in a gallery next to a little card that's identical to the painting, but is actually there to describe the painting. I'd do a whole series with different materials. Oil on canvas, Acrylic on wood, etc. See the photo illustration above for an idea of how it might look.

FEBRUARY 14, 2007

I see the Death Star

Whenever I walk through the Union Square subway station, I have to navigate through all these vertical I-beams that are all over the place. It always reminds me of something, but I couldn't figure out what. Finally it dawned on me. It's the first stage of the Death Star level in the *Star Wars* arcade game.

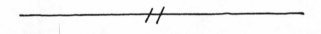

MARCH 29, 2007

Idea: Develop an F-Bomb

The term *F-Bomb* is used often these days to describe what we used to simply call the F Word. [...] Specifically, it describes the F Word when it's used unexpectedly. For example, if a caller on a radio show uses the F Word, the host might chastise him for "dropping the F-Bomb."

With that in mind, I think that if I were an evil dictator in a country developing a nuclear weapon, I would name my new weapon "The F-Bomb." Then I'd get a little giggle every time it was reported in the news that my country is threatening to drop the F-Bomb. As in, "Ironicsansistan tested a long-range missile today, heightening fears that it will follow through on its threats to drop the F-Bomb on South Ironicsansistan."

—————————— // ——————————

David Friedman, thirty-two, a commercial photographer in New York City, has maintained Ironic Sans since early 2006. But his first online project was in 1995, when he created a user-contributed list of must-see movies. Other online projects included a mock fansite for a fictional Saturday-morning cartoon about President Clinton as a second grader; an online experiment using a toy digital camera in ways it was never designed to work; and his own photography portfolio.

Realizing that separate Web sites for all his different ideas were getting expensive to maintain, he created Ironic Sans. (That "would be a great name for a serif font" someday, he notes, but in the meantime "it makes a good name for my blog.") There he has posted, for instance, a number of short videos: sixty seconds in the life of steam, sixty seconds in the life of landing gear, etc. He has also posted all the complaining notes that were slipped under his door by a downstairs neighbor, Sophina, years ago, and an interview with a guy who has seen almost every performance of *Saturday Night Live.*

"I get a lot of offbeat ideas," Friedman says. "Occasionally I share them with friends, but not everyone is interested in hearing them." Take the idea for a glass-topped desk that's also an ant farm. "It turns out only a small percentage of people would agree that an ant desk is a good idea. So now when I get these thoughts, when, say, I find myself wondering what a Godzilla-shaped building would look like in downtown Tokyo, I write them in my blog. There are enough people reading online who 'get' my sensibility to make it worthwhile. I've also learned that some great ideas are truly unique, and some are obvious enough that others have had them."

Born and raised in Phoenix, Friedman says he always felt like a New Yorker trapped in the body of an Arizonian. He had an urban relocation procedure in 1997, and now calls New York City his home.

IT'S RAINING NOODLES!

http://raining-noodles.blogspot.com/

The Kittens, They Die!

My mom dragged me to see a doctor specialised in Traditional Chinese Medicine (TCM) today, since throughout my exams I'd been breaking out in rashes. I fought against it with all the strength I could muster, because such a visit invariably results in me having to take some disgusting medicine. If you thought I was bitter enough about my ex, you really have to try TCM medicine for a whole new definition of that word. My mom won anyway, as all mothers do, and just a while ago I downed something that tasted lethal enough to exterminate the global population of termites. I feel like throwing up and the only thing that's stopping me from doing so right now is the awareness that if I actually puke my mom will drag me back to the TCM doctor for another prescription. What's the child abuse hotline?

Another reason why I prefer doctors specialised in western medicine is my dismal grasp of Chinese, a language often used by TCM doctors. I have written about this inadequacy of mine before here, but what I did not tell you is that whenever I speak Chinese, a few innocent kittens on the other side of the world die, and as a result I avoid the language whenever possible. It offends my kitten-loving sensibilities. However, this morning I had no choice, though it went well except for the dead kittens and the one embarrassing part where the doctor asked about some white thing, and I stared at her very blankly before looking at my mom for a translation. It turned out to be a pronoun referring to a certain type of monthly discharge.

The diagnosis was also given in Chinese: Hot blood. When the doctor said this line all I could think about was that I could have told you myself that I am both warm-blooded and hot-blooded, and why did my mom waste money for me to hear something I already knew? Apparently, though, it means something entirely different in TCM, and after one paragraph of explanation I nodded happily and pretended I understood, wordlessly of course. We don't want any more kittens to die, do we?

The doctor also told me to avoid "food that excites the taste buds" such as chili, and to switch to bland food. And refusing to eat anything mild or tasteless, I wanted to tell her that the rashes were actually only a physical manifestation of a strong emotional allergy to an ex-boyfriend, except that I didn't know how to phrase that in Chinese. I feel so wronged.

SUNDAY, NOVEMBER 26, 2006 @ 20:42

Of All the Things I Didn't Get to Write

Last night I dreamt that when I looked out of my window there was a river. It was a wide one and I remember identifying it as a braided stream, with mid-channel bars colonised by vegetation (pink flowers), but after staring at it for a while it suddenly morphed into miles of desert. I didn't think it was strange at that point, it felt so natural and peaceful to be admiring a vast sandy landscape. Out of the blue it occurred to me that one spot exhibited fluvial scarring that ceased more than four thousand years ago as well as more recent evidence of water presence, and when my mind decided that the glaciers were melting I abruptly began to quote word for word an entire page from my Geography lecture notes, one of those that utterly disgust me now because it turned out to be totally irrelevant during the recently concluded exams. After that it became hard to breathe, and instinctively I knew that those were greenhouse gases like carbon dioxide and methane. The last thought I remember having before I woke up is one that accurately pinpoints the source of my frustration today, that I never got to write these four words during the Geography exam: Cow fart produces methane.

MONDAY, NOVEMBER 27, 2006 @ 21:31

Foreign Encoding

Recently I've been spending most of my real life living the role-playing one, and an hour ago I was ready to write an entry about Maple Story [an online role-playing game with many players], which I have been playing for the past few days. Predictably I was distracted by the game and began taking random screenshots in which I deny my ability to speak English in French while making faces at NPCs [nonplayer characters].

[. . .]

Like most female characters, mine has a sugardaddy. I call him that because he supplies me with in-game currency and items without

me even asking, and in return every time he does a cool spell I paste
"Cool! ^_^" into the chat bar. He is also a genuinely nice person, and
when he did ask for my number I decided that he didn't deserve any
Bitch Treatment and gave him one of my two mobile phone numbers,
the one that runs on a prepaid card and that I give to people I don't
know very well.

I wasn't expecting Sugardaddy to call within the week because
typical males play this game in which they starve phone contact for
days and pretend to be wholly uninterested in the girl just so when
they finally call, there is a higher probability of the girl having waited
by the phone for hours and therefore sounding excited over the phone.

Unfortunately ever since my pretty illusions of dating were shat-
tered by one break-up over email, I've stopped waiting by the phone
for anyone, and the shock (as opposed to relief) in my voice must have
come across as hostility, because when we next chatted in Maple Story
he said I sounded uncomfortable. After I assured him that it wasn't

awkward at all for me, he asked, "What should I not say to make me sound not wierd?" and I didn't know how to answer.

Welllll . . . For a start, spelling it that way is sort of "wierd" . . . and so is the double negative . . . and the question itself. >_<

Also, I have started lying about the school I recently graduated from, because it intimidates my Maple Story buddies. Frankly it gets a little annoying; I don't see why I have to be treated like a supernatural untouchable being just because I was fortunate enough to attend an established school. [. . .]

Lately I realised that Maple Story players, like most online RPG [role-playing game] players, don't have a very good grasp of English. I'm not referring to the shortening of words or omission of vowels in strategic places, which Dudette [a friend] hates; her respect for the English language is so great that anyone who challenges the Oxford dictionary is committing blasphemy in her book, and she takes really long to read sth writtn lyk dis. [. . .]

In Maple Story, though, distortion of the language is taken to a whole new level, and for hours yesterday I stared at the screen cracking up whenever someone typed a line. There was a girl whose character didn't budge from one spot for ages, and when she finally replied to my question she apologised and attempted to explain herself, "I tok n click wil lag." And then there was the guy who typed, "GN ELIGN PL WT 4M!!!!!!!!!!!!!!!!!!!!" including all those exclamation marks. I eyeballed this for centuries trying to decide which language I was reading. Was he trying to tell me that he was drowning in a toilet bowl at home? The only conclusion I could draw was that this person most likely wasn't a native English speaker.

My brother, who has spent approximately two-thirds of his life in RPGs [role-playing games], took one look at that line and calmly translated, "Going to Elinia, please wait for me." I stared at him in admiration and asked him how he knew, was he psychic? He smirked and said, "Noob [i.e. novice] encoding."

It's Between the Devil and the Deep Brown Shit

Mum: "That's his. The other bowl of medicine is yours."

Me: "Yeah I can tell by the colour."

Brother: "How?"

Me: "Yours is vomit-y. See the yellow-brownish stuff? That's like bile."

Mum: "Yours is dark brown. Like shit."

Me: "I'd rather eat shit than eat vomit."

1,300-Word Complaint

One morning last week I woke up, switched to a random channel on TV, and started watching a table tennis game in the Asian Games. I realised that "Doha" was printed on the net. My brother entered the hall to ask why I was watching the Doha games, was I really that bored? I sleepily told him I needed something sane in my life and for God's sake, it's the Asian Games and not the Doha games! You don't call a Rolex-sponsored golf tournament the Rolex Tournament, do you? He gave me a look that approximated the face one makes when changing the dirty nappy of a baby with severe diarrhea, and pointed out that Doha was a place, not a brand. What year is it? I think I may have been living under a stone for maybe ten thousand centuries.

Lately I've been swamped with personal problems and for the past few days I have had the persistent, nagging conviction that I was going to fall over and die in the next minute or so. Obviously I am still alive, mournfully and pitifully alive, because the awfulness just took an exponential leap today and I have no idea where I should start, really.

Should I write an entry with a gradient of awfulness, from Awful to Dreadfully Awful to God Why Am I Not Dead Yet? This reminds me of a nightmare I once had, about me cooking alone (which is already a recipe for disaster) then eating the food I cooked, and with every bite the taste got increasingly worse. Then I managed to accidentally burn the kitchen down in a house that wasn't insured. Immediately, though, I realised that it was just a dream because if I bought a house, the first thing I would settle would be fire insurance. Duh!

It's graduation night tomorrow and I didn't intend to attend it until the overwhelming guilt finally won today. When my brother asked why, I told him that Dudette begged me to go because she needed a crazy friend to "laugh at things with." He simply replied, "Beg her not to beg you to go."

Anyway, today's last minute shopping for the prom was pretty horrifying. My mom picked out many pieces that I thought were more suitable as casual wear in her millennium, but I humoured her and tried them on. I hate dresses. I hate dress-shopping. And I hate dresses. Have I mentioned? I really hate dresses. [. . .] To add to my disgust, I wanted an S-sized dress but when I got home I realised that what I bought was in fact M-sized but erroneously tagged S. Tomorrow I'll have to make a trip down to the shop to exchange it for a new piece, size S, and I hate dresses so much I'm going to puke sequins and zips.

Yesterday morning my brother wanted me to wake up at 7 AM to accompany him on Maple Story, and even though it was already 3 AM that day, I agreed. He wasn't convinced that I could haul my heavy-weight ass out of bed as promised though, and because it's fun to make use of my subconscious fears I told him that he could hit my tummy with the heart-shaped cushion that Mr X gave me, knowing very well that I would sooner bleed to death than be reminded of my ex that way; after we broke up I used to pretend that the cushion was him and I would talk to it for hours whenever I felt lonely because talking to Mr X then would have yielded exactly the same reaction anyway.

As I expected, this morning I bolted out of bed at 6:58 AM for no reason, [. . .] as if I knew that in approximately two minutes something would happen to make me throw a major hissy fit. Seconds later my brother ran into my room, and when he saw me his face fell and got stuck to the floor, so disappointed was he that he was soclose! to gaining a secure advantage in the pillow war we started back in 1997.

[. . .]

I also wanted to complain about ten other different things including how my doctor is forcing me, this certified carnivore, to go vegetarian, but I'll probably turn fifty before I'm done. This one thing really can't be ignored, though: This afternoon my parents bought an apartment in the same town Mr X lives in. Yes, why not add to my grief by making me live in the same area as the person I am trying my bestestest to avoid? [. . .] I can think of many torture methods that would hurt less, such as hammering my arms onto planks of wood attached by rope to two horses running in opposing directions. Or plucking out my toenails one by one. Why must I be forced to relocate to his town? WHY???

FRIDAY, JANUARY 26, 2007 @ 19:52

. . . & One

Hello Prince Charming,

Umm. Shall we start with the cockroaches? When I told you that they were one of my greatest fears I had NO idea it would backfire this stunningly and inspire you to plan on throwing one of those vile things at me just so you get to watch my reaction. If you should ever put that plan into action one day, I suggest precautions such as reinforcement of all walls and windows, as well as life insurance. My intention behind pointing out my phobia of those disgusting creatures was in fact to indirectly help you identify the fire-breathing dragon you should slay. Like, dude, damsel in distress here. You do not point the dragon fire in her direction. If you should manage to wipe out cockroach-kind one day, I shall be your slave for eternity. As long as you don't kick a fuss when I squeeze toothpaste tubes at the middle.

I knew 2007 would be awesome; I just had no idea that this would turn out to be such a spectacular understatement. At times you give me mental indigestion and your brilliance makes my head explode several times a day. I painstakingly gather my brain cells to process the Awesomeness, and then you negate all my efforts with a simple move and they're splattered all over my walls again, brain cell wallpaper. On the sixth day of this year you decided that it would be a fantastic idea to inform me of your desire to shag me—subtlety evidently not your strong suit—and, having dated in the past only guys who indulged in euphemistic alternatives for "fuck," I had to give you brownie points for the refreshing candour. But the next time you plan on making me this enthralled and mortified at the same time, please buy me some Prozac and one month's supply of sleeping pills; I was in a hyperactive, besotted state for the next week, during which a record-high number of pillars strangely eluded my visual range. If you paid me a dollar for every pillar I kissed that week alone, I'd have enough to allow for my retirement next year. Not that I'm currently employed, but, bah. Technicalities.

Yeah, and the ratio of my age to yours corresponds to my waist-to-hip ratio. What this simply means is that approximately once every day I'm tempted to joke that you're old enough to be my father, although you technically aren't. Sometimes my cradle-snatched self gets lost in thought working backwards into the past, trying to figure out where you'd been all my life: When I went out with a boy for the first time ever, you were already in University; when I was negative two years old, you were flipping through medical encyclopaedias examining exclusively female terrain. Amazing.

Almost everyone I've told about you so far responded with surprise because we'd expected me to date someone three or four years younger, going by the arithmetic or geometric regression in my relationship résumé: The Ex a year younger, then Mr X two years my junior. I don't know what to make of our age difference; it is such a huge number and it offends my mathematical sensibilities because it has ruined a potentially peachy mathematical sequence. The only person who didn't bat an eyelid at this cradle snatching was Mr X, and I'd genuinely wondered what I'd done to make him expect insanity from me by default until I remembered my chainsaw, my pink and fluffy and absolutely! harmless! chainsaw. And the girlfriend he took after me, my successor, the one I sent a text message to at 1 AM saying that she had a cute butt, though I didn't reveal the fact that no one's posterior can probably compare to mine. My ass kicks all the rest.

This month has been crazy and kickass, and once again I enter the annoying stage of life in which every piece of clothing acquired is bought with a guy in mind, like my Mr X Jeans, the ones slyly calculated to reveal a gradually increasing amount of ass per second spent in them. Last week I bought skirts which by my standards are obscenely short, skirts others may consider only mini but nonetheless in my opinion resemble stingy fabric renditions of illegible Internet shorthand. These skirts, they place a nagging suspicion at the back of my head that the world is secretly experiencing a severe shortage of cloth, that the next big thing is Cloth Conservation. Also, the g-strings, which I suspect people wear only because it feels terribly uncomfortable—a wonderful excuse to take them off. Personally, I would rather use them to catapult stones at people I don't like. Yes, I do have a problem with having a string in my ass crack, but if it makes you happy, I'm delighted to wear it. As long as you buy me that pink Nintendo DS Lite you promised. Give and take, honey.

Besides walking into pillars and making absurd garment purchases, other stupid things I've done this week include writing your name in beach sand, looking up horoscopes, Google-stalking you, and living in your time zone, so that whenever someone asks me for the time I have to first derive local o'clock. In fact, it's 4 AM in Singapore as I write this, and my body clock is obviously screw-loose. Recently neither of us have been getting work done or decent sleep because you stay up to chat with me late into your early mornings, and I stay up to think about you until I forget that sleep isn't optional, and it's absolutely okay because people who're in love do lame and corny things like that all the time. It's perplexing, the way these emotions interfere with logic and reasoning, and if I weren't this intoxicated I would probably be angry with myself for being resigned to my newfound stupidity. But meh, ignorance is bliss.

The truth is, for too long I've been struggling against the urge to Fedex myself to wherever you are. Yesterday afternoon I had to hear it for myself, so I dialled Fedex's hotline and enquired if it would be possible to bribe them into mailing me to you. "My guy," I pleaded in a tiny voice, "I miss him." And the employee who took my call, a sweet lady overflowing with sympathy, replied that she too was powerless against immigration laws, though would it help if she got me the number of the local mental institution? I thanked her and told her I could remember my home telephone number perfectly well, and she said, "Have a nice day!" in a perky voice and hung up.

Maybe I should try other delivery services. This thing I'm feeling has a way of encouraging hope against hope. Silly, desperate, persistent hope.

Love,
Princess

P.S. No cockroaches please, or else no sex.

ANGELIQUE CHAN ▪ IT'S RAINING NOODLES!
http://raining-noodles.blogspot.com/

It's raining noodles! is the blog of a nineteen-year-old student in Singapore named Angelique Michelle Chan. "I live in secular, multiracial, multireligious, tiny Singapore," she writes, "where too much of the workforce is too busy to have sex." She says 99.9 percent of her things are pink.

Angelique is voluble about herself and her blog: "This blog chronicles moments I want to remember. It is my emotional piggy bank. . . . On most days I am head over heels in love with myself. I also love caffeine, dark chocolate, money, snow, pool, the Internet, roller coasters, horse-riding, long-haul flights with turbulence, pink, and Sunday. I detest tobacco, mushrooms, war."

Although she has posted her picture on her blog, she says she has never been stalked. "As for weirdoes . . . Well, I've had my fair share of hate mail from people with deep-seated psychological issues, albeit nothing seriously stalker-ish; I have a folder for such mail, just in case I need them for future reference (like if my house is mysteriously razed to the ground . . .) but other than that, I ignore them."

In 2006 she graduated from Raffles Junior College, where, she said, "I spent two very fulfilling years studying geography, literature, mathematics, and economics at the GCE A levels. In Singapore it's considered an 'elite' school attended by the rich and/or intelligent, and there's a paradox in that such prestige may be cumbersome in certain social situations," like the Web.

"Buried within me is a closet geek who believes that if men and women communicated in languages as beautifully precise as HTML or mathematics, break-ups would possibly become a thing of the past. Though I subscribe to existentialism, my worldview remains predominantly 'www.' My favourite vulgarity is 'double you tee eff.' I am the proud owner of huge eyebags. I am short but tall enough, fat but thin enough, happy but disgruntled enough, pacifist but assertive enough, wild but cautious enough, observant but self-absorbed enough. I am nothing and I am everything. I am alive."

JOHNNY I HARDLY KNEW YOU

http://jihky.blogspot.com/

WEDNESDAY, FEBRUARY 22, 2006

sitting in my mother's garden, and the moody blues coming from somewhere over the dam-lock, reverberating through the hills beyond the lake; you don't question. it matters a hell of a lot what happened before, and a pencil lies nearby and jon krakauer is quoting pasternak and still feeling guilty about the everest climb. I am eating two hot dogs, potato salad and drinking a beer. The "blue" flowers are in full bloom. Mom told me they are weeds, but i love them. On the other hand i feel ridiculous; so I rocked back on my heels and taught malcolm how to swim.

■ ■ ■

ouija board experiment #2876 (sometime in 1996)

Q: is there a spirit who would like to talk to us?
A: LLIJAH (. . .) ZOPOVERMR
Q: are you ELIJAH?
A: YES (. . .) WOVENOAKITL (. . .) MALAXMMP(. . .)
    IAMAMOMOMO (. . .) MATO MARY AMAWOMAN . . .
Q: Who are you, do you have another name?
A: ZNVZJ (. . .) ZAJ

Q: Is there a 3rd way you are called? Are you a spirit?

A: ZOET (. . .) JVK(. . .)YOU (. . .)YBJ

Q: ELIJAH, will you talk to us?

A: MASRTOKBK (. . .)LOHW(. . .)YES (. . .) XCGZSMA(. . .)
    MHMNSAB(. . .)LZCMUZ (. . .)M(. . .)M(. . .) GOODBYE

■ ■ ■

You know I've been channeling you all week? (Unfortu-nately, you're making my website not make sense anymore. Thanks a lot. Of course, it probably all makes perfect sense to you. Because you are a freak.)

[. . .]

my mother and my grandmother had a . . . tough relationship. "mom, do you miss grandma?"

"I've always missed her. She was never here." She paused next to me in the kayak. "but she said the best thing to me anyone's ever said, i was 4 or 5, and the way she gardened, she had a whole plan, that involved shading, light, color, timing: so the whole landscape would grow and shift and become things and then disappear. It was quite amazing. No one before or since could do that in the same way, I think. Anyway, we were standing together and i asked her about the colors and a certain area [. . .] and she turned to me and said, 'you're the only one who would be able to see that.' "

Mom grew quiet after that, and we paddled along in the sun.

■ ■ ■

"Hydrangea flowers vary with the species, some being white, while others may be pink or blue." These were deep red, and at 4 o'clock in the morning, they fell like rose petals in the courtyard. i thought they were roses. it took me approximately 20 minutes to figure out how the shower head worked.

In tokyo, we woke to crows. The crows are st. francis' friends and lovers. wolves, too. when francis died his friend, brother crow, followed him just two days later. stood guard while his heart broke. My father saw me across the street the day i left and said: it's like a movie, he said when i finally heard him and waved back and waited for him on the corner, two travellers or lovers [. . .] and it might be the last time he sees me.

■ ■ ■

now, i mainline trees, and water and country. trails and cows and bacon and eggs and rain and mist; sunrises over lakes and pine. my mother buys me new underwear and it moves me to tears. and a new battery powered toothbrush. "hey! it's a ladywand!"

"mom!"

"sale on aveeno™! . . . want some?"

■ ■ ■

My mom makes her garden and in her garden things grow (i am not kidding about this garden. it's breathtaking). The house is as big as my apartment here. nothing special, it almost disappears into the slope of the hill. The granddaughter of the original owners came by to see the house, and said right there in the middle of the garden. "why is it so beautiful here?" We went to the lake association picnic and everyone could see mom's garden from across the lake. "look at that."

so i was thinking that if i was in a film, a thriller, there would be a situation and i wouldn't know how the hell to get out of it. i'd be all, whoa, look stupid and then break all my ghost-busting equipment. for instance, i saw *serpico* recently, and besides being an amazing movie (sidebar: they used to make movies without soundtracks. none. no music ever), and one thing i have to say about sidney lumet is the women in *serpico* were seriously braindamaged. sample dialogue: i'm splitting. . . .

amazing!

Then pacino buys a puppy and that nearly derailed the entire movie for me. his whole life is very intense and i'm all, shmuck. who's walking the dog right now. is the dog lonely? who's feeding the dog? and then it ended and the last thing it said was "serpico is living somewhere in switzerland" and he was with the dog.

[. . .]

THURSDAY, MARCH 23, 2006

we were sitting on mom's floor having mac and cheese (the martha stewart kind, not kraft's, with wine and a salad to cleanse the palate, cause that's the way my moms do). keeping an eye out while the baby tear-assed around and danced and sang baby songs and ate cheerios he had thrown on the floor because they taste better that way. we were doing that thing where kelly was trying to have a normal conversation that didn't involve babies ("so jennie, how's anything in your life not involving babies?" "you want to talk about how cute my hair is?[. . .]") and mom was telling endless "when jennie and gabriel were babies" stories, and i wasn't paying attention or dying of embarrassment (for example, a story i don't remember is pottytraining. i was all scared of the toiletbowl, because it was bigger than me, so mom would hold my hand for balance and the first time i did it, we were like we will save it so daddy can see when he gets home. meanwhile mom took me to the store to buy big girl underwear and we got 50 pairs: the kind with the days of the week on it, the kind with polka dots, the kind for boys, the kind with little flowers. we got me all set up, and i was prancing around. and then we waited for dad to come home, and he came home, while i was prancing and leading the big band and he walks into the bathroom, says "NANCY, YOU FORGOT TO FLUSH" (ok WHO announces to their wife or girlfriend that they forgot something like that?) and he flushed it. apparently i went apeshit and had a really dramatic meltdown. dad realized as soon as he did it what had happened, and was INCONSOLABLE for a week. BESIDE himself. WE ALMOST BROKE UP. and that is the story of jennie's first poop. the end.) ok back to present time, mom had just told this story and i was CRYING i was laughing so hard, and chasing him all over the apartment, and picking him up and playing superman can fly. and then he got all serious and WALKED. way to shut down three adults in 0 seconds flat. "oh my god." and then it was all jubilation and yelling and jumping up and down and cheering. it was a motherfucking walkoff! AMAZING!

FRIDAY, JULY 07, 2006

i had done as much as i could to avoid pre–*superman returns* media watching. for whatever reason, i had made the mistake of clicking like an idiot through various links to see in no particular order: what the new superman looked like, what his suit looked like, the new colors, the stupid s symbol on the belt, if he was gay or not. you know what, the gays need to shut the fuck up. a quick review through my hand over my eyes of bryan singer's thoughts and feeeelings. big mistake. i had been completely crestfallen. my first reaction to seeing brandon routh was "WHATTHEFUUUCK."

then the teasers and the trailers started rolling out. the first time i saw the trailer i think i was just about to watch *the incredibles* or something and i heard john williams music and clark jumped over a cornfield and i got goosebumps and was a mess. but that was before i saw brandon routh. they were smart in the beginning and didn't show him. i could be wrong about this, but i don't remember any reveal, or maybe i blocked it out. i was just left dumbfounded because i was all, "omg. the FLYING" and was left to nervously speculate forever, because that was like a year before it was supposed to come out. they have the technology. they had better do that. because no matter how many times i see the original supes movies, i can never get over the complete disaster that is the flying. when i was 8 and first saw it, it was the same thrill i had seeing *x-men* for the first time. they did it right, and i think i must have been in a huge haze of gratitude because it was only later that i was all like, "WHAT ABOUT THE DANGER ROOM?" and "WHERE'S KITTY AND PETER?" [. . .]

i totally should mention that even as a snotty little 8 year old i had a problem with christopher reeve. big tall and gawky as hell, his arms were too long. but he was a genius. i didn't fully appreciate him until the 2nd movie and his hair got all blown-out and relaxed and right on seventies with the red chamois shirt. i admitted somewhere inside that yes, he was a strapping, handsome dude. and that smile. damn.

ok, so where i work? for the past months you'd be doing some awe-some task or another, like debating the purgatory-vs.-electromagnetic theory of *lost* (which have a lot in common, i think), and all of a sudden lights would dim, conversation would stop, someone would crank it up to 11 and you'd hear john williams music. the animators would get real quiet. once i peeked around someone's shoulder and saw superman fly. i thought, oh they just might have something. but brandon routh? yuk.

[. . .] so i saw *superman returns* last night, btw. i must say that eva marie saint is still amazingly beautiful. that was stunning. and marlon brando's voice? could have its own movie. i am sitting there hungrily devouring every signpost of clark kent mythology before i knew i was doing it: the corn fields, the farm, the old truck, the labrador retriever farm dog, the breaking sun over the plains. [. . .]

the plot was an annoying mess. but the flying. that day, one of the animators had stepped on the elevator and practically had a nervous breakdown trying to describe it. we were in a full elevator, and this man was almost dissolving with happiness. my friend turned to me, later, and said "i've never seen him show any emotion at all." i remained skeptical, because something told me that if they didn't do the flying right, all was lost.

you have to understand that i don't consider myself jaded at all, even though i work with animators and my brother is an animator and even if i can watch all these movies from *Titanic* to *LOTR* [*Lord of the Rings*] and see certain CGI [computer generated imagery] effects and wince with pain. how could whoever let that slide? that was not dope. omg, like when frodo puts on the ring and he goes into a diaphanous weird green world and i am squirming because it looks like a coney island stupid animatronic haunted house. like, ooh. terrifying. even in this *superman returns*, there were moments that were like that. certain inhuman, odd and jerky movements he made in the air that were clearly a computer program.

but there was something else. something that knocked me on my ass. and it was brandon routh. and it was the flying. both were absolutely quiet. dreamlike in the speed and scale. or at least they were so stunning to me that any cosmic fanfares signaling peak emotions were forgotten. i remembered all those repressed hopes. it was simple, really. it was the flying. in my dreams, not daydreams but deep, deep sleep dreams, iconic and shattering dreams, and this was truly bizarre, i have taken those same flights through the city searching for something, someone, getting back home wherever that is in the dreamscape, looking over my city. through its canyons and up into the cathedral of space, the slow zenith of an arc and suspended moment before i look back down, over and low in the middle of the hudson river. over and back along the coasts of the continent. seriously. it was as if this film had taken the exact blueprint of my movements, and speed and mapped them out of my dreams. the gentleness and impossible speed, the suspension of gravity. the strength i took from the sun's rays, how they entered my chest. the towering cloud formations, and gathering storms, lightning in the stratosphere and over horizons. everything.

i was trying to put my finger on it during the ride home and later as i lay flat out on my back on my floor with my cats on my chest. i lay there for a long time, like that.

isn't that amazing that we don't have that in this world. the abilities of superman. i mean, we do. but that very childlike desire to in actuality, in reality, fly of your own volition. that seems wrong to me. that that's "not" in the cards. and a little sad. yes, we can imagine that, and metaphorically take flight and whathaveyou. but it really is the start of all wonder, it's alpha and omega: to fly.

i thought, what if we did have a hero like that? in this world. not a savior, but a hero who could do those things (because my mind simply wouldn't jibe with the christ imagery), and i think even if the superman myth is based on all heroic myth, he's not a savior, and it would be really dangerous if he was? would we risk everything knowing somewhere we'd be saved? would our world's laws (physical and spiritual) be different? would we? or do we risk everything already knowing that we're kind of on our own? i think the question is garbled in the "does the world need superman" thread. that's not it at all. we certainly don't. but somewhere, at least i do, i need to know that i've taken to the air, and i inhabit that source of power and hope (because that's what it is . . .) and i can see them mirrored in a superman's eyes, in his look when he says to himself and the dog next to him, quietly and with no inflection except some sadness and open ended resignation, but only just . . . "well, i'm back." (he doesn't say that, but that's the feeling), and the puppy is like, "dude. the ball."

and brandon. damn. that kid. he was really astonishingly good. he was superman. a friend.

THURSDAY, JANUARY 11, 2007

many nights of insomnia with this one too, culminating in a strange dream of safety just last night. i was on a large plane, sort of a biosphere jet, it held people, populations, different stratas, on different levels. oh yes, the seats were there and the rows, but there were worlds also, and earth and ground and sky, it smelled of earth and summer and we were hurtling across the continent, or at least it felt as if that were so. i could see the moon. my mother was on the plane, and sara was there also. some minor characters from my past who morphed and wandered away like those people do in real life. shroudy figures.

halfway thru the trip sara went away somewhere, i was busy with something and she went up on the "road" and it was also a cathedral space. quite interesting, just above the level i was on. it was probably a country road, and i went way into the back of the plane and sat in the last section to be with my mother. suddenly, the sound of the plane changed, one of the engines had blown off, and there was an eerie silence or lowering of white noise tone of traveling overland and sea. it was the sound of space and something had nominally and logically, if logic really held in this space, and it didn't, so in other words it should have been terrifying but wasn't. "gone terribly wrong." or that's the "narrative" of that kind of thing. and my mother announced it in a very practical way. the engine's off. and i consciousness-jumped, was suddenly present in the moment of the dream and also a third party to it. and all of us waited it out. there was no panic, just all of us, the thousands of people all together on this ship, which really had infinite dimension but also was a jet—listening to the night hurtling outside its body.

there was no panic, because there was nothing that could be done and there was a long amount of time, longer than dreamtime usually allows to be in that moment. and then? i saw we were about 50 yards off the ground, having descended fast and steadily, and we crossed over a road, i saw the car lights coming towards us, a startled farmer probably, and we landed. and someone said, oh i thought we were over the ocean.

The author of the blog called johnny i hardly knew you is Jennie Port-nof. She is thirty-seven years old and has degrees from the University of California, Berkeley, and the Rhode Island School of Design. While at Berkeley, she helped June Jordan and nineteen other poets start Poetry for the People, a program that sponsors readings, workshops, and classes. She is a poet, an artist, and an editor of the poetry and fiction magazine *Fort Necessity*.

Her blog, which she began in 2005, "was a very bad attempt to keep a fourteen-year-old's secret diary, where, you know, I could think about stuff and rock my room. I also happened to link to all of my friends, who immediately knew who it was anyway, so that worked really well."

Before johnny, she blogged as "mr trinity." Why blog at all? "I started writing in this form because the internets, at base, is hilarious. I mean, seriously. It's, like, wait. What? Who writes like that? It opens everything up. Babel. It's really exciting. You can go deep down a rabbit hole if you really want to, anytime. There are people out there who I just think are gorgeous writers or live exceptional lives. They send me a message saying, 'Hi.' And somehow we make this funky public/private address thing work for the stranger parts of us or we dork out and make each other laugh. Sometimes it works, and sometimes you want to go live in a cabin and eat roots and berries." Her blog is now called jennie the lion.

julia {Here Be Hippogriffs}

http://julia.typepad.com/

MAY 31, 2006

The Adverbial Son

Hiya. How are things? Are you good? Happy healthy and whole? I hope so.

Personally I have been feeling a little sad, so I spent the past several days organizing my pantry, rearranging my kitchen cupboards, planting seedlings and annuals and hanging baskets, and putting away the winter clothes after washing all the summer ones. I still feel a little sad but now I know that I have dried mushrooms to last me forever so I can stop buying them. Would you like to hear all the luscious organizational details?

Of course not. Hence my prolonged silence.

From today:

After offering Patrick a lollipop (he accepted) the nice cashier asked Patrick how old he is.

"Actually, I am three. I am really really three."

"Three!" she said. "And do you like dinosaurs?"

"No, I certainly do not. I most definitely do not. No."

"Oh. What do you like?"

Patrick squinched his face up as if he was in pain (he was thinking) and said, "Fonts."

"Fawnts?" she asked, bewildered.

"Yes, I absolutely like fonts. Absolutely I do. Totally."

She looked at me for assistance but I just smiled at her. I was damned if I was going to explain. . . .

"Franklin Gothic," Patrick offered helpfully. Only he pronounces the word *go-thick*, like *go-kart*, whereas we say *gah-thick*, like *in-a-GA-dda-da-vida*. I am not entirely sure how he wound up all Canadian but whatever. "Courier. Baby Kruffy."

She looked confused. Or, as Patrick would say, very terribly really completely confused. "Thank you! Have a nice afternoon," I said, hauling Patrick into one arm while grabbing the bags and sprinting toward the door. "See you next time. Bye."

But I was not quick enough.

"Times New Roman!" Patrick shouted over my shoulder. "TIMES NEW ROMAN!

TIMES!

NEW!

ROMAN!"

So there is that.

P.S. I went to his preschool picnic and discovered that despite his idiosyncrasies Emily is in love with him. First the teachers told me. Next Emily's mother told me. Then there was the unpleasant yet suggestive squabble between Emily and Elise when Elise also wanted to tuck wilted dandelions into Patrick's hair. Finally Emily drug Patrick by his hand over to where her mother and I were sitting.

"THIS is Patrick!" she beamed. "I love him."

"She does," Patrick said, "she totally really does love me."

"You're kidding" is what I wanted to say. "How nice" is what I managed.

I find parents talking about so-and-so's "little girlfriend" creepy [. . .] so let's just say that Patrick obviously has a little friend (shall we say an admirer?) and I find it reassuring. How odd can he be, really, if a nice girl like Emily wants to introduce him to her mother?

JULY 31, 2006

Alrighty Then

Tonight's order will be chronological. The stream will be of consciousness. Bear with me. Having left Steve to his own devices for the past three days I am being heavily pressured to abandon the Internet (you! he wants me to abandon you!) and come downstairs to watch *SG-1* [*Stargate SG-1*] with him. An *SG-1* into which Ben Browder has not yet entered, I add darkly.

So this will have to be quick. Vite! Aprisa, aprisa!

I went to BlogHer [a blogging conference]. It was rather fun and rather ridiculous and I am quite glad I went although I do not know if I would ever go again. One thing of note for my infertile blogging friends: DO NOT EVEN THINK ABOUT IT. Do not go. Do not ever ever go to BlogHer. From the bib in the registration bag o' loot to the overwhelming mommyblogdaciousness of everything you will want to drown yourself in the pool after you poke out your eyes with the complimentary corkscrew. Seriously. No one's fault, nature of the beast, organic rather than intended but there it is. Trust me. [. . .] Thursday night my plane was delayed for three hours. I did the sensible thing and took my book to the closest airport bar. I had a glass of wine and read until a lifeguard from Huntington Beach decided to tell me his life story. He had come to Minnesota to surf Lake Superior (righteous!) and I think that is all we need to say about him. I eventually extricated myself and wandered back to my gate (F2), only to discover that it was eerily empty. I swore, delicately, and went to check the departures board. Where I discovered that my flight was now departing from G20. In three minutes.

I ran.

I ran and swore much less delicately and paused to gulp air and then ran some more. After about ten years of this I was rewarded for my Herculean efforts by the sight of a nice line of people still boarding at the new gate. Score. Then I realized I was going to throw up.

I was the last person on that plane with about thirty seconds to spare.

I would be lying to you if I told you that I did not immediately leap to the conclusion that I was pregnant. I mean, come on. I threw up! It is a sitcom-classic symptom. Then I used the airplane lavatory and discovered some discreet spotting. Spotting! At, like, nine days past possible unintended ovulation! Twelve little elves spelling I-M-P-L-A-N-T-A-T-I-O-N with their bodies could not have been any more clear.

But the next day the spotting got a little heavier and I wavered in my womanly certainty. Then Julie and I went to lunch in Palo Alto and I excused myself from the table to discover that I had vastly overestimated the power of the pantyliner (oh just look away if this grosses you out. honestly). I spent another few hours sort of kidding myself that it was anything other than a period before the frequent need for new tampons led me to throw in the towel and declare this ridiculous cycle a complete wash. Two days of bleeding seems conclusive, yes? Yes.

And yet . . .

I rolled over this morning and screamed as my breasts hit the mattress. So I did what any obsessive person would do, I took a home pregnancy test out of my trusty home pregnancy test cabinet and I tested.

And instantly saw a second line as black as the shades of Hades. I went for an hCG test today (embarrassed as hell, may I add), results back tomorrow.

So, yay, I guess! Also, whoops. Also, huh? Finally, yes, Virginia, apparently you can have sex twice on the day you get canceled with six follicles over 14 but under 18 and still get pregnant. Which looks sort of obvious when I write it out like that but it certainly did not seem obvious at the time.

I am . . . well, embarrassed but I said that already. Also, damn, I don't know. Too late to do anything differently now. Might as well enjoy it while I can. I am pregnant for the twelfth time. That must be good for something right?

[. . .]

AUGUST 29, 2006

12.6

You know those movies in which the main character is trying to accomplish some task that should be easy (the gorgeous *Run Lola Run*, Scorsese's *After Hours*, *Adventures in Babysitting*) and yet the hero/ine keeps getting thwarted? That was me trying to post today.

Do you want to tell me why, on a beautiful windless 74-degree day, our power went out for four hours? Or why, when it finally came back, my wireless keyboard would only respond to function keys?

The ultrasound was good. Better than good. Great. It was a great ultrasound. A solid week's growth. Heartbeat in the 140s. Last night I was too nauseous to sleep and this morning I threw up in the tub because it was that little scootch closer than the toilet so I was hopeful that things were still growing. I was, however, imagining one of those lose-a-day-or-two situations in which everything could be fine but . . . I hate that ominous *but.* Anyway, as I have said a million times before, I am pleased for now. Which is all one can ever ask for, really.

12 Dot Over

I had an ultrasound this afternoon with my OB. I was saddened (but not particularly shocked) to see that the fetbryo no longer has a heartbeat. It had grown a lot since last week so we assume that it must have died in the past day or so.

So.

Well.

Yes.

I feel quite peaceful, actually. The uncertainty of the past week was very hard for me. Hoping and yet hopeless, I felt utterly drained and panicky and . . . and just AWFUL. I know where we are now and I can live with it. Of the myriad horrible possible outcomes (postnatal death, stillbirth, genetically normal but irreparable defects, therapeutic termination) a gentle in-uterine loss at 11 weeks seems fairly kind in the scheme of things. Having accepted that this baby could not live (for whatever reason, although I suspect the CVS results will confirm an unbalanced translocation) I cannot help but be grateful that I was spared worse.

My OB said that at this stage miscarrying on my own is out of the question. She said the risk of winding up in the emergency room, bleeding profusely, is just too high. So I have a D&C scheduled for 7:00 AM (check-in time 5:45 AM, which is completely depressing because the only tiny shining light in this painful mess is the promise of the sweet sweet embrace of Morpheus and his general anesthetic and you know what? even *I* don't need general anesthetic at seven o'clock in the goddamned morning. four in the afternoon maybe. lunchtime perhaps. but DAWN? no) Wednesday morning.

Obviously we wanted this baby. Obviously it hurts to lose it.

I don't know how to end this post.

NOVEMBER 20, 2006

Knitting The Ravelled Sleeve

[. . .]

Last night I opened a bottle of red wine after reading that, in addition to all its other health benefits, researchers have just discovered that red wine helps fight diabetes. Steve's last physical indicated his glucose levels are on the high side of normal so I decided it was in his best interests to drink a few ounces. Then, because the bottle looked rather sloppy just sitting there with only half a glass missing, I finished the rest of it. Some time later, after arguing politics with the cat, having my way with Steve and successfully negotiating the bathroom floor (who left that tub there? very dangerous), I fell into the deep and peaceful repose of the pious, expecting to be fully restored to health and lucidity after a good eight or maybe ten hours. Imagine my confusion when I was awakened a mere 45 minutes later by the sound of fake crying coming from Patrick's room. I ignored it. He stopped and then started again just as I was about to fall back asleep. Eh-hehn-hehn, eh-hehn-hehn.

I stumbled up to his room.

"Ah, there you are, Mommy," said a pompous little voice in the darkness as I fumbled the door open. (He really talks like that for some reason. he says "ah" and "indeed" and he rarely uses contractions. very normal, is our Patrick.)

"I just thought of a story and I wanted to tell it to you."

What?

He's crazy, isn't he? You can tell me. My child is grapetastically insane.

"Patrick," I said, shoving him over in bed and climbing in beside him, since I was FREEZING (stupid Minnesota), "no. Too late. Very late. Dark. No talking. Shhhhh."

"But Mommy, I just thought of a story and I wanted to tell it to you. I did. Indeed I did. I just thought of it and I wanted you to . . . I wanted to tell it to you."

I shushed him again.

"But mommy mommy mommy mommy mommy mommy mommy mommy mommy mommy . . ."

"FINE. Tell me the story QUICKLY and then stop talking and go to SLEEP."

There was a long pause. Had he actually . . . fallen asleep?

"Mommy."

No, not asleep, offended. His tone was as of one wounded.

"Aren't you going to go get a pen so you can write down what I say?"

Crazy. Like Nero-crazy, I think.

JANUARY 31, 2007

Bor-heme

My name is Lucia but they call me Mimi.

[. . .]

Patrick returned to preschool on Monday, having been fever-free all weekend and after assuring me he felt fine. This did not prevent him from immediately announcing to the entire room "I AM SICK! I AM STILL VERY SICK!"

"Ha ha," I said. "You're fine. You were sick but now . . . HE'S ALL BETTER! NOT SICK ANYMORE! NOTHING TO SEE HERE!"

[. . .]

Speaking of Patrick, he is obsessed with me. After years, YEARS, of finding me to be a vaguely acceptable substitute provided it could be confirmed that Steve really (really and truly) was not around, I am suddenly Woman of the Year. It's like I am the winsome barista whose sunny smile brightens every day and Patrick is the taciturn loner who comes in each morning for a latte he never drinks but simply holds while he stares from a corner. Steve tried to let me sleep past 7:30 this morning but Patrick's cries of outrage and bereavement made it hard to enjoy the moment of solitude.

Steve and Patrick used to have a morning routine and an after dinner routine, neither of which involved me, but for the past several months Patrick has been insisting that I make him breakfast, I play with him after dinner, I give him his bath, and I put him to bed. Is this a stage? It's killing me. I love him more than the four mighty moons of Jupiter squished together but sweet sarah goodwife let there be spaces in our togetherness!

It doesn't help that Steve was gone last weekend and he will be gone again next weekend. Oh. I didn't tell you. On Friday he is going to meet his birth brothers for the first time. (Sensation!)

After Steve found his birthmother she gave him the information he needed to contact his birthfather, which he did about five years ago. There were a couple of emails exchanged but it eventually became obvious that the guy is not interested in pursuing any sort of relationship. So Steve let it go for a while. Then (suddenly to me but I guess he must have been thinking about it for a long time) while I was in DC with my mom he tracked down one of his birthfather's two sons and called him. After the initial shock (my dad did which? with whom? and you are . . . what now?) they apparently had a terrific conversation and Steve is flying to meet up with the one and surprise (as in: "surprise! I am your previously never heard of before ever until this very second half brother!") the other.

If you want MY opinion (although around here it is very clear nobody does) I think springing yourself like this on somebody is kinda risky. Steve, however, is positively giddy about the whole thing. I have rarely seen him so excited (Steve being the strong silent type) and it is very nice to see him all twitterpated.

Why are these biological ties so important to Steve that he is almost forty years old and still pursuing them? I truly do not know. But they are. And I respect this fact. I, for example, am fascinated by genealogy while my born into the same house raised by the same parents brother can think of few things more tedious and pointless than studying one's ancestry. He cannot even keep track of which states our great-grandparents came from or whether the family fought for the north or the south in that war of Northern Aggression.

Or, for another example, my brother likes bananas and I do not.

Apparently (and here is my pithy summation so you might want to grab a pen) . . . apparently people are just differently wired. So that while you might have no desire to seek your birth parents and cannot understand those who do, Steve is marginally obsessed by it.*

One can see how this complicates our reproductive decisions, yes?

Aaaaaaaaaaaaaaaaaaaaaand I am going for an HSG/mock embryo transfer tomorrow as we have decided to try yet another IVF/PGD

---

* Steve would probably object to the word *obsessed*. If I asked him. But I think it fits. So I won't.

cycle. Locally this time. In April. What the hell, eh? Remind me to tell you what the decision making factors were on this one. It involved a dart board and a handful of fortune cookies.

FEBRUARY 12, 2007

Compounding

I think between us we have put together a reasonable plan for dealing with the orange threat level currently in place at Patrick's preschool. Thank you for your thoughts—there is advice in the comments on that last post to cover every possible child, parenting philosophy and school situation.

Personally I decided on a three-pronged approach: talk to Patrick about how he handles being hit, talk to the teacher and director about Patrick's specific concerns with Butch, and then (possibly) attempt to neutralize the problem by having Butch over for some carefully supervised play.

Doesn't that all sound so mature and sensible? Well I thought so. I thought my plan was pretty good. Reasonable, effective, empowering.

Unfortunately the Witness, let's call him "Patrick," told me to get bent. Not in so many words of course but he assured me that everything at school is JUST FINE. That Butch is trying to be a nice friend. Yes, sure, he hits a lot . . . but sometimes he doesn't! And just the other day Butch and Tim were playing nicely with the cars!

"Did you play with the cars too?" I asked.

"No," said Patrick.

"Did you want to?"

"Yes," said Patrick, "but Butch told me to go away because Tim and Butch just wanted to play by themselves."

"And how, exactly, is this an example of Butch being nice?"

"He didn't hit Tim the whole time," Patrick said, like the modest but understandably proud psychiatrist whose patient has managed to go an entire week without killing anyone.

Patrick was so sincere in his desire to have me stop talking about it and he seemed so incredibly embarrassed by the whole thing that I wavered in my resolve. Maybe I should just let Patrick deal with it in his own way? Perhaps when Patrick said he didn't want to be hit anymore he was speaking metaphorically?

I was still waffling when I brought Patrick to school on Friday. We walked in, Patrick hung up his coat, showed me his latest art project and then skipped over to the archway separating the main room from the toy room. As he stood there Butch ran over, shoved Patrick to the ground, slammed his head into the floor and, lowering his face into Patrick's, screamed, "YOU CAN'T PLAY HERE! GO AWAY!"

So I drop-kicked the kid to fucking Namibia.

No, no. Of course not. I bellowed, horrified, "BUTCH!" followed by "You do not push Patrick and you do not yell at him!" And teacher A said, "I told you I would take the toys away if you cannot all play nicely" and director B said, "Now, now, that's not how we talk to our friends."

WHAT?

[. . .] "Take the toys away"? "Not how we talk to our friends"? Are these people HIGH? I was very upset. I am still upset. Is it me? Doesn't an unprovoked attack of considerable violence warrant . . . something? I know it was just my maternal instinct urging me to tie Butch to a rocket à la Wile E. Coyote and blast him to Pluto but surely one of the teachers should have done . . . something?

Meh.

I talked to them about it after school and they said blah and I said blah and ultimately I said please just try to keep Butch from hurting Patrick. It is all most unsatisfactory and in Patrick's version of the Friday morning smackdown Butch ran over to him and said, "You can play but just be careful with the toys." Freaking Stockholm Syndrome, that's all I can figure.

On a completely unrelated note I learned a very disturbing fact recently. When I volunteered at the preschool the teacher informed me that Patrick insists that we have a different rule at our house. Would you like to know what my child has told every adult willing to listen? He told them that at our house you don't have to wash your hands after using the bathroom if you do not actually SEE any pee on them. That's the rule at our house. He would follow his teacher around, palms outstretched, saying "Look! LOOK! NO PEE! I don't have to wash them! That's THE RULE!"

I have never been so embarrassed in my entire life.

So, officially, for the record, I would like to state:

WE DO INDEED WASH OUR HANDS AFTER USING THE BATHROOM WHETHER OR NOT THERE IS VISUAL CONFIRMATION OF PEE.

Thank you.

That is all.

Julia Litton, thirty-six years old, grew up in Washington, D.C., and moved north and west over the course of a decade. She now lives in the woods outside St. Paul, Minnesota, with her husband and their five-year-old son. She likes living closer to the coyote pack than to her neighbors but admits that she would kill for some decent Thai food.

She is obsessed with food and fertility. After several miscarriages, Litton learned that the cause was a genetic mutation carried by her husband. She left her job as a marketer of packaged goods so that she could "feel sorry for herself full-time," as she put it. But then, in 2002, their son was born. For the next few years she and her husband tried for a second child. After eleven miscarriages, she is expecting twins in early 2008.

Litton wrote an online diary for "an annoyingly restrictive parenting site" before setting out on her own in 2004. The banner she originally designed for her blog had an arrow pointing to the approximate location of the q32 breakpoint on the fourth chromosome with the legend "Here be hippogriffs." This, she explained, "is where Steve's translocation is, and it was a dumb inside joke based on the old maps that would slap up mythical beast warnings when they didn't really know what was going on somewhere."

Julia {Here Be Hippogriffs} is mostly about infertility but also about Julia's clever son, her dinner parties, her fights with her husband, and her occasional loneliness. She is amazed by the advice she receives from readers, who have diagnosed her son's speech problem and helped her decorate a bedroom wall. In 2006 she began writing The Infertility Diaries for *Redbook* magazine. In the summer of 2007 she was moved over to The Mom Moment blog.

Language Log

http://itre.cis.upenn.edu/~myl/languagelog/

JANUARY 16, 2006

The Birth of Truthiness?

Last week's great truthiness debate is still raging in some corners, despite the fact that both the American Dialect Society [ADS] and Comedy Central's *The Colbert Report* have probably milked about as much publicity out of the spurious squabble as can be expected. At the heart of the debate is the question of what sort of ownership Stephen Colbert (or rather the truculent on-air persona known as "Stephen Colbert") has over *truthiness*, the word first popularized on his show and later selected as ADS Word of the Year. Colbert was appalled when the initial Associated Press story on the Word of the Year selection didn't even mention him, instead turning to an ADS member, Michael Adams, for a quick gloss. (The AP's shoddy reporting has led, bizarrely, to Colbert calling the AP the "No. 1 threat facing America" . . . in an article by the AP.)

Though Colbert vehemently declared that he "pulled that word right out of where the sun don't shine," Adams defended his right to define the word by pointing out (both to Colbert himself and to the AP in its followup article) that *truthiness* can already be found in the *Oxford English Dictionary*. Colbert's rejoinder—"you don't look up truthiness in a book, you look it up in your gut"—is unassailably truthy. Nonetheless, we would be failing in our mission as wordanistas if we didn't try digging a little deeper into the roots of *truthiness*.

Since the *OED*'s lone 1824 citation for *truthiness* was first noted right here back in October, it's incumbent on us to investigate the source of this earliest known usage. The citation is taken from a book that was actually published in 1854 by Joseph Bevan Braithwaite, entitled *Memoirs of Joseph John Gurney, with Selections from His Journal and Correspondence*. Gurney (1788–1847) was an English banker who gained renown as a charismatic Quaker minister. [...]

The first of Gurney's uses, the one that made it into the *OED*, describes Amelia Opie (1769–1853), a family friend who, through Gurney's influence, decided to become a Quaker herself:

> Seldom has a more striking improvement been wrought in any one who has passed under my notice. Truly may it be said, that her valuable qualities have been sanctified; whilst her play of character has not been lost, but has been rendered more interesting than before. Every one who knows her is aware of her *truthiness*, and appreciates her kindness; and 'Quaker' as she is, and a determined one, she is still sought after by some of her old friends in high station.

[...]

[I]ts italicization in the text [...] suggests that Gurney was emphasizing the unusualness of the word, perhaps in recognition of its nonce status. I don't find any uses of *truthy* (or other derived forms) elsewhere in the text, so I doubt that this was a term in common use by the Quakers of the era. But certainly the word *truth* had a particular resonance for Gurney and his fellow Quakers. To this day, Quakers often call themselves "Friends of the Truth" and place great importance on truthful testimony. So for Gurney to trumpet Opie's "truthiness" must have been an innovative form of praise for a recent convert to Quakerism.

The second example of *truthiness* that I found in Gurney's writings, from a journal entry written in 1844, relates not to a personal quality but to the Scriptures themselves:

> How delightful have the Scriptures been to me of late seasons! I have been struck with the *truthiness* which is so evident in their apparent contradictions. These are generally capable of being easily reconciled; but they do indeed mark the genuineness and authenticity of the whole.

Again, the italicization of the word highlights its peculiarity. But here the usage seems positively (dare I say it?) Colbert-esque. Late in life, Gurney learned to take delight in the odd little contradictions found in the Scriptures. But these contradictions only reinforced his faith in the truth, or rather the *truthiness*, of the biblical text. Without those minor inconsistencies, the Scriptures would lack "genuineness and authenticity." So clearly Gurney was reaching for a concept beyond mundane *truth*. The Bible is no mere reference book, after all. As I'm sure Mr. Colbert would remind us, no one ever accused the Good Book of being "all fact, no heart."

[. . .]

Posted by Benjamin Zimmer

Engrish Explained

Illustrations of fractured English, particularly from East Asian countries, get passed around quite a lot online. There are even entire Websites devoted to collecting absurd examples. Most notable is Engrish .com, focusing on Japan, where English is frequently used as a design element in advertising regardless of whether the words make much sense contextually. Others revel in poorly translated English as it appears on hotel signs, menus, and the like. (One well-circulated compilation originally appeared in Richard Lederer's 1987 book *Anguished English*.) Such collections tend to get tiresome—even when not *explicitly* racist, they nonetheless partake in a long xenophobic tradition of ridiculing the English usage of nonnative speakers. Belittling the pidginized English of speakers from East Asia has an especially checkered past in American dialect humor.

Every once in a while, though, there is a presentation of "Engrish" that both amuses and enlightens. Jon Rahoi, an American living in mainland China, posted scans from an exceedingly bizarre restaurant menu—so bizarre that a commenter accused Rahoi of forging the whole thing with Photoshop. But "an anonymous professor of China studies" came to Rahoi's defense by demonstrating exactly how one evocative menu item ("Benumbed hot vegetables fries fuck silk") could have reasonably ended up that way through dictionary-aided word-for-word translation:

| 1313 | 麻辣韭菜炒干丝 | Benumbed hot vegetables fries fuck silk | 15元 |

Take #1313, "Benumbed hot vegetables fries fuck silk." It should read "Hot and spicy garlic greens stir-fried with shredded dried tofu." However, the mangled version above is not as mangled as it seems: it's a literal word-by-word translation, with some cases where the translator chose the wrong one of two meanings of a word.

First two characters: *ma la* meaning hot and spicy, but literally *numbingly spicy*—it means a kind of Sichuan spice that mixes chilies with Sichuan peppercorn or prickly ash. The latter tends to numb the mouth. "Benumbed hot" is a decent, if ungrammatical, literal translation.

Next two: *jiu cai*, the top greens of a fragrant-flowering garlic. There's no good English translation, so "vegetables" is just fine.

Next one: *chao*, meaning stir-fried, quite reasonably rendered as *fries* (should be *fried*, but that's a distinction English makes and Chinese doesn't).

Finally: *gan si*, meaning shredded dried tofu, but literally translated as *dry silk*. The problem here is that the word *gan* means both *to dry* and *to do*, and the latter meaning has come to mean *to fuck*. Unfortunately, the recent proliferation of Colloquial English dictionaries in China means people choose the vulgar translation way too often, on the grounds that it's colloquial. Last summer I was in a spiffy modern supermarket in Taiyuan whose dried-foods aisle was helpfully labeled "Assorted Fuck."

The word *si*, meaning *silk floss*, is used in cooking to refer to anything that's been julienned—very thin *pommes frites* are sold as "potato silk," for instance. The fact that it's tofu is just understood (sheets of dried tofu shredded into julienne)—if it were dried anything else it would say so.

Posted by Benjamin Zimmer

Googlefreude, Googleschaden, Schadengoogle . . .

Lynne Murphy, an American expat teaching linguistics at the University of Sussex, runs a wonderful little blog called Separated by a Common Language, exploring the differences (often quite subtle) between American English and British English. She recently held a Word of the Year contest with three categories: "Most useful import from American English to British English," "Most useful import from British English to American English," and "Best word invented by a reader of this blog." [. . .]

The winner of the last category, best word coined by a reader of SbaCL, is *Googleschaden*. This word's history began when Andrew Sullivan invented the similar *Googlefreude*, defining it on his blog as "the way in which pundits' past pontifications can now come back to haunt them." When a commenter noted this coinage on SbaCL, Paul Danon suggested *Googleschaden* might be more appropriate, "since that connotes the grief rather than the joy." An anonymous commenter followed up with *Schadengoogle*, "to make the parallel to *Schadenfreude* a little clearer."

[. . .]

Beyond the semantics of grief and joy, however, *Googlefreude* works better to my ear because it more closely follows how English speakers create new blends out of lexical material that is from a foreign source or is otherwise compositionally opaque. Previously I've posted about such blends as Jobdango, an employment Web site combining *job* with the last two syllables of *fandango,* and Infogami, a Web application combining *info* with the last two syllables of *origami.* The blend components -*dango* and -*gami* don't actually mean anything in themselves but are intended to evoke (at least vaguely) the full words *fandango* and *origami*. [...]

Most English speakers who use the word *Schadenfreude* do not actively analyze its composition into the German components *schaden + freude*. Rather, it's just a long Germanism with an unusual meaning, a meaning that remains crystallized in *-freude* when combined with other elements like *Google*. [...] (It seems important to maintain the metrical pattern of *Schadenfreude* in creating the blend.)

There have been other English-language riffs on *Schadenfreude* that maintain all but the word's first syllable. There's *blondenfreude*, defined by *The New York Times*'s Alessandra Stanley in 2002 as "the glee felt when a rich, powerful, and fair-haired businesswoman stumbles" (Martha Stewart being Stanley's case in point). [...] And Andrew Sullivan has been down this path before: in an online piece for *The New Republic* just before Election Day '04 he used *votenfreude*, which he defined as "the assimilation of other voters' agony." As with his later *Googlefreude*, Sullivan was unconcerned that the "agony" segment of the original *Schadenfreude* had been partially overwritten, and I doubt he would have considered *schadenvote* or *voteschaden* as possible alternatives. The *-(en)freude* segment appears to be crucial for such blends, regardless of whether the emphasis is on joy or grief. [...]

Posted by Benjamin Zimmer

FEBRUARY 15, 2007

Astronaut Drives Nine Hundred Miles Wearing ...

When NASA astronaut Lisa Nowak was arrested on Feb. 5 and charged with the attempted murder of her romantic rival, we were treated to nonstop media coverage of the bizarre story. Perhaps the bizarrest detail of all was that, according to the arrest affidavit, Nowak admitted to wearing a diaper on the 900-mile drive from Houston to Orlando so that she wouldn't have to stop along the way. In the wake of this mediathon, an interesting morphological question occurred to Jan Freeman [of *The Boston Globe*]. Sometimes Nowak was described as "wearing a diaper" on her journey, and other times as "wearing diapers." A current search on Google News suggests that "wearing diapers" outnumbers "wearing a diaper" about 3-to-1 in coverage of the Nowak story. But presumably Nowak wore just a single diaper during the trip (or else what would be the point, really?). So what's up with the prevalence of plural *diapers* for a single item?

The first thing to note is how limited the contexts are in which *diapers* can refer to a single garment:

She was wearing diapers.
She was in diapers.
She had diapers on.
She put on/took off her diapers.
She dirtied her diapers.

Clearly, the only frames that work are ones where the diaper is being *worn* by someone—a baby, an astronaut, whoever. Note too that in all of these examples, the morphologically singular *a diaper* would also fit, so the plurally marked form is not obligatory. The same also holds for the equivalent British English term: singular *a nappy* and plural *nappies* are both available for use in these contexts. Well-known diaper brand names also seem to follow this pattern: *Pampers, Huggies*, and *Depends* (for adult incontinence—Nowak's brand of choice?) all can take the ostensibly plural -s form even when referring to a single worn diaper. (*Pampers* and *Huggies* are already branded in the plural, while the *Depend* brand name is more often heard with an -s in frames like those above.)

Viewed historically, *diaper* and *nappy* were originally construed as singular, but plurally marked *diapers* and *nappies* in singular contexts became more frequent by the mid-20th century. An example from 1960 appears in the *OED* draft entry for *mess*, taken from A. S. Neill's *Summerhill* (a popular account of Neill's pioneering Summerhill School). The quote voices a boy's thoughts about his younger brother: "If I am like him and mess my trousers the way he dirties his diapers, Mommy will love me again." (That's from the U.S. edition—the U.K. edition [. . .] has *nappies* instead of *diapers*.) The parallel structure here is telling: "mess my trousers" vs. "dirties his diapers/nappies." The plurally marked *diapers* and *nappies* appear to be influenced by *pants* and *trousers*—words that almost always appear in the plural, or *pluralia tantum*, as they're technically known. Let's take a look at other *pluralia tantum* in the *pants/trousers* family:

> Outergarments: *pants* (orig. *pantaloons*), *trousers, slacks, breeches/britches, bloomers, jeans, dungarees, bell-bottoms, chinos, tights, shorts, trunks, Bermudas* (extended to brand names: [. . .] *501s, Wranglers, Calvins*).

> Undergarments: *underpants, long johns, skivvies, drawers, panties, knickers, boxers, briefs, undies, tighty-whities* (extended to brand names: *BVDs, Fruit of the Looms, Jockeys*).

The common theme is that all of these garments have two holes, one for each leg. For that reason, some have argued that the forms are best understood as duals rather than plurals, since the -s indicates duality or "twoness." [. . .] Considered as an individual piece of cloth, however, *diaper* remains resolutely singular (as in "Hand me that diaper"), since a diaper in its unworn state has no leg-holes and thus lacks duality.

Further evidence that *diapers* has taken steps towards the dual *pants* family can be found in constructions where duality is explicitly marked, as in "a pair of Xs." [. . .]

> It just doesn't seem Right Stuff macho to imagine John Glenn or Chuck Yeager in a pair of diapers (*Providence Journal*, 2/12/07).

> Nowak squeezed 900 miles out of a pair of diapers, exceeding the previous record of 220 miles or "I forgot the little man was still in the back seat." (*Bakersfield Californian*, 2/8/07).

[. . .] I've tried explaining all this to my six-month-old son Blake while I'm changing his diaper(s), but so far he's more interested in figuring out how to cram both hands in his mouth.

Update, 2/16: Diaper-related email has been arriving thick and fast. (Hmm, maybe that's not the best idiom to use when talking about diapers.) First, Bryan Erickson points out an element of the Nowak story that I had missed [. . .]:

> Complicating the entertaining *plurale tantum* analysis, the police report noted that the cops found a garbage bag in her car containing *two* soiled diapers—so she did change her nappy/nappies at least twice. . . .

Next we have a couple of informative emails from foreign correspondents, explaining some subtle usage differences between *diapers* and *nappies*. From Matthew Hurst:

> In your recent language log article about the astro diapers you state that one can say 'she had nappies on', 'she was in

nappies', etc. I don't believe this is correct (as a native brit). One can say 'she was in nappies' in the sense that during that period of her life she was in nappies, but one can't say that with the sense that at that point in time she was wearing the thing.

Posted by Benjamin Zimmer

Diapers, Diapers, and More Diapers

[...]

Now that I've had a chance to digest all of this *diaper*-talk, I see that there are some significant points that I neglected to address in my original post. I also didn't provide much historical documentation for singularly construed *diapers*, so I'd like to rectify those oversights in this post.

[...] Take, for instance, the 1960 quote from A. S. Neill's *Summerhill* that I provided (cited in the *OED*'s entry for *mess*) [...]: "If I am like him and mess my trousers the way he dirties his diapers, Mommy will love me again." A few commenters objected to my analysis of this quote, saying that this does not necessarily imply a single instance in which the younger brother is dirtying his diaper(s). [...] This is true also of other common collocations with the word *diapers*, such as "to be in diapers," "to wear diapers." [...]

The habitual sense of "wearing diapers" is extremely prevalent and may actually have been another contributing factor to the eventual construal of *diapers* with a singular sense. For at least a century or two, "being in" or "wearing" diapers has been taken as emblematic of the infant stage of life. This usage has lent itself well to political jabs at a younger opponent's inexperience. For instance, when Massachusetts governor James M. Curley ran for U.S. Senate in 1936, he had this to say about his opponent, Henry Cabot Lodge: "When my youthful rival was still wearing diapers I was serving the Commonwealth of Massachusetts in the halls of Congress." [. . .]

And in 1940, after 38-year-old Thomas E. Dewey announced his candidacy for president, Franklin D. Roosevelt's interior secretary Harold Ickes said that Dewey had "tossed his diapers into the ring." Or at least that's what was reported in the Sept. 15, 1941, edition of *Time*. When Ickes quoted himself in the next presidential campaign, he used *diaper* instead of *diapers*, according to *Time*'s Oct. 2, 1944, edition. ("Four years ago, I observed that Mr. Dewey had thrown his diaper into the ring. [. . .]") The interchangeability of *diaper* and *diapers* in the Ickes quote is, I think, further evidence that singular and plural forms of the noun often shade into each other.

[. . .]

Posted by Benjamin Zimmer

Benjamin Zimmer, age thirty-six, studied linguistic anthropology at the University of Chicago and taught at UCLA, Kenyon College, and Rutgers University. A few years ago he began to find what he calls "academic esotericism" too confining and in 2004 started writing guest pieces for Language Log, a group blog initiated by two linguists, Mark Liberman (University of Pennsylvania) and Geoffrey Pullum (University of California Santa Cruz).

Zimmer's first guest post, on "nonsense up with which I will not put" (a saying misattributed to Winston Churchill), began as a friendly e-mail exchange and eventually made its way into Liberman and Pullum's Language Log anthology, *Far from the Madding Gerund* (William, James & Co., 2006). After a few more guest posts, Zimmer joined Language Log as a regular contributor in 2005. There he specializes in what he calls "lexical detective work," tracking the history of words and phrases by searching newly available databases of digitized texts. In 2006 he became the editor for American dictionaries at Oxford University Press.

MATTHEW YGLESIAS

MATTHEW YGLESIAS

proudly eponymous since 2002

http://matthewyglesias.theatlantic.com/

7 / 4 / 0 4

Long Philosophical Rant About *Spider-Man 2*

This film's gotten nearly universal acclaim in the blogosphere and, indeed, it is a very good time. Lots of funny moments, some touching moments, good acting, a neat "look," one of the best credits sequences I've ever seen, quality emotional dynamics between characters, etc. That said, I think there's a rather big problem with the story. SPOILER.

The thing of it is that you can't—you just can't—make a whole film whose entire theme is that sometimes in order to do the right thing you need to give up the thing you want most in life and then have it turn out in the end that chicks really dig guys who do the right thing and the hero gets the girl anyway. Just won't fly. There's a long history in western thought that the moral life and the pleasing life are identical. It dates back to Plato or Aristotle or maybe both. The way the ancients put this, though, was pretty counterintuitive, and it had to do with the idea that in some sense you don't really want what you think you want. Hence all things in moderation and other Aristotelian platitudes. But whatever the defects of this view, it has the great advantage of being palatable, people are much more likely to do the right thing if you promise them that it will also make them happy.

Moving into the Christian tradition, they tie up the untidiness of this view with a little eschatological sleight-of-hand. It certainly doesn't seem like doing the right thing will always make you happy, so Christianity cleans things up by inserting heaven and hell. Going to hell forever would be a very bad thing indeed, and going to heaven a very good thing. Hence, despite appearances, it's in your self-interest to be good. Even Kant felt the need to attach this to his ethical system in order to ensure that everything comes out okay in the end.

But as we move forward into modernity, intellectual types lose their faith. But there's still a desire to come up with a moral system that people will want to follow. Hence we start hearing complaints that normative view X or Y is "too challenging" because morality, apparently, is supposed to be easy and it's just not cool for [ethicist] Peter Singer (and others) to go around telling us that it might suck to do the right thing.

One very interesting element of the first *Spider-Man*, however, is that it rejected what's known as the "doing-allowing distinction," which holds that it's one thing to do something wrong and another thing to stand aside as something bad happens. The former, or so we're told, is much worse than the latter. Clearly, morality is easier with the doing-allowing distinction. It's relatively easy to play by the rules, mind your own business, and not go around killing people. It's much harder to actually do something about the fact that people are dying every day all around the world, often in a way you could contribute to preventing (by donating to UNICEF or whatever). *Spider-Man* had it, however, that by not stopping the man who later killed his uncle, Peter was responsible for Ben's death. "With great power," we are told, "comes great responsibility." It's not just that Peter shouldn't use his powers to hustle people in ultimate fighting competitions, it's that if he fails to do everything he can to help others, then he is doing badly.

For most of the film, *Spider-Man 2* is very good at dramatizing the reality of this ideal. Being the good guy—doing the right thing—really sucks, because doing the right thing doesn't just mean avoiding wrongdoing; it means taking affirmative action to prevent it. There's no time left for Peter's life, and his life is miserable. Virtue is not its own reward; it's virtue, the rewards go to the less conscientious. There's no implication that it's all worthwhile because God will make it right in the End-Times; the life of the good guy is a bleak one. It's an interesting (and, I think, a correct) view and it's certainly one that deserves a skilled dramatization, which is what the film gives you right up until the very end. But then—ta da!—it turns out that everyone does get to be happy after all. A huge letdown.

7/4/04

Can the Klan Save Public Education?

One normally thinks of the Ku Klux Klan as a sort of far-right social mobilization. Nevertheless, I'm reading a book called *No There There: Race, Class, and Political Community in Oakland*, which reminds us that things are never so simple. Aside from its anti-black agenda, the Klan of the 1920s, especially in the North where the African-American population was small, was big into the evils of Catholic immigrants. As a result, the Oakland Klan busied itself campaigning for things like "the separation of Church and State" and good "free, universal public schools" in an effort to assimilate immigrants and limit the Church's political power. They were also, in the Oakland of the day, associated with campaigns against the corrupt "ethnic" political machine of West Oakland and did things like campaign for the awarding of contracts on a competitive [basis] or, even better, for the direct delivery of services. [. . .]

None of this is to rehabilitate the Klan in our historical memory or to suggest that liberals pick up racist nativism as part of our political strategy. It is to say, however, that in an era of rising movements for school vouchers, home schooling, the privatization of this and that, and a general effort to dismantle the public sector, it's worth thinking about the ways "left-wing" opposition to these measures can be given a nationalist gloss. Part of what happens if we privatize the education sector is that we dismantle the main vehicle by which people are socialized into American culture and society. Some conservative voucher-lovers would welcome this development, as it allows them to isolate their kids from American pluralism and have them raised purely within the context of (white, Protestant) Christian culture. Bringing first- and second-generation immigrants into play, however, changes this dynamic. Does the right really want a country in which immigrant parents live in immigrant neighborhoods and send their [children] to ethno-religiously segregated private schools at public expense? Some elements probably do, but others could be attracted by the notion that only real public schools can help build the civic identity whose continued existence is vital for the continued viability of the American project.

[. . .]

9/20/06

Dixie Jews

Revelations about George "Macaca" Allen's heritage have some folks wondering to me how a nice Jewish boy could have turned out to be such a Stars & Bars–loving racist. As I've been pointing out, it's contrary to stereotype, but Jews have a long history with the Confederacy. Over to your right, you'll see Judah P. Benjamin, who I'd thought was the first Jewish senator. He turns out to have actually been the second one, representing Louisiana in the Senate in the 1850s before resigning when the southern states seceeded. He then became the Confederate Attorney General (the USA had never had a Jewish cabinet secretary at this point) and later held some other CSA cabinet posts.

Benjamin's status as first Jewish senator turns out to be somewhat complicated because of the case of David Levy Yulee, who converted to Christianity before being elected to the Senate, but who had been a practicing Jew earlier in life. Yulee, too, was a southerner who also resigned his seat during the Civil War. So there you have it—the Confederacy was Good for the Jews.

Meanwhile, a note on nomenclature. Josh Marshall [the blogger behind Talking Points Memo] uses the term *crypto-Jew* with reference to Allen. That's always been my preferred term for folks in the Allen/Albright/Clark category of having Jewish ancestry but not knowing about it. Another crucial category is *stealth Jew*—persons like myself who are acknowledged Jews with very non-Jewish names. My successor at the paper I edited in college was a Jewish fellow by the name of Andrew Ujifusa so the *Independent* was, at the time, ground zero for the vast stealth Jew media conspiracy. Conversely, you have pseudo-Jews like Sam Rosenfeld—goys with super-Jewish names.

9/28/06

The Depends Theory of Geopolitics

I was interested to see GregPStone in comments mounting the argument that assuming the Iranians are, in fact, trying to build a nuclear bomb whose purpose is to mount a suicidal unprovoked nuclear first strike constitutes "erring on the side of caution."

There's something to be said for caution, but that's not what this is at all. Rather, it's erring on the side of panic, an approach that, stealing from [the blogger] Atrios, we might term the Depends Theory of International Relations. Running around constantly freaking out about everything, panicking, and fostering an atmosphere of paranoid alarmism isn't cautious at all. It doesn't make you safer. Primarily, it prevents you from focusing and setting priorities. It blinds you to real threats by diffusing resources and effort. It leads to mistakes, and imposes enormous costs. It makes it too easy for adversaries to throw you off your game at very little cost to themselves, while making it hard for friends and potential friends to trust you. It destroys your own credibility, leaving you, eventually, alone in the corner covered in your own piss.

[...]

12/12/06

Keep it Clean

Tom Edsall [in a guest column in *The New York Times*] writes about Hillary Clinton:

> Clinton's position at the head of the pack—a 20-point lead over her competitors—forces her campaign to shoot down a barrage of hostile challenges: Will voters trust a woman at a time of terrorist threat? Will the military accept a woman as commander in chief?

Look, I've been very critical of Senator Clinton in the past and almost certainly will be again in the future if she, as expected, mounts a presidential bid, but I'd like to think we could keep the discourse a little bit more elevated than that. There are much better questions to ask about Clinton's views on national security policy than whether she's too girly to handle it. Indeed, there's at least some indication that fear of this sort of misogynistic attack is part of what's motivated her to take such a hawkish line, which winds up being doubly or triply unfortunate. The fact that this sort of thing even gets discussed, though, points not only to the deep anti-feminist strains that remain in our culture, but also to the weirdly metaphorical nature of national security debates. The underlying presumption seems to be something like, you want a president capable of physically wrestling a terrorist to the ground and so a woman, or a man who's too effete, might not be able to get the job done.

1/30/07

"Democrat Party"

With a couple of articles out about the president's use of the incorrect "Democrat Party" locution, [blogger] Ezra Klein's question seems worth answering:

> Do we have any actual data showing that the term hurts Democrats? Particularly given that, in fact, the proper plural for Democratic people is "Democrats?" I'm not doubting that the right's intentions are malicious, but this bit of schoolyard-style word manipulation seems far below anything that will actually impinge on the electorate's preferences and sensibilities.

I disagree. Very strongly. Primarily, this is not a question of [Frank] Luntz-style linguistic manipulation, but a question of basic dignity and honor. It relates to Josh Marshall's "bitch-slap theory" of electoral politics. The key charge against liberals is that we're weak. Weak on Communism. Weak on crime. Weak on terrorism. Weak-minded, softhearted, weak, weak, weak. Well, what's the key sign of weakness: a person who won't stand up for himself.

To call someone by something other than the name he wishes to be called by is rude. To make a mistake is forgivable, but to persist—deliberately—in declining to use your adversary's proper name is rude and insulting. It's not a big deal unless you take standing up for yourself to be a big deal. When Democrats go on TV and let a conservative get away with the phrase *Democrat Party* it's signaling that Democrats are weak. They're too weak to stand up for themselves. They're too weak to have a sense of group solidarity or party loyalty. They're inclined to let things slide. They don't want to make a scene. They don't like to have a fight. They're weak. Is a political party that can't even protect its own name really going to keep America safe?

What's more, it establishes the conservative media as a truth-free zone. Presumably, if CNN cared about accuracy it would not employ people as regular commentators who can't correctly name America's older and larger political party. Nor would ABC, CBS, NBC, MSNBC, C-SPAN, NPR or any other media outlet. Yes, yes it would initially seem petty and bizarre of all these outlets to insist that people either name the party correctly or else not appear. But the fact that this would seem petty and bizarre is the point: *Democratic* is the correct word, and this isn't an obscure point. That everyone lets conservatives say *Democrat* over and over again is part of establishing mainstream acceptance of the idea that the conservative media operates in an accuracy-free zone. They're propagandists, and that's okay by the MSM [mainstream media]—no need to get things right!

More "Democrat"

To answer Spencer, *Democrat Party* is a slur just because it's wrong. Calling Spencer Spencer is appropriate. Calling me Spencer is insulting. Not because *Spencer* is an insult but because it's insulting to repeatedly call someone by the wrong name.

2/9/07

You Say "Mean," I Say "Kinda Crazy"

I asked yesterday what Rudy Giuliani's awesome national security credentials were supposed to be, and people replied that he seems mean and therefore tough and therefore good. Jonathan Alter makes an important point about this (via [blogger] K-Drum): As any actual New Yorker should recall, Giuliani's kind of crazy. Don't get me wrong, I thought he was a pretty good mayor! I was too young (16, I think) to vote to re-elect Giuliani in 1997, but I'm exactly the sort of liberal New Yorker whom he won over during his first term to be able to sweep to a crushing re-election victory.

It's worth recalling, though, that in his second term he basically went berserk. He'd always had [what Alter called a] "ridiculously thin skin and mile-wide mean streak" but in his second term that came to dominate everything. There were two basic directions in which it would have been reasonable to take that term. He could have tried to apply the hard-charging zeal he'd brought to reforming police procedures to some other significant area of urban policy. Alternatively, he could have focused on keeping his policies in place while trying to heal some of the wounds that implementing them caused. Michael Bloomberg has basically managed to do both. Giuliani, in essence, did neither. Instead, he picked a series of bitter-yet-pointless fights that served to reveal both a basic vindictiveness and a fundamental lack of interest in policies outside the realm of law enforcement.

These are not characteristics which, when combined with the gross opportunism we're now seeing on various cultural issues, are desirable in a president. Also recall his post-9/11 efforts to suspend the City Charter and extend his term in office, adding a dose of power-hunger into the mix.

3/6/07

The Joshua Generation

It's a few days old at this point, but Barack Obama's speech in Selma, Alabama, is worth a read. He faced a somewhat tricky task. A white politician goes to such an event merely to pay homage to the giants of the past and their struggle, and to pledge fealty to the contemporary leaders of the African-American community. Obama's task is to identify himself as a leader of that community. But worse as *the* leader—as the President of the United States. But this is presumptuous. What did Obama do? Are his accomplishments greater than those of the older generation that marched at Selma and elsewhere? No. His accomplishments are lesser. He is in a position to go further than they were not because of his efforts but because of their efforts. How to gain their support?

Obama, in his speech, aims for an analogy with Joshua. Not, compared to Moses, the greater leader of the Jewish people. But, rather, the successor; the one designated to build on Moses's work and lead the people into the promised land. Certainly, I'm not a grizzled veteran of the Civil Rights movement, so I can't say for sure how this will play, but it seems pretty clever to me.

I think it can also work as a larger metaphor. Progressives these days have a sometimes angsty relationship with the social movements of the 1960s and '70s. The sense that, ultimately, these movements failed and the Democratic Party came to disaster through its association with them is inescapable. And yet precisely what we don't want to do is mimic the smarmy neoliberals of the 1980s and 1990s, forever full of scorn, forever eager to blame the left for the right's malgovernment, forever looking to get ahead by knifing an ally in the back.

Arguably, Obama's hit on the right way to think about all this. The movements of yore accomplished a great deal and were absolutely right about the biggest issues of their time. But they made some mistakes. Mistakes that are dwarfed by the scale of their accomplishments, but nonetheless mistakes that carried a high price. Conveniently enough, 2008 could mark the end of 40 desert years launched by Nixon and capped by Bush. Enough time gone by for old wounds to heal, perhaps, and for a new generation of political leadership to redeem the promises of that earlier era.

Matthew Yglesias, sometimes called Big Media Matt, is an associate editor of *The Atlantic Monthly.* Previously he was a staff writer at *The American Prospect.* He is twenty-six years old and graduated with a degree in philosophy from Harvard College in 2003. There he was the editor-in-chief of *The Harvard Independent,* a weekly newsmagazine. He started blogging about American politics and public policy in 2002, which he calls "the dark ages of the blogosphere."

His blog, now at *The Atlantic,* is often noted for its evenhandedness and for its philosophical bent. Although he is generally viewed as a liberal blogger, he has fans on both sides of the aisle. He is cited by liberals such as Duncan Black and Kevin Drum and also by conservative writers like Glenn Reynolds and Andrew Sullivan. In fact, Sullivan dreamed up the Yglesias Award "for writers, politicians, columnists or pundits who actually criticize their own side, make enemies among political allies, and generally risk something for the sake of saying what they believe."

Yglesias writes not only about public policy and politics but also about basketball, particularly about the Washington Wizards. His father is the screenwriter and novelist Rafael Yglesias. His first book, with the working title *Heads in the Sand: Iraq and the Strange Death of Liberal Internationalism,* to be published by John Wiley and Sons, is about the Democratic Party's search for a post-9/11 foreign policy. His writing has appeared in *The New Republic, Slate, The Guardian, The Washington Monthly,* and other publications. He is a regular on BloggingHeads.tv.

MICROGRAPHICA

http://serializer.net/comics/micrographica.php

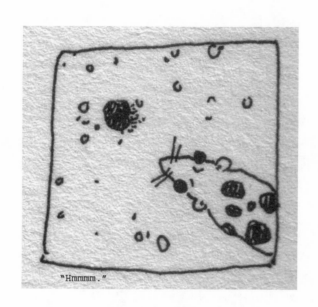

"Hey Moe, what do ya make of this?"

"Well, let me see it."

"Remember, I found it."

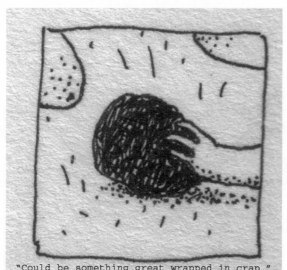

"Could be something great wrapped in crap."

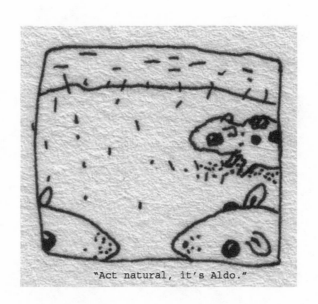

"Act natural, it's Aldo."

"Hi guys, whatcha up to?"

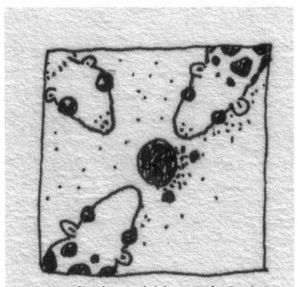

"I just found a sandwich on Manly Beach."

"We're real jealous, Aldo."

"Moe and me, we're late for a meeting."

"This place is a dump."

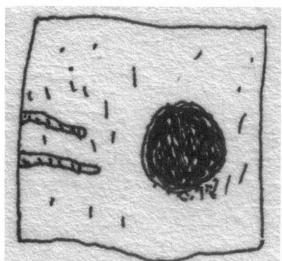

"Uh, ok, see you guys later."

"Roly-poly..."

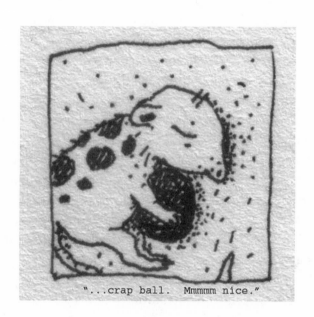

"...crap ball. Mmmmm nice."

Renée French, a forty-four-year-old artist who has kept an online comic called Micrographica at the comics Web site Serializer.com since 2005, may be the only person ever to utter these words about drawing very tiny pictures: "I can loosen up by making it small." Her Micrographica drawings are basically doodles drawn in a one-centimeter-square frame. "But when you blow them up they look tight," she says, explaining, "I'm a miniaturist. My hands are really steady. I can let myself go."

French, who has written and drawn some pretty disturbing comic books, including *The Ticking,* also writes and draws books for children under the name Rainy Dohaney. Two of her recent children's books are *Tinka,* a story about a sheep the size of a cupcake, and *My Best Sweet Potato,* about a stuffed animal named Woolyman, forever altered by a wash cycle. Last year *Micrographica* was published as a book (Top Shelf, 2007), and French's work was part of an exhibition at the Louvre about toys and comics.

Working in California and Australia, Ms. French says she used Micrographica "to calm myself down." The speech of the rodents, which is very simple and short, is liberating, she explains. Why not a written blog? As a child, she kept a journal in code. When her brother found it, she says, she "kicked him in the crotch—and then burned it." Therefore, she has no journal, because "I'd live in terror that someone would find it."

MIDNIGHT IN IRAQ

Midnight in Iraq

Not reading this is absolutely free.

http://midnight.hushedcasket.com/

Panties for a Dime

POSTED BY MIDNIGHT ON FEBRUARY 27, 2006

Our PX is a fascinating place. It appears to be staffed by locals with just a few American employees in the upper leadership positions. This makes for some interesting experiences. One of the first things I learned is that no matter what you want, it will be here tomorrow. Need a 3M plastic hook with a sticky back? They may be out of them, but the person stocking the shelf will assure you that tomorrow you may return to find the product you desire. Colgate toothpaste, coffee mugs, rabid two-headed koalas . . . tomorrow, tomorrow, it'll be here, tomorrow. You're only a day away.

The PX staff also appears to have the tendency to overestimate how much of a particular product they can sell. Sometimes this works to your advantage. For example, last week they had way too many tiny-sized women's running shoes (size 6.5 and smaller). They decided to blow them out for $18 a pair. The wife now has a beautiful pair of ASICS running shoes heading her way for a total cost of less than $25 shipped.

. . . and sometimes it's just weird. Panties. Lacy black women's panties. Underwear that looks too uncomfortable to pick up, much less wear in a combat zone. The PX has a rack full of these monstrosities

displayed strategically between the Under Armour and corn chips. Apparently $0.79 each was above the market price for these jewels, so now they are on clearance ("Camp Special") for $0.10 each. Now, my first reaction was disbelief that these are offered for sale, since their obvious intended use is outlawed in combat zones. This was followed closely by the thought that these were an incredible deal for a dime each! What do panties go for in the States? Hell, I don't know, but I'm guessing at least $1. Somebody could clean up if they're in the market for some women's underwear. So now I'm wondering how I can work this to my advantage. Send them back to the wife? No. Too weird, and the post office here is a royal PITA [pain in the ass]. No way am I standing in front of a postal Marine and inventorying a box full of panties to complete the customs form. With that option out the window I've almost given up. But they're 10 for a dollar . . . with no tax! The penny-saver in me just won't let this go.

Now I'm thinking practical joke material. I wonder what my roommate would think of a negligee explosion all over his rack, with pictures taken to capture the moment, of course. Yeah. That sounds good! I could even mail a picture of it back to his wife. Maybe I could put them on his head while he's sleeping and snap a photo. Hmm . . . more difficult, but the payoff is substantial. I'm liking this more and more. So if I'm going to pull this off, I have to buy 10–20 pairs of panties. Crap! There's Marines everywhere, of all ranks, and I want to stroll up to the counter with one score of panties in arm. This could only be accomplished after waiting in line for a few minutes, during which time I am sure to catch the glance of those standing to my front and rear. Great Odin's Raven, what if the cashier doesn't know the price!?! She'll start babbling to her supervisor in languages I've never heard of and waving these things in the air like a redneck on a Jumbotron. So there I stood, square between the Under Armour and corn chips, shopping basket in hand, trying to look like I was searching for the right type of deodorant, sweating bullets, and saying "Oh God, please take this cup from me." I couldn't do it. I left the PX disappointed in myself. The 19-year-old Midnight would have procured those panties without batting an eye. I am only a shell of my former self. For shame.

Junkyards of War

POSTED BY MIDNIGHT MAY 21, 2006
(ORIGINALLY PUBLISHED IN *THE NEW YORK TIMES* ON MARCH 26, 2006)

Last week I discovered the Camp Falluja junkyard. It was glorious.

As our HMMWV [Humvee] turned the corner and I caught my first glimpse of this vast expanse I heard the playing of "Hallelujah" and saw a radiant white light shine down from heaven upon the scores of deadlined vehicles, discarded parts and general detritus that filled the place. It was a sight to make any gearhead shed a tear. Gunny cursed out loud in excitement from the seat behind me. We had found our Mecca.

While my paycheck is currently earned by moonlighting as a professional warrior, I will always be an engineer at heart. There's just something about having to dig through piles of other people's rubbish to discover a nugget of gold that excites the thrifty engineer within.

The junkyard covers at least 25 acres.

My SNCOIC (staff non-commissioned officer in charge, second in charge of my team) is a gearhead much like myself. We both spent our high school days (his much earlier than mine) scouring junkyards in our hometowns for parts to boost the performance of our cars, to sell for profit, or to just build something cool. We both quickly agreed that while we were ecstatic about the find, we wished it was located at home, where we could put it to use on our personal projects. We then agreed—even more quickly—that our wives would be quite happy that it was not at home, but here in Falluja, preventing us from filling our garages with tons of metallic goodies.

We came there with an agenda—to look for a specific piece for the turret of our HMMWV. We found it in one of the first mounds we perused. One of my marines pulled the HMMWV up to our position and lifted the heavy steel apparatus onto the bed. With our primary goal achieved, anything we could find beyond that would be icing on the cake.

Looking inside an overturned hard shell for an unarmored HMMWV we discovered a 1,000-watt DC-AC power inverter. Score! We haven't tested it yet, but if it works it will find a home in a lucky HMMWV, or maybe be used as a spare in case another inverter breaks. We found lots of storage containers: metal, wooden, and plastic. Someone had dumped a mass of metal-lined plastic vats that are normally used for serving hot chow in the field. I wanted to turn them into weapons cleaning vats, but couldn't think of a place to procure solvent. I found many other things that I didn't have an immediate use for, but marked in my brain for a future trip. Next time I will bring my G.P.S. and make a log of where each particular goody is located.

Halfway through the trip we started to find even more interesting items such as a kevlar helmet (no doubt some marine got a thorough chewing-out for losing it), a light grey beret that one of my marines decided to wear for the remainder of our trip, and plenty of UXO (unexploded ordnance). It's generally considered dangerous stuff, as you can never tell if it's really a dud or if it's just biding its time waiting for the right gust of wind to set it off. Before we deployed we got a UXO brief that scared the bejesus out of me. The E.O.D. (explosive ordnance disposal) guys give you the brief, and they include plenty of graphic pictures of what can happen when you play with UXO. It's not pretty. I'm a big fan of all my appendages, so my marines and I follow the rule that if you don't know what it is, don't pick it up.

Unexploded ordnance. These particular pieces of UXO look to be artillery shells. Fun!

Expended Anti-tank (AT-4) rocket.

Nice tread on those brand-new tires . . .

The Camp Falluja junkyard is quite an expansive place, and it is definitely going to take more than one trip to fully appreciate all its recyclable glory. As we pulled back into work I could hear the theme from *Sanford and Son* playing in my head. If only we had been driving a red clunker instead of an olive drab HMMWV. Redd Foxx would have been proud.

Arab Life: An Outsider's View

POSTED BY MIDNIGHT JUNE 8, 2006
(ORIGINALLY PUBLISHED IN *THE NEW YORK TIMES* ON APRIL 5, 2006)

Since I have had the opportunity to see a few Arab homes, and to observe and interact at some length with the populace here in Falluja,

I thought it might be interesting to point out a few of the similarities and differences between the life we know and that of an Iraqi. Hundreds of customs and courtesies surround the Arab culture. Upon my arrival here, I didn't know what to believe and what to shrug off as nonsense. I quickly realized that most things I had learned from Ustatha Samir during "culture time" in Arabic class held true in the real world. It's always rather surreal to imagine life drastically different from American culture without actually experiencing it, but after seeing this small part of the Arab world with my own eyes, I know I'll never forget it. Let's start with the Arab home. Sandals will be strewn about in front of the door where their owners have left them for safe keeping. Closed-toe shoes are quite the anomaly here, even in the dusty environment of Iraq. It appears the locals' feet are quite accustomed to this and have hardened accordingly. Next, there will probably be a coat-hanger in the foyer where dishdashas are hung. Dishdashas are the long button-up robes worn by men, and are most often referred to as "man-dresses" by marines. It's difficult to explain, but the phrase *man-dress* doesn't really contain a negative connotation. It is simply a quick and easy way to describe a male's attire. (i.e. "Keep an eye on the MAM in the white man-dress.") That's an acronym we use: MAM (military-aged male). It means any male from his late teens to his late 50s. Insurgents are almost invariably MAMs, which I'm sure doesn't come as a surprise. That's right, we profile based on age and gender . . . and it works.

Further inside the house you'll find a "receiving room" that is usually the most nicely furnished and well-decorated room of the house. This room is used for entertaining and socializing with guests. It appears common for Iraqis to sleep in this room, although in my limited experience it appears sleeping may occur in almost any room except the kitchen. I'll get back to the kitchen in a moment, but first I must tell you about sleeping arrangements. No beds. None. Everyone generally huddles into the same room and sleeps on brightly colored blankets spread directly onto the floor. It appears the "sleeping gear" for one person consists of two blankets (one to lie on, one to cover up with) and a pillow. Some homes have large, brightly colored pads for the inhabitants to sleep on. Also, there doesn't appear to be an Arabic equivalent of pajamas. Everyone seems to sleep in his or her clothes from the day.

The kitchen usually has one stove, which consists of a large lattice grill over a propane burner. Sacks with grains of all types will be stacked in a remote corner amid racks of plates and glassware. There is also a refrigerator that will chill the day's leftovers. I don't believe Ziploc bags are a part of the equation. There will invariably be a stack of Muj-bread in some part of the kitchen.

[. . .]

Lastly: tea and tobacco. Both are extremely prevalent in Arab society. Elaborate metal teapots etched with ornate patterns adorn the receiving rooms of many households. I am not sure exactly how the tea is brewed, but I know that when served the tea leaves sit directly in your cup with no straining. The cup of home-brewed tea of which I partook was delicious. It was just the right blend of really sweet and really strong that I learned to expect of tea during my southern upbringing. Smoking doesn't happen quite as majestically, but it happens every bit as often. It also doesn't really appear to be a personal decision here; it actually seems as if everyone smokes. Almost every male keeps a pack of cigarettes on his person, usually in the breast pocket of his dishdasha. I am not sure where females keep them, but I have seen them quietly smoking indoors, out of the public eye.

The Conversation

POSTED BY MIDNIGHT JUNE 15, 2006
(ORIGINALLY PUBLISHED IN *THE NEW YORK TIME*S ON APRIL 22, 2006)

Not long ago I was out with a patrol on a "knock-and-talk" operation, visiting Iraqis in their homes to give and get useful information. We happened upon a large house situated across from a small mosque. I knew it was a mosque because I read the Arabic sign above the door and recognized the loudspeakers rising above its roof.

Some children were standing in the entryway to the house's courtyard, and they looked a little apprehensive as our Humvee pulled around the corner. As I exited the truck they moved away a bit and ducked back inside the courtyard, but still well within sight and hearing. I wanted to show them they had nothing to fear so I quickly shouted an Arabic greeting. That turned them around.

I approached them slowly and I began to speak with three of the boys, who turned out to be brothers. My conversation is transcribed below. Not everything is included, as there were lots of shrugs and hand signals used to make ourselves understood, but they seemed to understand most of what I was saying in modern standard Arabic, which is surprising given the Iraqi dialect. (A linguist later explained to me that children are usually taught modern standard Arabic in school, and, therefore, are probably the best at understanding me.) The older brother, Amar, led most of the conversation. I was thrilled to understand what he was saying and for him to understand me without the help of a translator.

Me: Welcome.
Them: Welcome.

Me: How are you today?

Them: Praise be to Allah.

Me: Good, praise be to Allah. Is that a mosque?

Amar: Yes, a mosque.

Me: It is a small mosque.

Amar: Yes, small.

Me: Do you play soccer?

Them: Yes, we play soccer.

Me: Good. Are these your brothers?

Amar: Yes . . . sisters. (He used the English word *sisters*, apparently excited he knew an English word.)

Me: Oh, not sisters. Boys are brothers. Girls are sisters.

Amar: Oh, brothers!

Me: Yes.

Amar: (Pointing to each) Ala, Abdullah, Amar.

Me: Good. I am pleased to meet you. (I used the formal word for *you*, which, literally translated means *your presence*. It's approximately the English equivalent of *sir*. They obviously liked this.) My name is Jeff.

Them: Jeff.

Me: I am from the state of Alabama in America.

Amar: Al-a-ba-ma?

Me: Yes, Alabama.

Them: Yes.

Me: (to Amar) Are you in elementary school?

Amar: No, I am in middle school. He (Abdullah) is in elementary school, and he (Ala) is in middle school.

Me: Oh. I graduated from the University of Alabama two years ago.

Amar: A university?

Me: Yes.

Them: Yes!

Me: Where is your mother?

Amar: In the house.

Me: And your father?

Amar: Abu Ghraib.

Me: Abu Ghraib?

Amar: Yes (putting his wrists together as if he was flex-cuffed), Abu Ghraib.

Me: Why?

Amar: I don't know.

Me: Did he shoot at Americans?

Amar: No. He has been in Abu Ghraib for one and a half years.

    (I later learned that their father was the sheik that ran the mosque across the street. He was involved in planting homemade bombs.)

Amar: Do you want to come into the house, where our mother is?

Me: No, I cannot.

Amar: Would you like some tea?

Me: Yes, I like tea.

Amar: OK.

I tried to ask them if life was difficult without their father, but I could only remember the words for *difficult* and *father*, which didn't make for a comprehensible thought. At this point they scurried inside to retrieve some tea. We had to leave before they returned, so I never got to drink with them.

Random Thoughts 20 July

POSTED BY MIDNIGHT JULY 20, 2006

[. . .] Over the course of deployment I have picked up a few Swahili (I assume) phrases from the Ugandan gate guards. *Jambo* is *Hey!* I started out using that as a greeting and then learned *Abadi* which means *How's it going?* They will usually then reply, *Mizuri, Abadi.* Which means *Good. How's it going with you?* It took me a while to realize they were returning a question to me, so now I follow up with another *Mizuri.* Just when I thought I had it licked, now one of them is following up the entire greeting exchange with something that sounds like . . . *alama.* It isn't the Arabic phrase *masalama* or *salam ayalickum,* so I'm stumped. I know those transliterations are probably horrible, but after learning how to write/read Arabic I pay very little attention to the proper spelling of non-western words in western characters, because the two don't mix. You can't technically spell Arabic words in western characters, so I just give it my best shot and call it a day. One day in a debate over the proper spelling of *Zaidon* (vs. *Zaydan*) I wrote it on a piece of paper in Arabic and said, "That, is how you spell Zaidon. Whether you want to transliterate it as *Zaidon* or *Zaydan* doesn't really make a difference. Use whatever makes you pronounce it correctly."

Someone crapped in a shower in Camp Grizzly. The barracks manager thinks it's probably a local national, perhaps an interpreter or one of the contracted local nationals. I don't know how he came to this conclusion. I can only assume turd forensics.

It's hot again this week. It had cooled down a little to the 107–109 range, but now it's routinely getting into the 115–117 range. Yes, you can actually tell a difference. I would have thought that once it gets hot enough you stop being able to discern a difference in comfort, but I haven't found that to be true, yet. Up to 110 is bearable without a lot of discomfort. After 115 walks outside are fairly uncomfortable. The couple times it's reached 119 it was almost painful when the hot wind would blow against my skin. I can't comment on any temps greater than that. Sunday it's supposed to be 119 again. Joy. [. . .] Tensions are high and whining is rampant as we wind down our time here, making leadership even more of a challenge. Determining the right time to explain the why behind the what and the right time to just say "Shut up, you're doing it" is sometimes more art than science. Perhaps the trickiest part is finding the correct use and position of the f-word, and which of its various prefixes, suffixes, and descriptors are most appropriate for the situation.

First Lieutenant Jeffrey Barnett is a marine officer from Huntsville, Alabama, who recently separated from the corps. He is twenty-six years old, and one of his many passions is video games. Midnight, his name in the gaming world, is also his blogging name. After graduating cum laude from the University of Alabama in Huntsville in August 2003 with a BS in mechanical engineering, he entered the Marine Corps and completed basic officer training with honors. Assigned to First Radio Battalion in Camp Pendleton, California, he deployed to Camp Fallujah, Iraq, in February 2006. He immediately started writing his blog Midnight in Iraq "as a way to communicate with my friends and family." In March 2006 *The New York Times* hired Barnett as a guest writer for the Frontlines blog.

On his Web site, Midnight once posted a conversation that he had with a journalism student at Rome University. Asked why he decided to serve in Iraq, he responded: "I am a product of September 11. To be quite honest I didn't really understand what was happening on that fateful Tuesday, but after I figured it out it ignited a rage in me that took me through two and a half years of training and thousands of miles to bring me where I sit right now. Make no mistake: I want to be here." He also noted, though, that he's fine with war protesters: "I'd hate to see this country trample on the First Amendment as it has the Second Amendment."

Barnett returned from Iraq in August 2006, and now his blog is called The Midnight Hour. It is posted on a Web site called The Hushed Casket, a video-gaming community that he cofounded in 2002 with a friend. In 2007 he separated from the Marine Corps, rejoined civilian life, and began writing for *The New York Times*'s Home Fires blog, detailing his homecoming and civilian transition experiences.

He now works for a defense contractor in Huntsville, Alabama, testing warheads and missiles. He has been married since December 2001.

NINAPALEY.COM

http://www.ninapaley.com/

FRIDAY, MAY 12, 2006

The Hostess with the Leastest

After much thought, I'm ready to post another animated chapter of *Sita Sings the Blues*: "Battle of Lanka." Only thing is, I can't afford the hosting if my site gets stormed again like it did last year. Anyone want to host this puppy? It's 31.6 MB. Yes, I tried Google Video, and it did upload, but it plays like crap, skipping 4 out of 5 frames. And yes, I know about bittorrent, but I've never had much luck with it myself and I always prefer clips that play online without any additional software. I guess I'm getting picky—artifact-laden compression and tiny picture sizes are as far as I'm willing to compromise; you'll have to pry that frame rate out of my cold, dead hands.

The Host with the MOST

[...]

I've just uploaded "Battle of Lanka" to the Internet Archive. I've long been a huge supporter of Creative Commons so this is a great solution.

"Battle of Lanka" was made about a year ago, and is chapter 4 in *Sita Sings the Blues*, after "Hanuman Finds Sita" and before "Trial By Fire." In this episode, Rama, Hanuman, and the monkey armies cross the sea to Lanka to conquer Ravana and the rakshasas, and rescue the captive Sita. Assisting me was Jake Friedman, the only anima-

tion apprentice I've ever had. [...] Jake animated much of the monkey-on-demon violence: monkey swinging ax, monkey throwing ax, monkey bashing demon with club, monkey kicking demon, etc.

[...]

There are several more episodes I haven't posted publicly, and I reformatted "Trial By Fire" for widescreen, as well as changing a few scenes, and haven't uploaded the new version. I don't want to post everything online before the film is done, but you can see stills from all 8 episodes.

SATURDAY, JUNE 03, 2006

More Miniature Madness

Age and Beauty

I've received some emails complaining about my character design for Sita. Specifically, her babe-aliciousness offends some sensibilities, like Sendhil's:

> . . . please do not portray Mother Sita in a skinny robe like an arabian belly dancer. It is insulting to us Hindus. I also went through all the letters of appreciation you have received from everyone Indians and others. I can only assure you that they are idiots who have not understood the meaning of *Ramayana.*

Sita's bodacious bod is in fact based on a grand tradition of devotional Hindu art. This tradition is pre-Mughal, but then so is the *Ramayana* itself. [. . .] No shame in the female form; fearing and hiding it is an idea imported to India relatively recently.

Speaking of ancient history, another correspondent, Suresh Kumar, would like you to know that the *Ramayana* is many millennia older than the 3,000 years I gave it. He's referring to whatever actual events the story is based on, not when it was written. I myself peg it closer to Valmiki's estimated era, since I'm working from Valmiki's version. Your mileage may vary.

[. . .]

Ow, my eyes

Before I became an animator, I was a cartoonist and illustrator. Illustration is, in general, easier than animation, because it usually involves making only one drawing that will be looked at for several seconds, as opposed to making 24 drawings that will be looked at for only one second. My illustrations were usually black-and-white line art. If color was needed, I added it digitally. I was considered fast.

This fake Indian miniature painting project, however, has brought me to my knees. I am humbled. Drawing takes time. Painting takes even more time. Who knew? All those years I was cranking out daily comic strips, I thought I was Ms. Speed Queen. HA! When I planned this painting phase of the project, I thought it would only take me a month to paint eighteen scenes. EIGHTEEN SCENES! And I thought each scene would include new renderings of characters and

architecture and trees and skies and clouds. HA HA HA! No, I'll be re-using every character, tree, and background I paint as many times as I can, to avoid re-painting anything. But even with repeats, this project is progressing humiliatingly slowly. And it's not like the quality is anywhere near real Mughal miniatures. I recently saw a real one belonging to an art-collector friend. The detail is mind-boggling even to my nearsighted self. I'm pretty sure Mughal miniature painting is what they did to make little children go blind before they had Nike factories.

SUNDAY, JULY 09, 2006

Great Minds

Once *Sita Sings the Blues* is finished, in 2008 or so, my next project may be writing *Seder-Masochism: A Self-Hating Haggadah*. This is partly a gesture of goodwill to remedy all those angry accusations that I've singled out Hinduism to pick on (if you've seen my comics, you'd know I've also picked on Catholicism, Judaism, and others), and partly a tribute to my favorite holiday growing up. I came up with the title, *Seder-Masochism*, many years ago in San Francisco, when I held my own seder with that name. Fast-forward to last week, when I googled the term to see how original it was.

It's not. [. . .] Oh, I still plan to use *Seder-Masochism* as the title of my Haggadah, if I ever write it. I did, after all, come up with it in parallel, rather than derivatively. As the great Jewish philosophers say: so sue me.

Cry me a river

I'm currently animating episode 9, wherein Sita pines relentlessly for her beloved, lost Rama. In this scene, Sita literally cries a river while Valmiki plays a tiny violin.

When this is done, I'll animate the final musical number, in which Sita returns to the Earth's womb. Since making this movie is primarily an attempt to heal my own broken heart, I see animating Sita's suicide as symbolically killing my inner Sita. Sort of like how ancient cave painters killed their imagined prey by drawing arrows on them. I've learned to love my Sita, but I look forward to a life in which she doesn't rule my heart.

The film project itself will continue to dominate my life until 2008, when it'll hopefully be done. After the 10 musical numbers, there remain the dialog scenes, and some crazy experimental shit to do.

"i know you did the sita version, but she doesnt go up onto a piano and start singing the blues, like wtf."

If concerned viewer Guyanese Princess is actually a woman, this marks my very first hate mail from the gentler sex. Truly, I have passed a milestone.

[...]

From: "Guyanese Princess"
Date: Mon, 07 Aug 2006

hi,
i saw your sita sings the blues shit. you have the nerve to make a movie
based on the ramayan like that. mata sita does not deserve to be dressed
like that with her breasts popping out. i have read the ramayan, it is not a
story trying to insult women, it is a story of the avatar of vishnu. i know
you did the sita version, but she doesnt go up onto a piano and start
singing the blues, like wtf. I AM A PROUD HINDU AND YOU ARE INSULTING OUR
RELIGION AND OUR BELIEFS. I DO NOT APPRICIATE YOU TO DO THAT STORY.
PLEASE

EITHER REMAKE THAT MOVIE, TAKE IT OFF YOUR
WEBSITE, OR MAKE A PUBLIC
APOLOGY
TO ALL HINDUS FOR THAT CRAP THAT YOU MADE.

[. . .]

Killing Sita

I've been working on Sita's triumphant suicide scene for over a month now. For those unfamiliar with the "Uttara Kanda" of the *Ramayana,* Sita's mortal incarnation ends when she calls upon Mother Earth to take her back into her womb. This is Sita's response to yet another wishy-washy rejection from Rama.

A lot of women hate this part of the story, but I love it. It's the Best Suicide Ever! Even though I'm working to a little Annette Hanshaw ditty called "I've Got a Feelin' I'm Fallin' " (she's fallin' straight into the Earth, get it?), Sita's assertion of power reminds me of "I Will Survive" by Gloria Gaynor. Except Sita won't survive, which is the point.

[. . .]

Long live Sita!

Born in Urbana, Illinois, Nina Paley moved to California in 1988 at age twenty to become a hippie, but ended up a cartoonist instead. Her strip "Nina's Adventures" spread to alternative weeklies around the United States. Seven years later "Fluff," a daily strip, was syndicated, but the monotony led to burnout. She turned to animation, making four short films in the late 1990s using different techniques. In 1999 she made the world's first cameraless IMAX film, *Pandorama*. In 2001 came *Fetch*, an "optical-illusionistic" piece. Next came *The Stork* (2002), a short "in which a serene natural landscape is bombed by bundles of joy."

Paley's husband got a job in Trivandrum, India, in 2002, and she moved with him: "Upon my arrival I was confronted with his midlife crisis, a complete emotional withdrawal. This left me without support in a city in which women were second-class citizens. . . . It was in Trivandrum I encountered the Indian epic, the *Ramayana*, for the first time." After a few months, Paley said, her husband left her and she ended up in New York teaching animation at Parsons School of Design and developing a strip for King Features. "The *Ramayana* took on new depth and meaning for me. It no longer resembled a sexist parable; rather, it seemed to capture the essence of painful relationships and describe a blueprint of human suffering."

One episode of the *Ramayana*, Sita's walk through a funeral pyre, inspired her short film *Trial by Fire* (2003). After another breakup in 2004, she decided to tell the whole *Ramayana* from Sita's point of view and began *Sita Sings the Blues*, a seventy-two-minute feature set to the music of 1920s radio star Annette Hanshaw. (You'll never hear "Mean to Me," the song to which Sita tries to immolate herself, the same way again.) Paley is thirty-nine years old.

OLD HAG

A little from the left...   ..A little from the right

BOOK REVIEWS,   **OLD HAG**   CULTURE,
SUNDRIES.   INTELLIGENTSIA.

http://www.theoldhag.com/

We sat through *Love, Actually* this weekend. It was so stunningly, pyrotechnically horrific that there was nothing we could do. Nothing, that is, except render this review in rhyming tetrameter:

Love, Actually *At Top Speed*

Laura Linney's zany brother
Keeps her from an artiste lover;
Liam Neeson grieves rhapsodic
With his prolix stepson moppet;
Emma Thompson's ample charms
Drive Rick to Man Another's arms
While Keira Knightley's slim confusion
Wins the heart of hubby's groomsman;
For the royals, there is plenty
post-empiric droit de senny:
Colin Firth is damply *tendre*
With Brazilian *femme de chambre;*
Naughty Hugh is all a-quiver
For the help—but he's Prime Min'ster!—
And, like Phoenix, 'ol Slick Willy
Rises from Bob's ash (the Billy).
Though an ad for Jergens lotion

Quite conveys this film's emotion
We'd have absolutely lied
If we did not admit we cried—
We are being purely factual
When we say it's Rubbish, Actual;
But Bill Nighy's pelvic torments
Are a bravura performance.

Posted by altehaggen on November 4, 2003

A Villanelle Composed Upon Jennifer Aniston's Answers To Her May 2001 Vanity Fair *Interview, With Catalina Island "Glimmering In the Distance"**

This was just very much meant to be.
There was something very familiar about it.
But you just never know. What will be, will be.

I didn't have a fantasy of what marriage would be like. I had
    no idea.
I was stunned when I was addressed as Mrs. Pitt.
This was just very much meant to be.

We said, 'This is going to be a grand experiment. We expose
    ourselves completely.'
Every question comes out—it's like, here's the key, have
    at it!
But you just never know. What will be, will be.

It's fun to be home. I'm such a nester, and we're ridiculous
    homebodies.
This is only a two-bedroom house, and now we're spilling out
    of it.
This was just very much meant to be.

Acting is so much fun I don't think I could give it up
 completely.
There are so many things I haven't explored yet.
But you just never know. What will be, will be.

I couldn't hate my hair more. It's just not me.
I'm taking every horse vitamin there is to make it grow faster—
 blue-green algae.
This was just very much meant to be,
But you never know. What will be, will be.

* Variant tercets that have no place in this poem but serve as
proof of my prescience:

1) There's been a real internal overhaul—about family, work,
 everything.
 I think I'm just starting to feel I can stop apologizing.
 Feeling stupid, feeling good enough, feeling inadequate,
 asking "What am I doing?"

2) Marriage brings up all the things I pushed to the back
 burner.
 God forbid you fall short of dreams, and you're a failure.
 Let them know it's all bullshit. Just be happy with who you
 are.

(We wrote this years ago, when we were obsessed with found
poems. Somehow, it seemed apropos.)

Posted by altehaggen on January 7, 2005

Wiretapping

Since it's, at best, a minor sin
To cock your ear and listen in
Should we condemn the NSA
For simply caring what we say?
Think: eavesdropping the global nation
Hardly counts as a vacation.
For all the dish you get on whether
Brit and Kev are done forever
There's teenage girls in a dispute
If Dave is hot or merely cute
In fact, it's comfort—albeit cold—
That someone's with us while on hold—
That when you pound the umpteenth digit
A G-man somewhere gets the fidgets.
Hey, misused funds are not in vain
If someone, somewhere feels our pain.
But since we're footing all the bills
For senators to hear our ills
Why can't we have those black ops guys
Divide their time and be our spies?
If citizens have lost this fight
The customer is always right.
We could insist the cats who oogle
Each email and every Google
Extradite that spyware scam
And neatly Gitmo all our spam.
Then, when that sly Bin Laden fox
Was found concealed in our inbox
We'll bounce him to that rich Nigerian
Who simply goes by "Mailer-Daemon."

White House overstepped its role?
Just tell them in their online poll!
Don't think "shaky jurisprudence"—
It's "Homeland Quality Assurance."

Posted by altehaggen on July 3, 2006

Ballad Of The Love-Scorned Anywoman

Would it trouble you, at my behest,
to put a stuttering heart to rest?
This trouble's neither great nor tall—
So look at me, at least, or call.
My number's listed in the book,
and much is said with scattered look,
or not. Not operating, then
fling out that stevedore, and pen
a captive letter, deeply felt,
as lush and fired as African veldt.
God's love, we never had a fight!
We Walked in Beauty like the Night!
or somesuch. As you used to say?
perhaps that was another day.
Perhaps you listed me along
with All Else In My Life That's Wrong:
the idling sound that's not quite sound,
the ruined roast, the basset hound
you wanted but never seemed to get.
And you had studied to be a vet!
Perhaps I'm left in flounced heap
with all else limitless and cheap.
Or backyard flung to sootwashed bin,
with other snot-strung cherubim.
But I digress, and I'm forlorn.

My hands are weeping, chewed-off, torn.
I'd send them to The One I Love,
If Hallmark made a helpful glove.
My needs are drippy, short and clear:
could you last lilt out, "My Dear?"
Can't do? Be kind, if we're to be free.
I sucked your dick; be nice to me.

Posted by altehaggen on January 21, 2007

LIZZIE SKURNICK ■ OLD HAG
http://www.theoldhag.com/

In 2003, after a series of "brutal firings and dashed dreams," Lizzie Skurnick, at the age of thirty, embraced what she calls the "then medium of the vaguely repentant fuckup" and started an anonymous literary blog, Old Hag. "This timid venture, mostly an assemblage of occasional verse, highly unsubstantiated assertions, and pun-happy headlines," she said, "led to an unprecedented branching out of career opportunities, a new group of friends, a changed city of residence, and a greatly enhanced sense of joy and optimism in the future."

Skurnick is a graduate of Yale University and has worked at the Book-of-the-Month Club and Simon & Schuster. She was also an editor and ghostwriter at 17th Street Productions, a teen book publisher, where she worked on projects such as the Sweet Valley series and *Alias* spinoffs. After receiving her masters in poetry at the Johns Hopkins Writing Seminars, she taught in the undergraduate and graduate programs at Johns Hopkins.

The Old Hag, now thirty-four, has been featured in *Forbes*, *The Washington Post*, *The Scotsman*, and *The Village Voice*. Skurnick is the author of ten novels for teens, and she reviews and writes for such publications as *The New York Times Book Review*, *The Washington Post*, and *The Baltimore Sun*. Her chapbook of poetry, *Check-In*, is available from Caketrain Books.

RADIO.URUGUAY

http://dgoutnik.net/

2 0 0 5 - 1 0 - 0 4

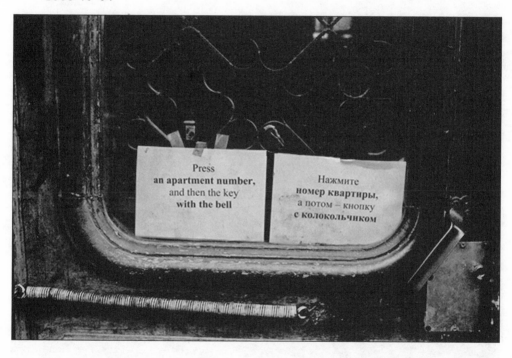

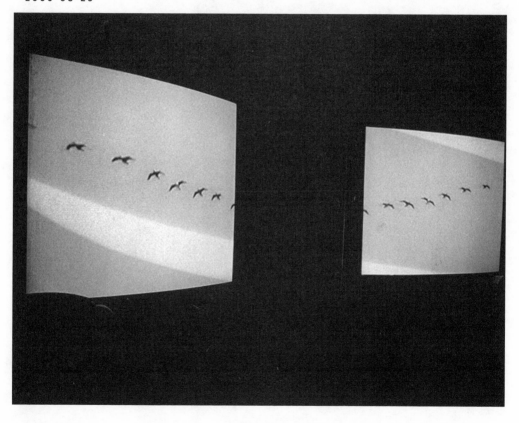

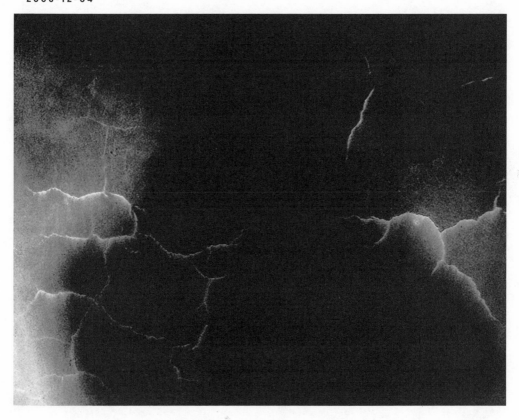

DMITRI GOUTNIK ■ RADIO.URUGUAY
http://dgoutnik.net/

Dmitri Goutnik's photoblog, which he began in 2004, won two prizes in the 2006 Photobloggies contest: Best Eastern European/Russian Photoblog and Best Black-and-White Photography.

ROOTLESS COSMOPOLITAN

Rootless Cosmopolitan
Analysis and commentary by Tony Karon

http://tonykaron.com/

WEDNESDAY, JULY 20, 2005

Free Mandela (From the Prison of Fantasy)!

Monday was Nelson Mandela's 87th birthday and on these shores I sometimes feel he's in need of rescuing, trapped in some pretty bizarre narratives that have nothing to do with his own story or politics. Full disclosure: I freely admit that Nelson Mandela is the only politician for whom I've ever voted; that I celebrate him as a moral giant of our age; and that I proclaimed him my leader (usually at the top of my tuneless voice, in badly sung Xhosa songs) during my decade in the liberation movement in South Africa. That may be why the "Mandela" I've encountered in so much American mythology is so unrecognizable. Herewith, the three most egregious versions:

Mythical Mandela #1: "Like Gandhi, Martin Luther King, and Nelson Mandela . . ."

How many times have [. . .] you heard that phrase to describe some politician, somewhere, opting for pacifism in the face of a nasty regime? Don't take it from me, try a google search on that exact phrase.

I understand the compulsion to link figures of great moral authority, but this is a little misleading. Nelson Mandela was never a pacifist.

When the Gandhi route of non-violent civil disobedience brought only violence from the state, Mandela declared, "The time comes in the life of any nation when there remain only two choices—submit or fight. That time has now come to South Africa. We shall not submit and we have no choice but to hit back by all means in our power in defence of our people, our future, and our freedom."

He played a leading role in setting up the ANC's guerrilla wing, and traveled abroad to gather support, even undergoing guerrilla training himself in Algeria, from the commanders of the FLN who had recently ejected the French colonials.

Mandela was no terrorist, however: Under his leadership, the movement's armed wing targeted symbols and structures of minority rule, and combatants of its security forces, never white civilians or any other non-combatants. And most important, he saw it as always, immediately and ultimately, subordinated to the political leadership.

In these beliefs he remained consistent and proud. Even as the mass non-violent opposition reasserted itself, under ANC guidance, in the 1980s, he reiterated its connection with the armed wing, writing in a smuggled message from prison that "between the hammer of armed struggle and the anvil of united mass action, the enemy will be crushed." (Of course it didn't ever work that way—the armed struggle was never particularly effective, and mass action combined with international sanctions did more to topple the regime.) [...]

Myth #2: The "Mandela Miracle"

Google *Mandela* and *miracle* together, and there are at least 86,000 citations. This idea has entered American shorthand as follows: South Africa would have exploded in a racial war, and white people would have been driven into the sea, had it not been for the "miraculous" generosity of spirit of Nelson Mandela, who supposedly restrained the vengeful hordes.

Oy, where to begin?

The assumption that black people would seek violent revenge for the violence they had suffered at the hands of white people is pretty racist. (Remember Gandhi's arch put-down when asked by a journalist what he thought of Western civilization: "That would be a fine idea," or words to that effect.)

But let's not even go there. This myth ignores the political culture of the ANC, which Mandela helped form, and which also formed him, and was never dependent on his own, or any other individual's, strength of character. [...] [T]he ANC [...] was always a non-racial movement that had substantial white membership [...] whose policies distinguished between white minority rule and white people. It would be remiss of any historian to understate the role of the South African Communist Party in nurturing this culture. I've written some pretty nasty things about the SACP in the past, but nobody can deny that not only were they the first, and for a long time the only, organization in South Africa advocating black majority rule; inside the ANC they played the leading role in shaping the analysis and strategy based on non-racialism and drawing whites into the struggle against colonial-style minority rule. [...]

And, paradoxical as it may sound, it was the Leninist realpolitik of the ANC's communist intellectuals that led the movement to embrace the path of a negotiated, compromise solution with negligible "rejectionist" backlash.

Of course communist discourse had a downside: I remember cringing when freed Robben Island prisoners would tell me things like "In Moscow, comrade, when you come out of the subway, there's just piles of fruit there, really good fruit, and it's just there for anyone to take, free, for everyone. . . ." And I nearly fell off my chair when reading a statement Mandela released to the media in Cape Town from prison late in 1989 proclaiming German reunification such a spectacularly bad idea that if released from prison, he would personally fly to

Germany to try and stop it. Uh, let's just say he was a product of a different age, shall we?

But the broader point here is that it was not some epiphany on the part of Nelson Mandela that led South Africa to its inspiring outcome. [...]

Myth #3: Marcus, Malcolm, Mandela, and Me– It's a Black Thing, You Wouldn't Understand

When I first saw that on a T-shirt being sold in Chinatown in 1991, I laughed out loud. (And actually, when watching Spike Lee's *Malcolm X* movie at an ANC fund-raising premiere in Cape Town, I'll never forget how the audience of Mandela loyalists erupted in raucous laughter when their good-natured leader appeared in the final *Spartacus* scene, intoning, "I am Malcolm X." The implication that their leader was inspired by a figure entirely unknown in the South African liberation movement discourse was pretty funny.)

Louis Farrakhan was probably a little surprised when he visited South Africa in 1995 and received a verbal dressing down from Mandela over his separatist politics.

My own favorite encounter with the Marcus-Malcolm-Mandela myth came one night in 1997, at a media party where I was chatting with a well known hip-hop scribe and his girlfriend, who ended up giving me a ride home in their rented limo. I should have known trouble was coming when the girlfriend said to me "So, what was it like coming to America and meeting FREE black people?" I told her that I had worked in the struggle, and although the black people I met there were viciously oppressed by a colonial regime, their minds were always free.

But the scribe and his girlfriend simply could not accept that I, a white boy—a Jew, to boot—had been in the ANC. "Mandela didn't work with white people," he insisted. Uh, actually, of the eight men on trial with Mandela in 1964, three were white (all of them Jewish, actually).

[. . .] Neil Aggett was killed in security police detention, just like Steve Biko. David Webster was murdered by a police assassin, just like Matthew Goniwe. Of course the vast majority of the people waging the struggle and bearing its sacrifices were black. But there were always a handful of whites alongside them. And so I went on, but none of this was making any impression.

Finally, the limo driver turned around, exasperated. He was Palestinian, he informed us, from Ramallah, where he'd been active in the Popular Front for the Liberation of Palestine, a leftist faction of the PLO. "And we always had Israeli Jews in our organization," he said. "Not many, but always a few. Because we were against Zionism, not against Jews."

And so it went on: the South African Jew and the Palestinian leftist trying, in vain, to explain Mandela's basic non-racialism to the hiphop philosopher who preferred the Mandela of his own fantasies. [. . .]

What Arab Holocaust Deniers Should Learn from Mandela

No, this is not another one of those idiotic diatribes by Americans or Israelis who know nothing about Nelson Mandela, but use their fantasy picture of him to add authority to their claims that the Palestinians should embrace whatever Israel deigns to offer them. For the record, in making peace with the apartheid regime, Nelson Mandela did not significantly compromise on the ANC's core demand. [. . .]

Still, there is a very, very important lesson that the Palestinian national movement and its Arab allies—and certainly those in Iran who claim to speak on its behalf—have failed to learn. Mandela made it his business, as a responsible leader of a national liberation movement fighting apartheid's unique form of colonialism, to understand the motives of the system's die-hard supporters. Not simply their tactics and strategies, but the historical narrative within which they constructed their system of minority rule as an "historic necessity" by which they could justify the suppression of others. Because all systems of oppression are ultimately founded on fear. [. . .]

When Mandela stood in the dock in 1964 and told the court that one of his prime sources of inspiration for waging guerrilla war was the great Boer War general Deneys Reitz—whose book *Kommando* was an early manual worthy of Giap—he was not simply being cute. He was telling the Afrikaners that he connected with their own national liberation struggle waged against the British, and that he was representing his own people in a narrative they should understand from their own experience. The Boers built the system that guaranteed their privileges and power on the basis of the common historical experience of the Afrikaners at the hands of the British—and for those of you who didn't know, the very term *concentration camp* was actually a British invention during the Boer War. The highly mobile Boer guerrilla forces were more than a match for Britain's large conventional formations, saddling up and riding into battle and then simply disappearing back into the civilian population. So the British responded by simply rounding up that civilian population, burning their farms, and imprisoning them in what they called concentration camps, where 26,000 Boer women and children died of starvation and disease.

And it was that sense of victimhood and outrage at the hands of the Brits that drove the Afrikaner-Nationalist ideology of Mandela's foes. Both from prison and in power, Mandela never belittled or dismissed their experience; instead he honored the suffering of the Boers and their courage and ingenuity in their war against Britain. Mandela's message, in essence, was "we understand your suffering, but we were not your oppressors, and you have nothing to fear from us; your suffering cannot excuse the suffering you have imposed on us."

Mandela went out of his way to incorporate Afrikaner suffering, and even Afrikaner national pride, in his articulation of a new national identity. The ANC government celebrated the centenary of the Anglo-Boer War in 1999, commemorating it as part of the legacy of South Africans' fight for freedom. And five years earlier, Mandela had donned that most potent of symbols of Afrikaner pride—the Springbok rugby jersey—to cheer on the national team at the Rugby World Cup, a gesture more powerful than any words could convey to many ordinary Afrikaner people fearful of their place in Mandela's new South Africa.

The reason we're talking about this, of course, is that Iran is hosting an international gathering of Holocaust deniers, as if assembling a rogues' gallery of neo-Nazis and Ku Klux Klansmen to "negate" the experience of history can somehow strengthen the Palestinian cause. [. . .] And in inviting Palestinians and Arabs to deny the Holocaust, Ahmadinejad is doing their cause a profound disservice. Ahmadinejad's Holocaust denial is hardly unique. It has been echoed even in recent weeks by representatives of Egypt's Muslim Brotherhood, and even Mahmoud Abbas. [. . .]

To deny the Holocaust because of the way it has been exploited is like denying that the attacks on the World Trade Center took place because you don't like the Patriot Act or the way 9/11 has been used to cow a frightened nation into supporting the invasion of Iraq. Arab Holocaust denial is a feeble-minded distortion that puts its adherents into the bizarre company of people who today would just as soon butcher Muslims to get them out of Europe as they once did to Jews (or, indeed, of the diseased minds in the Zionist camp who spend all their time bashing out emails and journal articles purporting to show that there are no Palestinians. [. . .])

But that's not the worst of it: Arab Holocaust denial also evades [. . .] the fact that not only did the Holocaust happen to the Jews of Europe, but because it happened to the Jews of Europe—and because of the reaction by other Western powers before and after the fact—the Holocaust profoundly changed the Arab world. Indeed, in this sense, the Holocaust may have been one of the most important historical events shaping Arab history over the past century.

[. . .] The vast majority of the world's Jews before World War II had rejected Zionism and its idea of colonizing Palestine in order to build a Jewish nation-state as a fringe movement of zealots. [. . .] The vast majority of Europe's Jews had identified themselves with the parties of the Left (and also secular liberalism in the case of elements of Western Europe's more prosperous Jewish communities)—they were socialists and social democrats, Bolsheviks and Bundists. [. . .]

And, of course, among the massive Jewish population of the main Arab cities of the time, such as Cairo and Baghdad (and also Tehran, of course, which is not Arab, but Persian), there was no statistically significant presence of a Zionist movement at all. [. . .]

The Holocaust wiped out the pre-war (mostly anti-Zionist) European leadership, and the Zionists were ready to take advantage of the opportunity presented by universal horror at what had transpired in the camps to make a case for a Jewish state in Palestine—a cause for which they had fought long before the Holocaust, but in which they hadn't won the support of a majority of European Jews. Ben-Gurion notoriously remarked, circa 1938, "Were I to know that all German Jewish children could be rescued by transferring them to England and only half by transfer to Palestine, I would opt for the latter, because our concern is not only the personal interest of these children, but the historic interest of the Jewish people." Indeed, Ben-Gurion warned that as a result of universal outrage at the Kristallnacht pogrom, other nations might be moved by conscience to open their doors to Jewish refugees—"Zionism is in danger!" Ben-Gurion warned.

Indeed, after the war, the Zionist movement actively agitated to ensure that the survivors of the Holocaust were transferred to Palestine, and nowhere else. Morris Ernst, a Jewish adviser to President Roosevelt, wrote later of a plan he devised and had pressed the U.S. president to accept that would throw open the doors of the U.S. to at least 150,000 survivors. "It would free us from the hypocrisy of closing our own doors while making sanctimonious demands on the Arabs," Ernst wrote, in reference to the fact that Arabs in Palestine were being told to make room for the survivors, while the main Western powers kept a tight restriction on Jewish immigration even after Auschwitz. When he proposed the plan to Zionist activists in Jewish organizations, he was shocked at the reaction: "I was amazed and even felt insulted when active Jewish leaders decried, sneered, and then attacked me as if I were a traitor . . . "

[. . .] [My] point is simple: The memory of the Holocaust is such a powerful ideological tool for Zionism precisely because of its reality— it speaks to the collective memory of Ashkenazi Jews of our fate in Europe, and it pricks the conscience of the perpetrators and those who preferred to turn away.

To respond by trying to deny the reality of the Holocaust is as profoundly immoral as it is idiotic—creating a kind of binary game in which if Israel says mother's milk is good for babies, the likes of Ahmadinejad will convene a symposium to prove the superiority of formula. The point about the Holocaust is that it happened to the Jews of Europe, and afterwards, as a result of the efforts of the Zionist movement and some combination of shame and latent anti-Semitism in the West, many of its survivors had no choice but to go to Palestine, where they were willing to fight with every fiber of their being for survival, without the luxury of considering the history and context into which they'd been thrust.

In the war that followed, Palestinian Arabs, who had been 55% of the population and had controlled around 80% of the land, now found themselves displaced and dispossessed, confined to a mere 22% of Palestine (the West Bank and Gaza), and prevented by a series of ethnic-cleansing laws passed by the State of Israel at its inception from reclaiming the homes and land from which they'd mostly fled in legitimate fear for their lives.

So, the Holocaust, in a very real way, reverberated traumatically in Palestinian national life: It was the narrative that fueled the ferocity with which many of those who drove the Palestinians from their homes in 1948 approached the struggle. And, as Morris Ernst wrote in his reference to "sanctimonious demands on the Arabs," the Palestinian Arabs had been asked to pay a steep price for Western guilt over what had befallen the Jews of Europe.

Ahmadinejad ought to pay attention to one particular guest, a Palestinian lawyer from Nazareth called Khaled Mahameed, who runs a small Holocaust exhibit at his office in Nazareth, and argues that it is essential that the Palestinians understand the Holocaust because in it lies the root of their own suffering. Addressing the Israelis on the basis of an understanding of their experience was essential for the Palestinians to make progress in their own national struggle, he argues. He was invited to the conference after writing to Ahmadinejad, telling him that the Holocaust was an historical fact that should not be questioned, and that doing so only played into the hands of right-wing Zionists. Indeed, the Zionist establishment doesn't quite know what to make of Mahameed, because he's directly challenging Ahmadinejad at the same time as [he's] making clear that the Holocaust has been abused in order to justify suffering inflicted on the Palestinians. That's how a Palestinian Mandela would put it—the Holocaust, in fact, is part of the legacy of suffering that is the common history of Israel and the Palestinians.

TONY KARON ▪ ROOTLESS COSMOPOLITAN
http://tonykaron.com/

Tony Karon, a forty-six-year-old journalist from Cape Town, South Africa, has lived in New York since 1993. He is a senior editor at TIME.com, where he has worked since 1997, covering the Middle East and international issues. He writes op-ed pieces for the Israeli newspaper *Haaretz* and did a stint at FOX News ("measured in months," he says, "I swear!").

After college he worked in South Africa as an editor in the "alternative" press and as an activist for the banned African National Congress. After Mandela was released, he gave up that work, explaining: "If you'd been French under occupation, you might well have joined the resistance, but that didn't mean you'd remain active in party politics after the Nazis were gone—that was how it was for many of my generation of South African activists." He then worked for a couple of newspapers and did "a mad array of freelance gigs."

Karon began his first blog shortly after 9/11, writing mostly for friends. That blog evolved into Rootless Cosmopolitan, which covers not only the "war on terror" but also soccer, pop culture, and food. The name for the blog derives from Stalin's "euphemistic pejorative" for Jews in the 1940s, and Karon, "an African Jew with roots in Eastern Europe and before that France," says he now wears it as a "badge of honor."

"I'm not at all religious, and certainly no Zionist," he writes. "But I am proudly Jewish. . . . All of the great Jewish intellectual, philosophical, moral, and cultural exemplars I can think of were products not of a separate Jewish existence, but of the Diaspora . . . Maimonides or Spinoza; Marx or Freud; Einstein or Derrida; Kafka or Primo Levi; Serge Gainsbourg or Daniel Barenboim; Lenny Bruce or Bob Dylan."

Alex Ross: The Rest Is Noise

Articles, a blog, and a book-in-progress by the music critic of *The New Yorker*

http://www.therestisnoise.com/

Applaud away

On Saturday night I went to see the New Jersey Symphony in Trenton. [. . .] Something delightfully odd happened during Stenhammar's Piano Concerto No. 1, with Neeme Järvi conducting and Per Tengstrand, an intense young Swedish virtuoso, at the piano. After the first movement, there was the usual smattering of applause mixed with assorted "hushes." Tengstrand looked toward the audience encouragingly, as if pleading for applause. Then he reached for a microphone and began to talk. He explained that he'd intended to say something about this unusual work—unheard in America for more than a hundred years—but as he walked out onstage he forgot. So he decided to speak up in the middle of the concerto. Highly irregular, yet it did not harm the piece. It was refreshing to have a brief respite and change of mental gears before the Scherzo. I'm not recommending the inter-movement lecture as a regular feature, but it exemplifies the kind of (mildly) free-spirited behavior that classical concerts need more of. The historical record suggests that composers of the pre-1900 period would be horrified by modern concert etiquette. Accustomed to applause between and even during movements of a large-scale work, they'd assume that audiences hated their music or had no comprehension of it. Are we more serious, more cultured, than Mozart, Beethoven, and Brahms? All those who consider themselves more serious than Brahms have every right to shush their neighbors after the first movement of the D-minor Concerto.

—*January 10, 2005*

More applause

Re: The post on intrasymphonic applause [...], Felix Salmon reminds me that he and Terry Teachout [both bloggers] debated this matter back in 2003. Terry, pro-applause, quoted the great conductor Pierre Monteux: "I do have one big complaint about audiences in all countries, and that is their artificial restraint from applause between movements of a concerto or symphony. I don't know where the habit started, but it certainly does not fit in with the composers' intentions." Felix worried that the culture of applause could get out of hand, leading to intrusive clapping after every movement and indiscriminate standing ovations such as you find on Broadway. [...] I wouldn't necessarily want applause after *every* movement, but that's the way audiences did it before 1900, and classical culture was far healthier in that period. [...] Is it a paradox that composers of past eras wrote so much astounding music while audiences, by our standards, "misbehaved"? Or was there a direct relationship between the unruliness of the audience and the greatness of the music? [...]

It's an interesting question, how this silent routine got started. In my article "Listen To This," I alluded to the strange behavior of audiences at the premiere performances in *Parsifal* in 1882. I think it began there and then spread to orchestral culture. From Cosima Wagner's diary: "When, after the second act, there is much noise and calling, R. comes to the balustrade, says that though the applause is very welcome to his artists and to himself, they had agreed, in order not to impinge on the impression, not to take a bow, so that there would be no 'curtain calls'. . . . At the end R. is vexed by the silent audience, which has misunderstood him. [. . .] Two days later: "After the first act there is a reverent silence, which has a pleasant effect. But when, after the second, the applauders again are hissed, it becomes embarrassing." Two weeks later: "R. had a restless night. He feels so languid that he does not attend the performance, just appears during the intermissions, and the only thing he hears all through is the flower scene, since the excellence of the performance always refreshes him. From our box he calls out, 'Bravo!' whereupon he is hissed." [. . .] I can't think of a better example of nincompoop pseudo-seriousness than the idea of a Bayreuth audience inadvertently hissing Richard Wagner himself.

On a related matter, see my short piece "Concert Rage." People who "shush" are just as annoying as people who chatter and crinkle cough-drop wrappers; no, more annoying. Often I hear a "shush" wafting down from the upper gallery without hearing whatever minor disturbance caused it. [. . .]

—January 10, 2005

Applause mailbag

Re: my applause posts, Peter Rolufs writes from Tokyo:

Considering "the direct relationship between the greatness of the audience and the unruliness of the music" I was by all means disturbed when a "young lion" of jazz at New Orleans's leading club Snug Harbor made a sarcastic remark between songs about the audience not listening. [. . .] Well, there was a bit of a din, but I for one was concentrating full-on as the music was sublime, and by golly the din fit right in. The lion's dad would have known better, I thought. [. . .]

Actually, I wrote "the unruliness of the audience and the greatness of the music," but that's just the point, ain't it? Greatness and unruliness are often interchangeable. On the too rare occasions I make it to a jazz club—as, for example, when I saw Cecil Taylor at the Iridium last spring—I feel I'm in audience heaven: informality and seriousness are in perfect balance. [. . .]

—January 18, 2005

Absolutely final applause post

Mozart writes about the 1778 premiere of his Paris Symphony: "Just in the middle of the first Allegro there was a Passage I was sure would please. All the listeners went into raptures over it—applauded heartily. But, as when I wrote it, I was quite aware of its Effect, I introduced it once more towards the end—and it was applauded all over again." Mozart here describes an atmosphere similar to that of modern jazz clubs. [. . .]

—January 24, 2005

Applause: the nightmare returns

When I said [. . .] that I had produced my "absolutely final applause post," I meant, of course, that I had written my absolutely final applause post in the Year of the Monkey. It is now the Year of the Rooster, and I am free to resume. Explosive new information on the history of classical concert etiquette has come over the transom, which I will need a few more days to digest. In the meantime, I'd like to quote a brief item that Emanuel Ax recently posted on his Web site:

> . . . I really hope we can go back to the feeling that applause should be an emotional response to the music, rather than a regulated social duty. I am always a little taken aback when I hear the first movement of a concerto which is supposed to

be full of excitement, passion, and virtuoso display (like the Brahms or Beethoven concertos), and then hear a rustling of clothing, punctuated by a few coughs; the sheer force of the music calls for a wild audience reaction. On the other hand, sometimes I wish that applause would come just a bit later, when a piece like the Brahms Third Symphony comes to an end—it is so beautifully hushed that I feel like holding my breath in the silence of the end. I think that if there were no "rules" about when to applaud, we in the audience would have the right response almost always. [...]

—*February 13, 2005*

Applause: A Rest Is Noise Special Report

Here is everything I have been able to discover about the history of applause between movements of symphonies and concertos, a topic which has taken over my blog like a crazy weed, and which I now intend to spray with Brahms. [...] Bernard Sherman has been very helpful in pointing me toward sources. [...] Descend into the quagmire at your own risk.

To recap: Up until the beginning of the twentieth century, applause between movements and even during movements was the sign of a knowledgeable, appreciative audience, not of an ignorant one. The biographies of major composers are full of happy reports of what would now be seen as wildly inappropriate applause. [...]

The great change in audience behavior began, I believe, at the premiere performances of Wagner's *Parsifal* at Bayreuth in 1882. [...] By around 1900, a portion of the public had embraced the idea that certain works should be heard in rapt silence. [...] The "Bayreuth hush"—the silence that descends on the house before the performance begins—became the gold standard of audience sophistication. One young acolyte who absorbed the Bayreuth ideal—which, we know, Wagner himself discouraged—was Anton Webern. In a diary devoted to his "Bayreuth Pilgrimage" of 1902, he wrote: "Hardly has the crowd left the temple when laughing and idle chatter start again, when each one inspects the other's wardrobe and behaves as if he had not experienced something that transports our kind out of this world. And then! There was, on top it, applause!"

Was Webern's hero Gustav Mahler responsible for the "ban on applause"? I hinted as much in a previous post, but I was confusing symphony with opera. Mahler, like Toscanini, opposed the "claques" that delivered explosions of applause to favorite singers and routinely stopped performances in their tracks. He worked hard to root out that often corrupt practice, to the point of hiring detectives to patrol the theater. But he does not seem to have been exercised about applause during symphonic performances. He certainly welcomed the increasing rounds of applause that greeted each movement of his Third Symphony at its Krefeld premiere in 1902. (Richard Strauss tipped the audience in Mahler's favor by applauding ostentatiously after the first movement.) [. . .] Toscanini, likewise, evidently did not care much about the issue, as the scholars Harvey Sachs and Mortimer Frank report to me. Applause can be heard after the first movements of concertos on the NBC Symphony broadcasts. No doubt if the practice had displeased Toscanini we would have heard about it.

So who is the culprit? Barney Sherman came forward with the apparent answer: Leopold Stokowski. A surprising development, given Stokowski's well-earned image as the showman of music, the populist preacher, Deanna Durbin's costar, and so on. But, at the end of the 1920s, he convinced himself that applause during symphonies intruded on the divinity of the concert experience, and he began trying to convince audiences to stop. From Oliver Daniel's biography *Stokowski: A Counterpoint of View:*

When the audience burst into spontaneous volleys of applause after the pizzicato movement of the Tchaikovsky Fourth Symphony during a concert on November 8, 1929, Stoki turned, signaled for silence, and explained that his remarks were not intended as a rebuke for their appreciation. "But," he added reflectively, "I have been considering this matter of applause, a relic from the Dark Ages, a survival of customs at some rite or ceremonial dance in primitive times" [. . .] (pp. 278–79).

As Herbert Kupferberg's *Those Fabulous Philadelphians* reveals, Stokowski then went even further, proposing that audiences stop applauding altogether:

> [. . .] He didn't make this suggestion casually: on November 22, 1929, in the green room at the Academy, he actually held a secret meeting of 100 women—if there is such a thing—to announce his revolutionary idea. [. . .] "But how are we to let you know we appreciate your programs?" one bewildered matron asked. Stokowski's blue eyes took on a faraway look. "That is of no importance," he said. "When you see a beautiful painting you do not applaud. When you stand before a statue, whether you like it or not, you neither applaud nor hiss" [. . .] (p. 78).

Do not assume that Stokowski did this in a spirit of modesty. The kind of concert that he had in mind would hardly have concealed his role as the genius of the scene. In another meeting with the women of the Academy he said: "It has been the dream of my life to have a Temple of Music. This very minute I have the plans for such a temple completed at my House. Each of the audience would sit alone in a stall-like seat. No one would see his neighbor. . . . Just before the music begins the light will be slowly dimmed so that the entire temple will be in darkness and the audience will be literally drenched in beautiful music" (Kupferberg, p. 75). Stokowski actually made a trial run at the Temple of Music, and it turned out that the darkness was not quite total, as Abram Chasins relates: "Stokowski ordered the house lights extinguished and allowed only infinitesimal lamps over the orchestra stands, while a huge spotlight played upon the conductor from below so as to project mammoth shadows of his flashing, expressive fingers and hands onto the walls and ceiling of the stage" (Chasins, *Leopold Stokowski*, pp. 104–5).

It's not surprising that conductors were intent on stamping out spontaneous clapping. [. . .] Silence is the measure of the unbreakable spell that Maestro is supposedly casting on us. [. . .]

The other factor that deserves to be mentioned is that just a few weeks before his no-applause experiment Stokowski conducted the first commercial radio broadcast of a symphonic concert (Oct. 6, 1929). [. . .] The notion of a Temple of Music, each listener cocooned in solitude, is a mirror image of the new, non-communal modes of listening that radio and recording were in the process of creating. [. . .]

Stokowski's campaign against applause aroused immediate opposition. [. . .] The composer Daniel Gregory Mason spoke out against it in his 1931 book *Tune In, America*, which I quoted in "Listen To This." Mason, a sometimes obnoxious, sometimes constructive polemicist who was arguing for a less hidebound concert experience, began a chapter on audience behavior by talking about different philosophies of rearing children—the "repressive" method and the "responsibility-delegated method." The silence campaign, he said, represented

the repressive method with a vengeance. It deprives the audience not only of all active participation in the artistic experience, such as might well be thought essential to the healthy progress of art itself, but even of psychological and physical relief after the strain of attention. [...] After the Funeral March of the *Eroica*, someone suggested, Mr. Stokowski might at least have pressed a button to inform the audience by (noiseless) illuminated sign: "You may now cross the other leg" (p. 52).

Mason notes that the pianist-conductor Ossip Gabrilowitsch took another view, announcing his approval for "those countries in the south of Europe where they shout when they are pleased and when they are not, they hiss and throw potatoes."

[...]

The no-applause rule was slow to spread. It was not in force in Vienna in 1938, when Bruno Walter conducted Mahler's Ninth Symphony in one of the last concerts before the Anschluss. [...] Here is one of the most "serious" audiences that ever existed. Many of those in the hall had attended Mahler's legendary Viennese performances. Some had known Mahler personally. Yet they applauded during this most searching and death-haunted of Mahler's works. [...] You can also hear intermittent applause on American orchestral broadcasts into the 1950s. A very kind reader sent me a tape of a 1954 Boston Symphony broadcast of the Bartók Second Violin Concerto, with Tossy Spivakovsky as the soloist and Pierre Monteux conducting. There is warm applause after the first movement, none after the second. [...]

That's as far as I've gotten in my investigation. How and why the Rule became universal in the fifties and sixties remains to be discovered. It was probably tied to the influence of technology on listening habits: these were the years of the LP, with neat bands of silence between each movement. It was almost certainly related to the transmogrification of classical music into a purely "highbrow" form of entertainment, as opposed to the middlebrow, music-for-the-masses ethos that had prevailed in the 1930s and 1940s. I cannot divine any strong musical reason for it. [. . .]

—*February 18, 2005*

Alex Ross was born in 1968 in Washington, D.C., where he studied composition and played piano and oboe. At Harvard College he worked at the radio station (presenting György Ligeti's *Poème Symphonique for 100 Metronomes*) and played keyboard in the noise band Miss Teen Schnauzer. From 1992 to 1996 he was a critic at *The New York Times*, and since 1996 he has been the music critic for *The New Yorker*. His first book, *The Rest Is Noise: Listening to the Twentieth Century*, a cultural history of music since 1900, has just been published by Farrar, Straus and Giroux.

Ross said he started his blog The Rest Is Noise in 2004, after "falling under the spell of several blogs by fellow writers, notably those of Terry Teachout, Sasha Frere-Jones, and Kyle Gann." He finds the informality of the blogosphere liberating: "You can test theories, find like-minded colleagues, indulge in whimsy or irrelevance, and offer up quotations or factoids without feeling the need to comment." And for readers, he says, reading about an opera singer who fears forgetting her lines or a harpist who scorns the people who hire her for weddings can humanize classical music.

Despite their reputation for being terminally hip, blogs, he said, have really been a boon to the "socially challenged" (read: nerdy) form known as classical music, which is all but ignored by major print media. "The music can find its audience without having to pass through advertising filters that tailor everything to the taste of eighteen- to thirty-year-olds." Ross, who is pushing forty, lives in Manhattan. He is married and has two cats.

THE SMOKING GUN

the smoking gun

http://www.thesmokinggun.com/

Bush Received Weapons Cache From Jordan

Collectibles, DVDs, bling highlight foreign leader gift list

JUNE 15, 2006—President George W. Bush received a $10,000 sniper's rifle, six jars of fertilizer, eleven antique handguns, ten pounds of dates, and a DVD of *Singin' in the Rain* from various foreign leaders, according to a report filed today by the U.S. Department of State. The annual report from the Office of Protocol, excerpts from which you'll find below, covers gifts provided in 2004 to federal employees by "foreign government sources." Included in Bush's haul (which gets sent to a government archive) were assorted Dallas Cowboys merchandise from Saudi Arabia's Prince Bandar, a $125 braided leather whip from the Hungarian prime minister, and a copy of *The Worst-Case Scenario Survival Handbook* from the Sultan of Brunei. The Asian leader also gave Bush DVDs of *Singin' in the Rain* and *To Kill a Mockingbird*. Jordan's King Abdullah gave Bush $12,000 worth of antique weapons, including a pistol dating to 1780, and a $10,000 Dakota Arms sniper's rifle. He also provided the president with six jars of "various fertilizers" valued at $60. As the State Department report notes, the circumstance "justifying acceptance" of these foreign gifts is "non-acceptance would cause embarrassment to donor and U.S. Government." The

AGENCY: WHITE HOUSE OFFICE AND THE NATIONAL SECURITY COUNCIL—Continued
[Report of Tangible Gifts]

Name and title of person accepting the gift on behalf of the U.S. Government	Gift, date of acceptance on behalf of the U.S. Government, estimated value, and current disposition or location	Identity of foreign donor and government	Circumstances justifying acceptance
	Weapon: 9″ stainless steel and gold-tone knife with malachite handle and stamped with the seal of the Kingdom of Bahrain. Recd—November 29, 2004. Est. Value—$400. Archives Foreign.		
President	Athletic equipment: 34″ black and brown wooden Sam Bats baseball bat engraved "Texas Rangers, Prez 43, George W. Bush, Future Commissioner MLB, Presented by The Right Hon. Paul Martin, Ottawa, Canada, November 30, 2004." Recd—November 30, 2004. Est. Value $111. Archives Foreign.	The Right Honorable Paul Martin, PC, MP, Prime Minister of Canada.	Non-acceptance would cause embarrassment to donor and U.S. Government.
	Accessories: pair of 3/4″ white and yellow 14kt gold maple leaf cufflinks. Recd—November 30, 2004. Est. Value—$800. Archives Foreign.		
President	Household accessories (3): 21″ x 44″ x 20″ dark wood table ornately inlaid with bone; and 22″ x 22″ x 20½″ dark wood end table ornately inlaid with bone (2). Recd—December 4, 2004. Est. Value $1400. Archives Foreign.	His Excellency Pervez Musharraf, President of the Islamic Republic of Pakistan.	Non-acceptance would cause embarrassment to donor and U.S. Government.
	Weapon: 52″ x 8″ antique muzzle loader (circa mid-1800s); held in a 20″ x 62″ wooden shadowbox with a 4″ x 3″ plaque engraved "Presented by General Pervez Musharraf, President, Islamic Republic of Pakistan." Recd—December 4, 2004. Est. Value—$725. Archives Foreign.		
	Clothing: cream wool traditional Pakistani coat embroidered with a satin ornate design. Recd—December 4, 2004. Est. Value—$175. Archives Foreign.		
	Accessory: 10″ cream wool traditional Pakistani hat. Recd—December 4, 2004. Est. Value—$65. Archives Foreign.		
President	Weapons (11): Maynard Revolver; Colt Revolver (circa 1884); Colt Police Revolver (circa 1860); Remington Double Derringer Pistol; Sharps Flint-Ignition Pistol (circa 1780); Winchester Lever-Action Repeating Carbine (circa 1866); Colt Navy (circa 1851); Pistol from Lowell, Massachusetts (circa 1858); Colt Derringer, Sharps 4 Barrel Pocket Pistol; and Wesson and Harrington Pocket Revolver (circa 1871); all held in a 23″ x 43″ hinged wooden box. Recd—December 6, 2004. Est. Value—$12,000. Archives Foreign.	His Majesty King Abdullah II of the Hashemite Kingdom of Jordan.	Non-acceptance would cause embarrassment to donor and U.S. Government.

AGENCY: WHITE HOUSE OFFICE AND THE NATIONAL SECURITY COUNCIL—Continued

[Report of Tangible Gifts]

Name and title of person accepting the gift on behalf of the U.S. Government	Gift, date of acceptance on behalf of the U.S. Government, estimated value, and current disposition or location	Identity of foreign donor and government	Circumstances justifying acceptance
	Miscellaneous (6): 4″ jars of various fertilizers; held on a 12″ x 15″ wooden revolving display. Recd—December 6, 2004. Est. Value $60. Archives Foreign. Weapon: 50″ x 8½″ black Dakota Arms sniper rifle with an 8″ scope; held in a metal hinged box embroidered on the inside "To My Dear Friend, George W. Bush, Abdullah II" with a Jordanian crown and the Great Seal. Recd December 6, 2004. Est. Value—$10000. Archives Foreign.		
President	Jewelry: 18kt yellow gold Cartier Santos 100 watch with a square face, Roman numeral hour markers, and a brown alligator band. Recd—December 16, 2004. Est. Value—$4200. Archives Foreign. Accessories (12): variety of E. Marinella silk ties. Recd—December 16, 2004. Est. Value—$1620. Archives Foreign.	His Excellency Silvio Berlusconi, President of the Council of Ministers of the Italian Republic.	Non-acceptance would cause embarrassment to donor and U.S. Government.
President	Miscellaneous: 20½″ x 16″ red and white leather chest with hinged lid; padded interior with a two-tiered leather lined wood tray. Recd—December 17, 2004. Est. Value—$280. Archives Foreign. Consumables: ten pounds of Tunisian dates. Recd—December 17, 2004. Est. Value—$60. Handled pursuant to Secret Service policy. Consumables (6): bottles of Les Vignes de Tánit wine (2 Rose, 2 Blanc, 2 Rouge). Recd—December 17, 2004. Est. Value—$48. Archives Foreign. Consumables (8): liter bottles of Tunisian olive oil. Recd—December 17, 2004. Est. Value—$28. Handled pursuant to Secret Service policy.	His Excellency Zine El Abidine Ben Ali, President of the Republic of Tunisia.	Non-acceptance would cause embarrassment to donor and U.S. Government.
President	Household: 3½″ x 4″ round frosted glass containers with "Savour Jordan." Recd—December 22, 2004. Est. Value—$30. Archives Foreign. Miscellaneous (2): myrtle flower scented candles. Recd—December 22, 2004. Est. Value—$20. Handled pursuant to Secret Service Policy.	Their Majesties King Abdullah II and Queen Rania al Abdullah of the Hashemite Kingdom of Jordan.	Non-acceptance would cause embarrassment to donor and U.S. Government.

Tunisian president gave Bush $60 worth of dates. First Lady Laura Bush received an $1150 Chanel purse from the French president's wife and a $12,500 Mounier & Bouvard clutch from the King of Morocco. Vice President Dick Cheney scored a $400 set of white gold cufflinks "with Arabic lettering symbolizing good fortune and health" from the Jordanian king, while former Secretary of State Colin Powell received a Bulgari necklace set from Saudi Arabia's Prince Faisal. At $24,500, the gold and diamond jewelry was the most valuable gift from a foreign official. While Defense Secretary Donald Rumsfeld received some nice bottles of wine, his most unique gift came from Jordan's King and Queen, who gave Rummy a $380 aromatherapy gift set. Though Rumsfeld could surely use the aromatic relaxation, the item was transferred to the General Services Administration. [. . .]

"A School Is No Place For A Gun"

Columbine killer wrote cautionary H.S. report before massacre

JULY 7, 2006—One of the Columbine High School gunmen prepared a report on the danger of guns in schools more than a year before carrying out a deadly attack on teachers and fellow students. Eric Harris's December 1997 school report was included in more than nine hundred pages of Columbine-related documents released yesterday by Colorado investigators. In grading the Harris report, a copy of which you'll find below, a Columbine teacher judged it "thorough & logical" and gave the paper a 69 out of 75. Noting that "a school is no place for a gun," Harris concluded that the use of metal detectors and an increased police presence "are a great start to fight against guns in school." On April 20, 1999, Harris and Dylan Klebold—armed with shotguns and semiautomatic weapons—murdered twelve classmates and a teacher before killing themselves. [. . .]

Guns in

Schools

*Thorough &
logical. A few
formatting problems/
however. Nice job.
69/75*

By:

Eric Harris

period 4

12/10/97

Mr. Webb

Eric Harris
12/10/97

Guns in School

In the past few weeks there has been news of several shootings in high schools. A student in Texas killed three fellow classmates and injured many more when he fired at a prayer group before school. This student had several other weapons with him when he was apprehended, showing how easy it was to bring so many weapons to school and not be noticed. Students who bring guns to school are hardly ever detected. This is shocking to most parents and even other students since it is just as easy to bring a loaded handgun to school as it is to bring a calculator. The problem of guns in school is a major one faced by many parents, teachers, and citizens these days. Solutions are hard to come by in such a situation because of how widespread the problem is and how different each school in each town can be. Students can get weapons into school too easily and they have to much access to weapons outside of school.

A. Weapons in school are hard to detect and students have ways of getting out of searches or other ways of detection.

    1. One example of students avoiding detection is a 1990 survey conducted by the Centers For Disease Control (CDC) which found that one in 20 high school students carried a gun in school during the past month (CDC).

    2. Students can use their backpacks, purses, or even projects to bring weapons into school.

    3. Metal detectors can be avoided by using other school entrances.

B. Students have access to many weapons and can obtain a gun from many places.

    1. The low price of junk guns (as low as 69 dollars) brings these guns within the economic reach of children (Gun Digest, 288).

JC-001-026352

Eric Harris
12/11/97

Works cited

Centers For Disease Control. "Weapon Carrying Among High School Students." Morbidity and

Morality Weekly Report. Vol. 40 No. 40. 11 Oct. 1991.

Gun Digest 1995, 49th Annual Edition. Northbrook, Il. DBI Books, Inc., 1994. 288.

Harrington, Donna. "Blown Away." The American School Board Journal. May, 1992. 22.

"Junk Guns." On-line. Available: www.gunfree.org/csgv/bsc_jun.htm. 9 Dec. 1997

Sixteen Other Fidel Castro Operations

U.S. military developed kooky plots to oust Cuba's charismatic leader

AUGUST 1, 2006—Now that Fidel Castro has ceded power due to illness, the end of the Cuban president's 47-year rule may be nearing—something that the U.S. government has sought for decades. In fact, American military leaders once drafted memos detailing various proposed plots to destabilize Castro's government and topple its charismatic leader. The formerly Top-Secret U.S. Army records, copies of which you'll find below, describe 16 separate "operations" with code names like "Operation Bingo" and "Operation Dirty Trick" (the latter scheme would have tried to pin the possible failure of the *Mercury* manned orbit flight on Cubans and other Reds). But the most inspired of Uncle Sam's kooky Cold War–era plans was "Operation Good Times," which would have sought to disillusion Castro's constituents via the distribution of "fake photographic material." Specifically, the proposed doctored images would have shown "an obese Castro with two beauties" in a lavish residence complete with "a table brimming over with the most delectable Cuban food." A caption would have noted that, "My ration is different." The sight of the well-fed revolutionary, Army officials concluded, "should put even a Commie Dictator in the proper perspective with the underprivileged masses."

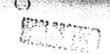

(g) Resupply and replacement activities.

Properly executed, the above could overthrow the Cuban Government in a matter of hours, providing the plan is implemented within the next six months.

11. Operation GOOD TIMES:

a. **Objective:** To disillusion the Cuban population with Castro image by distribution of fake photographic material.

b. **Concept:** Prepare a desired photograph, such as an obese Castro with two beauties in any situation desired, ostensibly within a room in the Castro residence, lavishly furnished, and a table briming over with the most delectable Cuban food with an underlying caption (appropriately Cuban) such as !!My ration is different." Make as many prints as desired on sterile paper and then distribute over the countryside by air drops or agents. This should put even a Commie Dictator in the proper perspective with the underprivileged masses.

12. Operation HEAT IS ON:

a. **Objective:** To create the impression with Castro Government that certain dyed-in-the-wool Red pilots are planning to defect, thus causing a detrimental tightening of security.

b. **Concept:** It is known that many Cuban refugee pilots are personally acquainted with many of the present CRAF pilots. Accordingly, by utilizing all sources available, determine by name those pilots considered to be dedicated Castro Reds. Then by use of agents, communications, etc. inject into the Castro intelligence system the fact that these pre-designated Reds are planning to defect for monetary and/or ideological reasons. Security crackdown should help destroy Castro image and also impose unacceptable restrictions on routine training activities.

4
Incl 5/4

Rudy Giuliani's Vulnerabilities

Secret study cited "weirdness factor" among candidate weaknesses

FEBRUARY 12, 2007—As he campaigns for the Republican presidential nomination, Rudolph Giuliani will have to contend with political and personal baggage unknown to prospective supporters whose knowledge of the former New York mayor is limited to his post–September 11 exploits. So, in a bid to educate the electorate, we're offering excerpts from a remarkable "vulnerability study" that was commissioned by Giuliani's campaign prior to his successful 1993 City Hall run. The confidential 450-page report, authored by Giuliani's research director and another aide, was the campaign's attempt to identify possible lines of attack against Giuliani and prepare the candidate and his staff to counter "the kinds of no-holes-barred [sic] assault" expected in a general election rematch with Democratic incumbent David Dinkins. As he tried to win election in an overwhelmingly Democratic city, Giuliani needed "inoculating against" the "Reagan Republican moniker," the vulnerability study reported. "The Giuliani campaign should emphasize its candidate's independence from traditional national Republican policies." The final six words of that sentence are underlined in the study. Additionally, the Giuliani report noted that the candidate needed to make it clear to voters that he was "pretty good on most issues of concern to gay and lesbian New Yorkers" and was pro-choice and supported public funding for abortion. "He will continue city funding for abortions at city hospitals. Nothing more, nothing less." Giuliani's stance on these issues, of course, may leave him vulnerable today with an entirely different electorate. The campaign study was obtained by *The Village Voice*'s Wayne Barrett in the course of preparing *Rudy!,* an investigative biography of

Giuliani. In its preface, the study notes that it is "tough and hard-hitting. It pulls no punches." Perhaps that is why Giuliani, as Barrett reported, ordered copies of the vulnerability study destroyed shortly after it was circulated to top campaign aides. He surely could not have been pleased to read that his "personal life raises questions about a 'weirdness factor.'" That weirdness, aides reported, stemmed from Giuliani's 14-year marriage to his second cousin, a union that he got annulled by claiming to have never received proper dispensation from the Catholic Church for the unorthodox nuptials. "When asked about his personal life, Giuliani gives a wide array of conflicting answers," the campaign report stated. "All of this brings the soundness of his judgment into question—and the veracity of his answers." The internal study also addresses prospective charges that Giuliani dodged the Vietnam draft and was a "man without convictions" because of his transformation from George McGovern voter to a Reagan-era Justice Department appointee. "In many ways Rudy Giuliani is a political contradiction. . . . He doesn't really fit with the Republicans. Too liberal. Giuliani has troubles with the Democrats, too." [. . .]

"Obama Bin Laden" Fails To Register

Government turns down Florida man's conflated trademark bid

FEBRUARY 13, 2007—Government officials have rejected a Florida man's bid to trademark the term *Obama bin Laden,* ruling that the conflation of the names of a U.S. Senator and the world's leading terrorist was "scandalous" and wrongly suggested a connection between the politician and the mass murderer. In a February 6 decision, U.S. Patent and Trademark Office attorney Karen K. Bush informed applicant Alexandre Batlle of her decision not to register the trademark. [. . .] Last month, Batlle, a 28-year-old Miami Beach resident, filed an application to trademark the term for use on hats, shirts, pins, and bumper stickers. Along with citing Trademark Act sections dealing with "scandalous refusal" and "false association," Bush noted that the application was also refused because "the record does not include the written consent of Barack Obama and Osama bin Laden, the names of the living individuals identified in the proposed mark." Batlle, who paid $325 to file his trademark application, told TSG that he does not plan to appeal the USPTO decision, adding that he wanted to use the "Obama bin Laden" handle to "make a quick buck." Batlle, who described himself as "more of a Democrat myself," planned to sell t-shirts through obamabinladen.net, which he registered on January 19, the same day he filed his trademark application. Batlle shared with TSG artwork for one shirt, which features Obama carrying an assault rifle and wearing a turban. The Illinois Democrat is accompanied by Hillary Clinton, who appears to be leashed and wearing a modified burqa. [. . .]

WILLIAM BASTONE ■ THE SMOKING GUN
http://www.thesmokinggun.com/

The Smoking Gun is the Web equivalent of old-fashioned investigative reporting. The editor of TSG, William Bastone, age forty-six, is the guy who digs up the dirt and presents it in nice tidy packages. Every week TSG publishes anything it can get through the Freedom of Information Act. The most famous post is still probably the one from 2006, in which TSG revealed that *A Million Little Pieces*, the Oprah-approved memoir by James Frey, was actually fiction. Frey said he was in jail eighty-seven days; his records, posted by TSG, showed it was five hours.

The Smoking Gun has been muckraking for ten years. In April 1997, Bastone, a *Village Voice* reporter, Daniel Green, a freelance journalist, and Barbara Glauber, a graphic designer who owns a firm named Heavy Meta, founded TSG. From the beginning Bastone was the editor in chief. That means, he says, he makes "all calls in terms of what we cover, how we report stories, how they are played, etc. And I've probably written 95 percent of all TSG material."

Bastone started at *The Village Voice* in 1984, when he was a student at New York University. He rose from intern to contributing writer to staff writer. An investigative reporter, he covered City Hall, criminal justice issues, and New York's five Mafia families. In 2000 he left the *Voice* to work at TSG full-time. That was the year that Court TV, a basic cable network with 80 million subscribers, bought the site.

The Smoking Gun, which now has more than 3.5 million visitors monthly, has put out two books: *The Smoking Gun: A Dossier of Secret, Surprising, and Salacious Documents* (Little, Brown and Company, 2001) and *The Dog Dialed 911: A Book of Lists from The Smoking Gun* (Little, Brown and Company, 2006). Bastone, a lifelong New Yorker, lives in Manhattan with his wife (Barbara Glauber) and seven-year-old son.

Unδεr Οδυssευs

http://www.underodysseus.blogspot.com/

μ′

I spent most of the day lying on my stomach.

Odysseus still hasn't stopped by. —He did send some grapes over with Misenus, however.

Attached was a note:

Dear Eurylochus,

I hope that your butt is better. That is really really terrible. It made me really sad to hear that your butt was hurt. I have been really busy. Sorry I have not visited you. I hope that you like the grapes.

Your General,

Odysseus

Amazing. It's obvious the General penned this one himself. —I guess I could take that as a sign of sincerity.

Anyway, I have a feeling that Odysseus feels a bit guilty for blowing me off right before the battle. No doubt he wanted to be seen leading the charge with Achilles. —Especially since Ajax was there.

Whatever.

In other news, Elpenor and Epeius are having troubles.

Elpenor stormed into my tent today screaming: "I can't do it anymore! I just can't work with that pompous asshole. I won't do it. Who does he think he is?!"

When I calmed Elpenor down, he explained that "the pompous asshole" was Epeius. According to Elpenor, Epeius has been acting like "Zeus' gift to men" ever since he won the Patroclus Honor Games boxing match.

I tried to change his mind, but Elpenor was adamant. When I reminded Elpenor his duty was an order and not a request, tears welled up in his eyes and he started ranting about how I had no idea what he was going through.

[...]

I'm sure it was just a spat.

Ironically, Epeius stopped by later this evening looking very calm. Epeius coolly explained that he and Elpenor had some disagreements, but he assured me it would have no effect upon the Wooden Horse construction.

Epeius then gave me what should have been Elpenor's daily report in his usual mouth-breathing manner.

I really need to get those two back together again.

posted by Eurylochus at 11:31 AM on Apr 3, 2006

μβ′

[...]

My ass was feeling much better this morning, so I decided to go with Odysseus to watch Achilles challenge Hector. —I guess I'm glad I did.

[...]

I sat with Odysseus, Agamemnon, Menelaus, Ajax, Nestor and their respective aides. —I was surprised to see Menelaus there. He was looking a bit pasty, and one of his staffers was always making sure to block his sun.

Anyway, Agamemnon's staff brought lunch, and as the rest of our envoy set up, we enjoyed some bread, cheese and wine.

Oddly, I didn't see Achilles ride up with our troupe.

Soon after we had set up, the huge gates of Troy cracked open. —To our surprise, King Priam stepped out, accompanied only by his sons Hector and Paris.

Paris stayed by the doors. However, Priam and Hector casually walked up to our little camp. Seeing them approach, Agamemnon stood up, waved, and politely called them over. —This was worth getting out of bed for.

[...]

When Achilles approached, Agamemnon placed his hand on Achilles' shoulder and said: "King Priam, it seems we have a duel. We shall give your brave son rest before he fights, and we thank you for your hospitality until he is readied."

"Ah, I'm ready now! I'll kick his ass now!"
shouted Hector, but Priam waved him silent
once again.

Priam replied. "Give us until the sun is just
as far setting as it has risen now, King
Agamemnon. Then we will have our duel."

Agamemnon nodded.

At that, Priam led a very agitated Hector
back into the gates of Troy. —Achilles stared
at him coolly.

Several of our men shouted: "Achilles!
Achilles . . ." but it faded out before it became
a rally.

We went back to lunch.

[. . .]

It wasn't until Hector's arrival was
announced that Achilles got to his feet.

Once again, Hector arrived with Priam and
his brother Paris. Priam and Hector were
wearing armor, and Paris was wearing some
sort of white flowing thing and a helmet.

Paris' outfit was a bit strange, but what
really got everyone's attention was Hector's

armor. Hector's breastplate had a big cheesy "Alpha" on it. —He was wearing Achilles' armor which he had peeled off the corpse of Patroclus.

The sight of Hector wearing Achilles' armor brought loud boos and jeers from our entire camp. When Achilles saw it, it drove him mad.

[. . .]

Now, in all seriousness, I have seen many fights in my lifetime. —I have never seen a fight like this one.

[. . .]

I couldn't do it justice to describe the battle in full. However, Hector and Achilles slashed, jumped, rolled and punched like they were having some kind of physical debate.

[. . .]

Watching this melee, I realized that Achilles probably had no intent to hit Hector with that initial javelin throw. More likely, it was just another way of cursing Hector before their sparring began.

[. . .]

At first there was total silence.

Achilles then yelled: "Yes! Yes! Yes!" and pumped his fist into the air.

This was punctuated by a shrill "Noooooooooo!" from Paris.

Achilles, then quickly regaining his composure, [. . .] walked out of the ring, followed closely by a group of his Magnesian pals.

Everyone else just stood and stared at the body of Hector, who was lying twisted, with Achilles' sword still stuck in his throat.

Paris ran to Hector's body first, followed slowly by Priam. The two knelt down, and all became silent once again.

After nearly a full minute, Agamemnon gently approached King Priam and his fallen son.

Agamemnon spoke in such a compassionate tone that even I began to feel emotional.

Agamemnon placed his hand on Priam's shoulder and said: "There will never be another like him, King Priam. And as such, all of us will mourn this tragic loss. Today, we are without one of the greatest warriors to walk mortal soil, Hector, Son of Pr—"

Agamemnon was cut off by the thunder of horses.

Achilles and several of his Magnesian men charged into the circle.

In just a matter of seconds, Achilles tossed a rope loop about Hector's leg, pulled it tight, and rode off, dragging Hector from Paris' lap and across the plain towards our encampment.

As Achilles rode off, we could hear him shout: "Yes! Yes! Yes!"

This made things *very* uncomfortable.

Once again, Paris let out a shrill "Noooooooooooo!"

Priam screamed as well.

[...]

Achilles 'posted' Hector's body just outside the Magnesian encampment, where the celebrations are nearly out of control.

Once again, Achilles' actions must have
really pissed off Agamemnon.

Although Agamemnon has command of this
army, Achilles has command of its heart.
The Commander-in-Chief must know this.
That must piss him off all the more.

Polites just came in. —He wants to know if I
think five bottles of wine is too much for one
of Hector's sandals.

posted by Eurylochus at 1:16 PM on Apr 6, 2006

μγ′

The party is over, but Hector is still hanging
there.

I hope Achilles takes him down soon. I can't
leave my tent without looking at his bloody,
naked corpse. —I don't think it becomes us
Achaeans to do stuff like that.

Anyway, it was a pleasant day, nonetheless.

It seems that Elpenor and Epeius have
worked out their differences.

Elpenor stopped by this morning to give me
his report. Epeius waited for him outside.
Elpenor was in a good mood, and I heard

the two of them giggling about something
when they left.

Polites came by after lunch, and he asked
that I come down to the beach to have a look
at something.

Apparently, Macar and one of our naval
officers, Baius, fashioned a small fishing
skiff into a nice little sailing boat.

Although it will hold only about six people, it
looks like a miniature bireme, complete
with a carved nymph at the bow.

I was really impressed by their
craftsmanship. Macar and Baius had even
gone so far as to fix some bronze plates
along the bulwark. On these, they stamped
the name of their craft: *Li'l Tethys*.

Unfortunately, the sea was a bit too rough
for sailing today. However, they promised to
take us out tomorrow if the weather
permits.

posted by Eurylochus at 7:43 AM on Apr 8, 2006

μδ′

We went sailing today. It was really nice.

Macar and Baius took us out just after
breakfast. There was a cool, steady breeze

across the water this morning, and the *Li'l Tethys* really cut through the waves.

Standing at the bow [. . .] Macar could [not] have looked more pleased. —I've never seen him with such a genuine smile.

Polites brought some bread and wine along, and we stopped off at one of the small rock islands for lunch.

While we were there, a Minyan ship sailed in. We threw some rocks and pissed them off. —It was a good time.

Hector's body is still hanging about. He's looking pretty nasty.

Some dogs were pulling on his foot yesterday, so they elevated him quite a bit. Now you can see him from most anywhere in the camp.

When Hector was first put up, he looked pretty ragged, like some old clothes or something. Now his skin is kind of shiny, and his belly is getting big.

I really wish they would take him down.

Odysseus came by and asked if I wanted to go hunting tomorrow. I guess Diomedes' pal

Sthenelus has some dogs, and they want to take them out. He said that Achilles might be there.

I had to decline.

My ass was good enough for sailing. However, I don't think I am ready for a day on horseback just yet. Besides, Sthenelus is kind of a prick, and I hate the way Odysseus gets when he is around people like him.

I suppose it was a nice gesture, nonetheless.

Anyway, although he walked right by it, Odysseus didn't say anything about Hector's rotting corpse.

It kind of bothers me that we are hanging Priam's son on a pole just to make Achilles happy.

posted by Eurylochus at 5:29 PM on Apr 10, 2006

με΄

Priam visited us today.

He rode up with about ten Trojan generals, carrying a flag of truce. —Paris wasn't there.

It seems they were first headed towards Agamemnon's camp, but after catching sight of Hector on a pole, they rode over to the Magnesian camp instead.

[. . .]

Machaon attempted some sort of formal greeting. However, upon dismounting, Priam walked up to Machaon, grabbed him by the neck, and flung him to the ground.

Priam then looked up to his bloated son and started screaming: "Where is that sonofabitch Achilles?! Mother of Zeus, I'll have his eyes! Where is that bastard Achilles?!"

Although hundreds of Achaean soldiers had gathered around, not one would come within twenty meters of the Trojans. Even Machaon scurried away when he got to his feet.

As for the Trojan generals, I don't think they knew what to do either. Priam was the only one who dismounted. No doubt, the Trojans didn't want to start trouble. However, their king was on the ground crying. . . .

It was Glaukos who spoke first: "You sick fuckers! How could you fuckers be so sick!? You put Hector on a fucking pole? What is this shit?!"

During Glaukos' tirade, Agamemnon,
Nestor and Ajax rode up.

Upon seeing their horses enter the circle,
Glaukos yelled: "Who the fuck are—" But,
realizing it was Agamemnon, he cut himself
short.

Seeing our Commander-in-Chief, Priam
shouted once again: "Where is he,
Agamemnon?! Where is that bastard
Achilles?! How could he do this?! How could
you let him do this?!"

Without saying a word, Agamemnon
climbed down from his horse, walked up,
and embraced Priam. Strangely, Priam did
not resist. —He just sobbed.

I then heard a sniffle from Nestor. —For
some reason he was getting choked up too.

Anyway, in a very gentle tone, Agamemnon
explained to Priam that Achilles was not
present because he had gone hunting.

Agamemnon did order our men to take
Hector down, however.

Hector had been raised up somewhat like a
flag. When the rope attached to him was
untied, he dropped quickly, making

somewhat of a squishy thud. —Hector had ballooned to nearly twice his size.

Standing over the bloated body of Hector, Agamemnon announced that Priam's son would be returned tomorrow, in a grand funeral procession fit to restore his honor.

[...]

Priam thanked Agamemnon for his kindness. He then kneeled and kissed the puffy forehead of his dead son.

The Trojans left in silence.

Agamemnon ordered some unlucky men to carry Hector to his camp.

I heard a wheeze of gas come from Hector as these guys lifted him up. —One of the bearers vomited.

The rest of the day was uneventful.

I don't think Achilles and the hunting crew have come back yet.

posted by Eurylochus at 6:31 PM on Apr 11, 2006

μς′

Bad news. —Achilles torched Hector's body.

The hunting crew returned sometime late last night. Apparently, Achilles was pretty pissed when he found Agamemnon had taken his trophy.

Some Magnesians told Achilles what had happened, and upon hearing this, our Champion decided that Priam was not going to get his funeral parade.

Not long before dawn, Achilles and a group of his Magnesian buddies stole Hector back from Agamemnon's camp.

Then, in somewhat of an ironic gesture of respect, Achilles burned Hector in a funeral pyre down by the beach.

[. . .]

The Commander-in-Chief flipped.

When I got to the scene, Agamemnon was swinging a charred femur, screaming at Achilles at the top of his lungs: "What is this?! What the fuck am I going to do now?! Am I supposed to send Priam his son in a box?!"

"It was a hero's burial, Commander,"
Achilles responded calmly.

Agamemnon was furious: "A hero's burial?!
You torched him in spite, Achilles! I let you
stick him on a pole! I let you have your fun!
But this?! Why did you have to do this?!"

Agamemnon pointed the leg-bone at
Achilles: "You are going to bring a grave
wrath upon us, Son of Peleus. . . ."

"Couldn't you just let Calchas kick them
around, Commander?" Achilles quipped.

"You sonofabitch!" Agamemnon shouted,
tossing Hector's femur at Achilles.

Agamemnon then drew his sword.
—Everyone gasped.

Nestor spoke up: "King Agamemnon, let us
not forget ourselves. We are Achaeans. We
are all Achaeans here."

At that, the Commander-in-Chief paused.
He slowly sheathed his sword. —Achilles smiled.

[. . .]

I didn't hear anything else of it today.

The sun set about an hour ago.

I have to imagine things are getting pretty tense inside the walls of Troy right about now.

posted by Eurylochus at 6:22 PM on Apr 13, 2006

μη΄

No Trojan attack today.

I did almost get to see Ajax and Odysseus fight, however.

This morning, Odysseus dropped by again. There was a meeting between a handful of Agamemnon's closest commanders this afternoon, and he wanted me to be there to take notes.

I have to say, I was a bit flattered by Odysseus' invitation, and I happily accepted.

The meeting took place during lunch in Agamemnon's tent. —That was interesting enough. I had never been in Agamemnon's tent before. It isn't so much one tent as it is a series of tents, all connected to one another.

Even more impressive, the Commander-in-Chief's place was filled with beautiful women. Well, maybe not filled, but there were at least five pretty maids that waited on us. —I think I'd almost forgotten what pretty women looked like.

[. . .]

Anyway, I sat between Odysseus and Nestor. Menelaus wasn't there. —No big surprise.

The food was great. However, Nestor doesn't have many teeth, and as he kept talking at me during lunch, half of his food ended up on my shoulder. —That kind of killed my appetite.

Besides that, when Nestor saw I had papers and ink, he started drawing all these maps and diagrams of the stuff he was babbling about. —He left me with almost no room for my notes.

After we had eaten, Agamemnon started things off by saying that the Trojans were preparing an attack. He said we had a new spy in Troy, and that this guy had told us that Priam was awfully pissed about what happened to Hector. (Some spy!)

Apparently, the King of Troy is planning a grand battle to finally settle this thing.

At that point, Achilles spoke up: "Well, let them bring it! Let's do it! Mother of Zeus, I'm sick of this beachhead!"

At that, Agamemnon frowned.

Odysseus then spoke: "Achilles, I admire your bravery, but don't forget, we are building the Horse . . ."

Ajax then interrupted: "Oh, fuck the *Horse*, Odysseus! Do you *really* think the Trojans are going to fall for that?!"

[. . .]

After the luncheon was adjourned, I walked with Odysseus back to his tent.

I asked the General what he wanted me to do to prepare our men for battle, but he just kept asking me questions about the Horse.

Among other things, Odysseus asked me if I thought the Horse was too tall, whether I thought it looked too much like a Horse, if I thought the Trojans knew we were building it, and whether I thought that it would hold enough people.

I could tell he was upset by Ajax's criticism. Perhaps Odysseus was also anxious because Agamemnon hadn't gone so far as to actually defend the project. —Maybe the Commander-in-Chief has his doubts as well.

Anyway, I got no advice concerning the upcoming battle.

When I asked when he was going to inspect
the men tomorrow, Odysseus looked
confused and said: "Why? I am sure they
look just fine, Eurylochus."

I then reminded Odysseus that Agamemnon
warned us the Trojans could come as early
as tomorrow night.

He then nodded and said: "Oh, yes, yes.
Sure, I'll have a look at them, right after
breakfast."

As I turned to leave, the General stopped
me: "Hey Eurylochus, could you send that
Lieutenant Epeius over to my tent?"

I nodded and left.

I then went to tell Epeius that Odysseus
wanted to discuss the Horse with him.

Elpenor was not pleased.

posted by Eurylochus at 6:33 PM on Apr 17, 2006

vγ′

I had a look at the horse again today.

I'm beginning to think Epeius and Elpenor
might be going overboard. —They've tacked
some brass plates on as "hooves," and Epeius
has started work on a huge saddle.

Epeius and Elpenor were obviously proud,
and they should be. —The Horse looks great.

I'm just not so sure it needs to be so fancy.

Anyway, the Horse has no head as of yet, but
the body is close to completion. Elpenor said
they squeezed twenty-five guys in it the
other day. —However, those guys weren't
wearing any armor.

I told them they were doing a great job.
Since they offered me lunch, I didn't
mention the excessive frills.

Of course, lunch was fantastic.

On the way back to our camp, I ran into
Polites and Euryalus.

Polites waved to me and said: "Eurylochus, I
haven't seen you in three days!"

—He was waving the thumb and two fingers
that remained on his right hand.

Polites thought it was hilarious.

[...]

posted by Eurylochus at 7:31 PM on May 2, 2006

Mark Katakowski, thirty-two years old, writes Under Odysseus: the journal of a soldier serving under Odysseus during the Trojan War. The soldier is Eurylochus. And Under Odysseus is Katakowski's fiction. "I suppose that sounds obvious, but I receive many e-mails from confused readers who think otherwise." While it is based on the Richmond Lattimore translations of the *Iliad* and the *Odyssey,* he says, "Under Odysseus is a palimpsest. That is, it's a work on top of, or inside of, another established work.

"I was flipping through the *Odyssey* one day," Katakowski says, "when I realized the famous exploits of Odysseus, all his adventures, the Lotus eaters, the Cyclops, etc., were all related by him alone.... Maybe the men who were serving under him would have seen things differently. Maybe Odysseus's story was all bullshit." Why did Katakowski make Eurylochus the narrator? "Eurylochus is close enough to Odysseus to get an insider's account of Homer's hero. However, in the chain of command, Eurylochus is still 'under Odysseus' and therefore subject to his whims. It's a uniquely difficult place to be."

Katakowski is a postdoctoral fellow in neuroscience at the Henry Ford Hospital in Detroit, Michigan, specializing in the treatment of stroke and brain tumors. "Please don't hold that against me," he says. He writes during his lunch breaks.

When UO is done, Katakowski plans to edit it and publish it in print. He is also writing a book inspired by James Joyce's *Ulysses*—yes, yet another *Odyssey.* He says, "I was reading *Ulysses* when I thought: Damn, this is different! It's not fun to read at all, but wow, this is really different! Anyway, it motivated me to start writing something with no boundaries."

HOW TO FIND BLOGS

Start, of course, with the blogs you like best in this book. Go to your computer and find them on the Web by searching for the blog by name or by entering its Web address, or URL (I've listed the URL with each entry). Once you're on a blog you like, you'll sometimes see (often on the right-hand side of the screen) a blogroll—a list of other blogs that this blogger likes. Click on some of those links. If you find a new blog that you like, put it in your favorites list so you can easily find it later.

To find the most popular blogs, go to a Web site like *The Truth Laid Bear*, http://truthlaidbear.com/ecosystem.php, whose colorful ranking system of more than seventy thousand blogs runs from Higher Beings to Insignificant Microbes. Or you can go to *Technorati*, which tracks millions of blogs. There, at http://technorati.com/pop/blogs, you'll also find a list of the top hundred blogs (ranked by how many other sites link to them).

If you want to find out what bloggers are saying on a certain topic, you can use Google's blog searcher, http://blogsearch.google .com/. Just as with plain Google, you enter a keyword and then search. (Note: if you're reading a blog on a certain subject and then want to explore the same blog further, click on the title of the blog to get to its main page.)

Another way to start your blog search is to go directly to some of the very large blogs and online magazines like *Slate*, http://www .slate.com/; *The Huffington Post*, http://www.huffingtonpost.com/; *Design Observer*, http://www.designobserver.com/; *Metafilter*, http:// www.metafilter.com/; *TPM Café*, http://www.tpmcafe.com/; *Crooks and*

Liars, http://www.crooksandliars.com/; *Science Blogs*, http://science blogs.com/; *ArtsJournal*, http://www.artsjournal.com/; or *Boing Boing*, http://boingboing.net/. These sites use many bloggers, refer to lots of other bloggers, or give you appetizers from various blogs along with the links to those blogs.

Yet another gateway to the blogs is through what bloggers disparagingly call the MSM (mainstream media). If you read about an intriguing blog in a newspaper or hear about it on the radio, note the name and find it when you're at your computer. If you're reading the article online, just click on the link. Also, remember that bloggers love to feast upon articles in MSM rags like *The New York Times* and *The Wall Street Journal.* And lucky for you, some newspapers and magazines not only have blogs of their own but are also happy to feed other bloggers' snarky tendencies by including a list of the most-blogged-about articles in their online editions. For instance, at http://www .nytimes.com/gst/mostblogged.html you'll find what the bloggers have to say about *New York Times* articles.

Helpful hint: If you find strange words and abbreviations while looking for blogs, check out *Wikipedia*, http://www.wikipedia.org/, an online encyclopedia that gets constantly expanded and edited by its readers. It may not be totally reliable but it almost always has something of what you're looking for.

ACKNOWLEDGMENTS

I hope I can remember every person who helped me, knowingly or not, by e-mail, by phone, or in person, with this anthology. First thanks go to Harry Cooper, for his time and judgment, and to Julius Boxer Cooper, for his sweet presence. Thanks also to my folks, Florine Boxer and Phillip Boxer, for their curiosity and title suggestions, and to my sister, Susan Boxer, for her great ear.

Next come some of my friends and relations, most of whom don't give a hoot about blogs but who have nevertheless talked to me about them and have promised to give a hoot soon: David Adams, Emily Benedek, David Berreby, Joe Castiglione, David Dorfman, Carroll Eastman, Michael Frank, Sarah Funke, Shari Hersh, Larry Jacobson, Steven Levitsky, Liz Mineo, Mica Pollock, Sam Robinson, Julia Rothwax, Dan Silver, Evan Spring, Peter Stein, Bill & Joyce Thorn, and Herman & Sophia Travis.

Thanks also to the people I know (and a few I don't) who actually read blogs and, in some cases, offered me the names of their favorites: Alex Balk, Steve Boxer, Tim Christenfeld, Louis Cooper, Scott Diperna, Angela Forster, Dwight Garner, Steven Guarnaccia, Barry Gewen, Celia & Kate Gilbert, Steve Heller, Ariel Kaminer, Jodi Kantor, Jessica Krash, Nick Lemann, Gina Maranto, Judith Shulevitz, Choire Sicha, Rebecca Skloot, Andre Sternberg, Lawrence Weschler, Paul Wilson, Bob Wright, and Gary Young.

I am very grateful to all the book-loving people who were directly involved with the strange and complicated task of turning blogs into print: Deb Garrison, Marty Asher, Lisa Weinert, Caroline Zancan,

David McCormick, Joy Gallagher, Stephen McNabb, Cathryn Aison, Bob Bull, Mark Abrams, Anke Steinecke, Nicole Pedersen, and Tiffany Yates.

My greatest thanks, of course, go to the bloggers in this book—Pamela Merritt, Richard Posner & Gary Becker, Nick Currie, Sean Carroll, Samuel Pepys & Phil Gyford, "El Guapo," Delly Hayward, David Rees, Jessica Morgan & Heather Cocks, "Francis Strand," Jill Posey-Smith, Raed Jarrar, David Friedman, Angelique Chan, Jennie Portnof, Julia Litton, Benjamin Zimmer, Matthew Yglesias, Renée French, Jeffrey Barnett, Nina Paley, Lizzie Skurnick, Dmitri Goutnik, Tony Karon, Alex Ross, William Bastone, and Mark Katakowski—who have been generous, game, patient, and brave.

BLOG CREDITS

AngryBlackBitch selections reprinted by permission of Pamela Merritt.

Becker-Posner Blog selections reprinted by permission of Gary S. Becker and Richard Posner.

Click Opera selections reprinted by permission of Nick Currie.

Cosmic Variance selections reprinted by permission of Sean Carroll.

El Guapo in DC selections reprinted by permission of the author, known as El Guapo.

Eurotrash selections reprinted by permission of Delly Hayward.

Get Your War On selections reprinted by permission of David Rees.

Go Fug Yourself text reprinted by permission of Jessica Morgan and Heather Cocks.
Go Fug Yourself photo of Blu Cantrell: Gregg De Guire/Getty Images
Go Fug Yourself photo of Anne Hathaway: Frederick M. Brown/Getty Images
Go Fug Yourself photo of Sarah Brightman: Dave Hogan/Getty Images

How to Learn Swedish in 1000 Difficult Lessons selections reprinted by permission of the author, known as Francis Strand.

I Blame The Patriarchy selections reprinted by permission of Jill Posey-Smith.

In The Middle selections reprinted by permission of Raed Jarrar.

Ironic Sans selections reprinted by permission of David Friedman.

Its raining noodles! selections reprinted by permission of Angelique Chan.

Johnny i hardly knew you selections reprinted by permission of Jennie Portnof.

Julia {Here Be Hippogriffs} selections reprinted by permission of Julia Litton.

Language Log selections reprinted by permission of Benjamin Zimmer.

Matthew Yglesias selections reprinted by permission of Matthew Yglesias.

Micrographica selections reprinted by permission of Renée French.

Midnight in Iraq selections reprinted by permission of Jeffrey Barnett.

Nina Paley.com selections reprinted by permission of Nina Paley.

Old Hag selections reprinted by permission of Lizzie Skurnick.

Radio.Uruguay photographs © Dmitri Goutnik reprinted by permission.

Rootless Cosmopolitan selections reprinted by permission of Tony Karon.

The Rest Is Noise selections reprinted by permission of Alex Ross.

The Smoking Gun selections reprinted by permission of William Bastone.

Under Odysseus selections reprinted by permission of Mark Katakowski.

All photographs and illustrations, with the exception of the three photographs in Go Fug Yourself (credited above), the Abu Ghraib photograph, the photograph of Michelangelo's *David*, and the documents that appear with The Smoking Gun, are reprinted by permission of the respective bloggers.